T3-BPX-406

Colección Támesis

SERIE A: MONOGRAFIAS, 156

WHITE INK

ESSAYS ON
TWENTIETH-CENTURY FEMININE FICTION
IN SPAIN AND LATIN AMERICA

STEPHEN M. HART

WHITE INK

ESSAYS ON
TWENTIETH-CENTURY FEMININE FICTION
IN SPAIN AND LATIN AMERICA

TAMESIS BOOKS LIMITED
LONDON

EDITORIAL TÁMESIS, S.L.
MADRID

DISTRIBUTORS

Spain: Grupo Distribuidor Editorial, S.A., Ferrer del Río 35, 28028 Madrid

United States and Canada: Boydell & Brewer Inc., PO Box 41026, Rochester, NY 14604, USA

Great Britain and rest of the world: Boydell & Brewer Ltd, PO Box 9, Woodbridge, Suffolk, IP12 3DF, UK

First published 1993 by Tamesis Books Limited, London

ISBN 1 85566 031 8

British Library Cataloguing in Publication Data
Hart, Stephen
    White Ink: Essays on Twentieth-century Feminine
    Fiction in Spain and Latin America. – (Coleccion
    Tamesis, Serie A: Monografias; Vol. 156)
    I. Title II. Series
    863.609
    ISBN 1-85566-031-8

The paper used in this publication meets the minimum requirements of American National Standard for Information Sciences – Permanence of Paper for Printed Library Materials, ANSI Z39.48-1984

Printed in Great Britain by
St Edmundsbury Press Ltd, Bury St Edmunds, Suffolk
for
TAMESIS BOOKS LIMITED
LONDON

CONTENTS

	Pages
Abbreviations	ix
Preface	xi
INTRODUCTION	1
I. THE NOVEL OF DEVELOPMENT	9
Carmen Laforet: *Nada*	13
Mercè Rodoreda: *La plaça del Diamant*	19
Clarice Lispector: *Perto do coração selvagem*	28
II. THE PATRIARCHAL PRISON	36
María Luisa Bombal, *La amortajada*	37
Rosario Castellanos: 'Lección de cocina', *Album de familia*	45
Elena Garro: *Los recuerdos del porvenir*	53
III. FAIRY TALES	63
Ana María Matute: *Primera memoria*	65
Carmen Martín Gaite: *El cuarto de atrás*	71
Esther Tusquets: *El mismo mar de todos los veranos*	78
IV. SEXUAL POLITICS	88
Isabel Allende: *La casa de los espíritus*	91
Marta Traba: *Conversación al sur*	99
Montserrat Roig: *L'hora violeta*	107
V. GENDER TROUBLE	116
Luisa Valenzuela: *El gato eficaz*	117
Cristina Peri Rossi: *La nave de los locos*	124
Rosa Montero: *Temblor*	131
CONCLUSION	140
LIST OF WORKS CONSULTED	143
INDEX	155

for Dany

ABBREVIATIONS

ALEC	*Anales de Literatura Española Contemporánea*
AmH	*The American Hispanist*
BHS	*Bulletin of Hispanic Studies*
CAm	*Casa de las Américas*, Havana
CL	*Comparative Literature*
EC	*España Contemporánea*
ER	*Estudis Romànics*
FMLS	*Forum for Modern Language Studies*
HJ	*Hispanic Journal*
HR	*Hispanic Review*
KRQ	*Kentucky Romance Quarterly*
LF	*Letras Femeninas*
LALR	*Latin American Literary Review*
MLN	*Modern Language Notes*
PMLA	*Publications of the Modern Language Association of America*
RCEH	*Revista Canadiense de Estudios Hispánicos*
REH	*Revista de Estudios Hispánicos*
RHM	*Revista Hispánica Moderna*
RLC	*Revue de Littérature Comparée*
RI	*Revista Iberoamericana*
RoN	*Romance Notes*
RR	*Romanic Review*
SiN	*Sin Nombre*
SpSt	*Spanish Studies*
TSWL	*Tulsa Studies in Women's Literature*

PREFACE

I take this opportunity to thank Professor Margaret E. W. Jones, Dr Verity Smith and Professor J. E. Varey for taking the time to read the manuscript; for their intellectual rigour, expressed as much in their suggestions for amendment as their correction of my fallible spelling, I remain very grateful. I can only hope that some of their wisdom will have filtered into what follows. Any mistakes to be found in this book, though, are mine, not theirs.

S. M. H.

INTRODUCTION

In the eleventh chapter of his *Poetics*, Aristotle defines *agnorisis*, a crucial element in the plot of any tragedy, as 'the change of fortune in the action of the play to the opposite state of affairs'. He gives two examples to illustrate this idea, one from *Lynceus* and the other from *Oedipus*, explaining with regard to the latter text that 'the messenger comes to cheer Oedipus and to remove his fears in regard to his mother; but by showing him who he actually is he accomplishes the opposite effect'. This reversal, as Aristotle continues, is predicated on a 'recognition' which 'is a change from ignorance to knowledge, bringing about either a state of friendship or one of hostility on the part of those who have been marked out for good fortune or bad'.[1] The recognition which Aristotle identifies at the centre of Greek tragedy is undeniably androcentric since it involves a man's self-awareness; yet, in terms of rhetorical reversal, it is as good a figure as any other to describe the type of knowledge actively or obliquely engendered in the modern feminine Hispanic text. The passage from ignorance to knowledge projected in the texts studied in this book involves self-awareness, as in Oedipus's case, but it also involves recognition of an ideology (patriarchy) which is perceived as existing in an objective sense as well; just as important, the *agnorisis* created in the modern feminine Hispanic text crosses the gender lines drawn so taut in Aristotle's text.

Women's writing in Spain and the Americas neither follows the path of a gradually increasing crescendo, nor that of a sudden, unexpected 'boom'; rather it seems to have evolved in fits and starts, with some periods lying fallow (the eighteenth and the first half of the nineteenth centuries), and others demonstrating unparalleled growth (1976 to the present). In the interests of providing a rule-of-thumb sketch, I would propose the following groupings to characterise women's writing in Spain and the Americas:

[1] Aristotle, *Poetics*, translated by Leon Golden (Tallahassee: University Presses of Florida, 1981), p. 19.

1

1400–1530: ERA OF FRAGMENTS

Leonor López de Córdoba (1362/3–c.1412)	Teresa de Cartagena (c.1420–c.1470)	Florencia Pinar (c.1470–c.1530)	Isabel de Villena (1430–1490)

1550–1700: THE DAWN

Santa Teresa (1515–1582)	María de Zayas (1590–1661)	Sor Juana (1651–1695)

1835–1905: THE STUNTED FLOWERING

Gertrudis Gómez de Avellaneda, *Sab* (1841)	Cecilia Böhl von Faber, *La gaviota* (1849)	Rosalía de Castro, *Cantares gallegos* (1863)
Pardo Bazán, *Los pazos de Ulloa* (1886)	Clorinda Matto de Turner, *Aves sin nido* (1899)	Catarina Albert, *Solitud* (1905)

1906–1935: THE ERA OF DECANONIZATION

Delmira Agustini (1886–1914)	Gabriela Mistral (1889–1957)	Alfonsina Storni (1892–1938)	Juana de Ibarbourou (1895–1975)	Concha Méndez (1898–1986)

1936–1975: LOW RENAISSANCE

María Luisa Bombal, *La amortajada* (1938)	Clarice Lispector, *Perto do coração selvagem* (1941)	Carmen Laforet, *Nada* (1944)	Ana María Matute, *Primera memoria* (1960)
Mercè Rodoreda, *La plaça del Diamant* (1962)	Elena Garro, *Los recuerdos del porvenir* (1963)	Rosario Castellanos, *Album de familia* (1971)	Luisa Valenzuela, *El gato eficaz* (1972)

1976–PRESENT DAY: HIGH RENAISSANCE

Carmen Martín Gaite, *El cuarto de atrás* (1978)	Esther Tusquets, *El mismo mar* (1979)	Montserrat Roig, *L'hora violeta* (1980)	Marta Traba, *Conversación al sur* (1981)
Isabel Allende, *La casa de los espíritus* (1982)	Cristina Peri Rossi, *La nave de los locos* (1984)	Rosa Montero, *Temblor* (1990)	

The four authors mentioned under 'The Era of Fragments' are important in terms of chronological primacy, although biographical details as well as the works themselves are only known to us in a piecemeal fashion.[2] The three writers listed under the title 'The Dawn' of women's writing in Spain and the Americas signal the emergence of women's writing, but their work was followed by a vacuum; the quality of at least two of these writers (Santa Teresa and Sor Juana Inés de la Cruz) has not been surpassed to date. The individuality of their genius is suggested by the fact that their works ushered in a barren period for women's writing for the following century and a half.[3] And even when women began writing again in the second half of the nineteenth century, it was no more than a 'stunted flowering', since these writers were hampered by their adoption of the masculinist mode of Realism. This is graphically suggested by the fact that two of the authors mentioned, Cecilia Böhl von Faber and Caterina Albert, both felt the need to adopt male pseudonyms (Fernán Caballero and Victor Català, respectively) to further their writing careers. To write during the second half of the nineteenth century, it seems, was still to be inscribed under the sign of patriarchy.[4]

No less significant an obstacle was faced by those representative female writers I have grouped as connoting the Era of Decanonization.

[2] See the expert detective work carried out by Alan Deyermond, 'Spain's First Woman Writers', in *Women in Hispanic Literature: Icons and Fallen Idols* (Berkeley, Los Angeles and London: University of California Press, 1983), pp. 27–52.

[3] Serrano y Sanz meticulously examines women's writing during this period from 1401 to 1833, and includes much evidence of letter writing, but outstanding literary works are infrequent during this period; *Apuntes para una biblioteca de escritoras españolas desde el año 1401 al 1833*. 4 vols. Originally published in 1903. Now reprinted in the *Biblioteca de Autores Españoles* Series (Madrid: Atlas, 1975).

[4] For an excellent discussion of women writers in nineteenth century Spain, see Susan Kirkpatrick, *'Las Románticas': Women Writers and Subjectivity in Spain, 1835–1850* (Berkeley: University of California Press, 1989).

While their male contemporaries were busy establishing genealogies and inheritances in the form of generations (such as *modernismo*, the Generation of 1898, the Generation of 1927), the significant female writers of this period were pushed to the outer limits of non-identity. Concha Méndez, for example, though writing in Spain at the same time as the Generation of 1927 and on the same themes, was not and has not been accepted into membership of that generation.[5] The four other poets listed in this group, Agustini, Mistral, Storni and Ibarbourou, all from the Cono Sur, are generally denied canonic status, and are simply placed in the anonymous grouping called *postmodernismo*, a movement which is as good an example as any of what Hélène Cixous calls a 'nonname' (see below).

Another type of gender secrecy, more implicit than explicit, has also tended to keep women writers of this period in the shade, namely, dominance by their 'more famous' literary husbands. Examples in Spain are Josefina R. Aldecoa (1926), the wife of Ignacio Aldecoa; Clementina Arderiu (1899), wife of Carles Riba; María Teresa de León (1904), wife of Rafael Alberti; María de la O Martínez Sierra (1874–1974), wife of Gregorio Martínez Sierra. While being married to an already established writer might be thought to provide greater opportunity in the sense of introductions in literary coteries to potential publishers, in some cases it proved to have a dispositive effect. It is now clear, for example, that many of the novels which Gregorio Martínez Sierra originally passed off as his own were in fact penned by his wife.[6] Marriage to a famous writer has occasionally led to a wife's work being seen as an accompaniment in a *minor* key to the *major* work of her husband (as in the case of Clementina Arderiu-Carles Riba). Times have changed, of course, since then; nothing could be further from this idea of gendered dominion than the more recent marriage between Marta Traba, the novelist, and Angel Rama, the cultural historian. Their cultural influence in their respective fields was notably more balanced than some literary marriages of the past (before their tragic death in the 1983 Madrid aircrash which took the lives of many Latin-American writers).

The period from 1936 to the present day, both in Spain and the Americas, is one which has witnessed a steady growth in women's writing. To this group of writers, which I have called a Renaissance,

---

[5] In an important article José-Carlos Mainer goes some way towards righting the masculinist assumptions about the Generation of 1927; see his 'Las escritoras del 27 (con María Teresa de León al fondo)', *Homenaje a María Teresa de León* (Madrid: Universidad Complutense, 1989), pp. 13–39.

[6] Patricia O'Connor, *Gregorio and María Martínez Sierra* (Boston: G. K. Hall, 1977), pp. 59–67.

could be added a vast number of other names such as Gloria Fuertes, María Victoria Atencia, Clara Janés, Ana Rossetti, Juana Castro (Spanish poets), Alejandra Pizarnik, Nancy Morejón, Olga Orozco, Claribel Alegría, María Sabina, Adélia Prado (Latin-American poets), Ana Diosdado, Maribel Lázaro, Pilar Pombo (Spanish dramatists), Dolores Medio, Elena Quiroga, Adelaida García Morales, Concha Alós, Marina Mayoral, Carmen Gómez Ojea, Ana María Moix, Carme Riera, Helena Valentí, Maria-Antònia Oliver, Isabel-Clara Simó (other Spanish novelists), Elena Poniatowska, Silvina Ocampo, Armonía Sommers, Marta Lynch, Sylvia Bullrich, Giaconda Belli, María Luisa Mendoza, Angeles Mastretta, Marta Jara, Beatriz Guido, Rosario Ferré, Lygia Fagundez Telles (other Latin-American novelists).[7] The omission of a

[7] The bibliography on women's writing is growing daily. What follows is only the barest minimum which might serve as an introduction: Caridad L. Silva Velázquez and Nora Erro-Orthman, *Puerta abierta: la nueva escritora latinoamericana* (Mexico: Mortiz, 1986), contains good bibliography pp. 267–340; *Woman who has Sprouted Wings: Poems by Contemporary Latin American Women Poets*, edited by Mary Crow (Pittsburgh, PA: Latin American Literary Review Press, 1987); *La mujer por la mujer*, edited by Juana Robles Suárez (México: Pepsa Editores, 1975); Naomi Lindstrom, *Women's Voice in Latin American Literature* (Washington, DC: Three Continents Press, 1989); *Knives and Angels: Women Writers in Latin America*, edited by Susan Bassnett (London and New Jersey: Zed Books Ltd., 1990); *Latin American Women Writers: Yesterday and Today*, edited by Yvett E. Miller and Charles M. Tatum (Pittsburgh, PA: Latin American Literary Review, 1977); *Women, Culture and Politics in Latin America: Seminar on Feminism and Culture in Latin America*, ed. Emilie Bergman, *et al.* (Berkeley: University of California Press, 1990); Jean Franco, *Plotting Women: Gender and Representation in Mexico* (London: Verso, 1989); *Women's Writing in Latin America: An Anthology*, edited by Sara Castro-Klarén, Sylvia Molloy and Beatriz Sarlo (Boulder-San Francisco-Oxford: Westview Press, 1991); Lucía Fox-Lockert, *Women Novelists in Spain and Spanish America* (Metuchen, N.J., and London: Scarecrow Press, 1979); *Continental, Latin-American and Francophone Women Writers*, edited by Eunice Myers and Ginette Adamson (Lanham, MD: University Press of America, 1987); Janet Pérez, *Contemporary Women Writers of Spain* (Boston: Twayne, 1988); *Feminine Concerns in Contemporary Spanish Fiction by Women*, edited by Roberto C. Manteiga, Carolyn Galerstein and Kathleen McNerney (Potomac, Maryland: Scripta Humanistica, 1988); Biruté Ciplijauskaité, *La novela femenina contemporánea (1970–1985): hacia una tipología de la narración en primera persona* (Barcelona: Anthropos, 1988); *Women Writers of Contemporary Spain: Exiles in the Homeland*, ed. Joan L. Brown (London and Toronto: Associated University Presses, 1991); Katharina M. Wilson (ed.), *An Encyclopedia of Continental Women Writers* (New York and London: Garland Publishing, Inc., 1991), 2 vols.; Carmen Conde, *Poesía femenina española (1950–1960)* (Barcelona: Bruguera, 1971); Patricia O'Connor, *Dramaturgas españolas de hoy: una introducción* (Madrid: Espiral Fundamentos, 1988); *Litoral femenino: literatura escrita por mujeres en la España contemporánea*, edited by Lorenzo Saval and J. García Gallego (Granada: Litoral, 1986); *On Our Own Behalf: Women's Tales from Catalonia*, edited and with an introduction and notes by Kathleen McNerney (Lincoln and London: University of Nebraska Press, 1988); *Feminist Readings on Spanish and Latin-American Literature*, ed. L. P. Condé & S. M. Hart (Lampeter: Edwin Mellen Press, 1991).

discussion of their work does not imply a negative evaluation of its quality. Gone are the days when an attempt to be all-inclusive might have been thinkable, let alone possible. The works chosen for analysis in this study were selected on the basis of the presence of one of the five structuring elements (*Bildungsroman*, the patriarchal prison, the fairy tale, sexual politics, and gender trouble) which I would suggest are recurrent themes of contemporary women's writing in Spain and the Americas. The present study has centred on the novel since this is the genre in which women's writing in the Spanish-speaking world has boomed in the modern period.

A brief look at literary scholarship on the novel in the English- and French-speaking world tends to suggest that women writers elsewhere have also favoured this genre. Various reasons for this have been proposed. Michael Danahy has argued that ever since the novel first emerged in France, 'it has been associated, mysteriously, curiously, but inevitably, with women – a desire to please and appease them as readers, honor them as subjects, and absorb their talents as writers'.[8] Henry James's view adduced to explain the wealth of gifted female novelists (novel as the domestic genre par excellence, women write novels with the noses close to the everyday texture of life) has been influential. Other critics, such as Ellen Moers, Richard Bolster and Germain Brée have extended and refined James's insight.[9] Cora Kaplan, however, has warned against an over-literal adoption of the Jamesian view of women's writing:

> If fiction has been the most successful genre for women writers it is not, as has been often suggested, because the novel makes use of the domestic scene, or the life of the feelings, or 'trivial' observations, all those things supposedly close to women's experience, but because its scene is that world of social relations, of intersubjectivity, in which the author can reconcile to some extent her speech and her silence and be the first to explore and expose her bisexuality without the threat of losing her feminine identity.[10]

[8] *The Feminization of the Novel* (Gainesville: University of Florida Press, 1991), p. 4. A similar phenomenon has occurred in Italy; women's writing has boomed in the 1980s and the most popular genre there, as elsewhere, has been the novel; see Carol M. Lazzaro-Weis, 'From Margins to Mainstream: Some Perspectives on Women and Literature in Italy in the 1980s', in *Contemporary Women Writers in Italy: A Modern Renaissance*, edited by Santo L. Aricò (Amherst: The University of Massachusetts Press, 1990), pp. 197–217.

[9] The opinions of these critics are quoted in Michael Danahy, *The Feminization of the Novel*, pp. 35–37.

[10] *Sea Changes: Essays on Culture and Feminism* (London: Verso, 1984), pp. 82–83.

Kaplan's observation goes some way to removing the limiting focus of domesticity from arguments about women's fiction. Her last (implicit) point about the importance of reaching an awareness about 'feminine identity' is one which we shall see is crucial. Kaplan's view on bisexuality, however, needs to be qualified. Though applicable in the case of a number of women writers, and particularly the work of the Spanish novelist, Esther Tusquets, and the Uruguayan-Spanish novelist, Cristina Peri Rossi (see Chapters 3 and 5), it is not applicable to all and sundry. Nevertheless, Kaplan's comments are helpful as a basis for future discussion. Her suggestion that women writers use the verbal medium as a means of reconciling 'speech and her silence' is a fruitful one.

The title of this book is taken from a passage in Hélène Cixous's article 'The Laugh of the Medusa', in which she attempts to isolate the specificity of women's writing:

> In women's speech, as in their writing, that element which never stops resonating, which, once we've been permeated by it, profoundly and imperceptibly touched by it, retains the power of moving us – that element is the song: first music from the first voice of love which is alive in every woman. Why this privileged relationship with the voice? Because no woman stockpiles as many defenses for countering the drives as does a man. You don't build walls around yourself, you don't forego pleasure as 'wisely' as he. Even if phallic mystification has generally contaminated good relationships, a woman is never far from 'mother' (I mean outside her role functions: the 'mother' as nonname and as source of goods). There is always within her at least a little of that good mother's milk. She writes in white ink.[11]

In this passage, as in the rest of her text, Cixous is searching for metaphors to define feminine writing which, here as elsewhere, eludes her grasp. In their 'motherly' role, as Cixous suggests, the female writer functions as 'nonname' and simultaneously 'source of goods'; thus she gives of herself through writing and yet also loses her linguistic identity, her name, as a result. The 'white ink' with which Cixous identifies women's writing is based metaphorically on a mother's milk, which can only be gender-specific. Yet to write in white ink also means that the female writer is doomed to the curse of invisibility, that invisibility which Virginia Woolf also proposed as the hallmark of women's writing. In a celebrated passage from *A Room of One's Own* (1929) Woolf imagines

---

[11] 'The Laugh of the Medusa', *New French Feminisms: An Anthology*, edited by Elaine Marks and Isabelle de Courtivron (Brighton: The Harvester Press, 1981), pp. 245–64 (p. 251).

the life of Shakespeare's sister, whom she gives the name of Judith. Unlike her brother William, Judith remained at home, she was not sent to school, and had no chance of learning grammar and logic. As Woolf continues, perhaps 'she scribbled some pages up in an apple loft on the sly, but was careful to hide them or set fire to them'.[12] Subsequently she tried to live out her dream of acting in a theatre but became pregnant with the actor-manager's child and, as Woolf imaginatively concludes, 'killed herself one winter's night and lies buried at some cross-roads where the omnibuses now stop outside the Elephant and Castle'.[13] Judith Shakespeare's vision of the world never found its way to the printed page. It remained, Woolf suggests, an epitome of women's writing, as an invisible body within the literary canon, white on white, as opposed to the black on white of her brother's work.[14]

Woolf's point is well taken, though it applies more specifically to those writers whose works appeared before the Renaissance of women's writing, namely (in Spain and Latin America, at least), before 1936. Since that time the visibility of women's writing has increased to a degree which no doubt would have been unimaginable to Virginia Woolf.[15] And yet, as we shall see, the sexual fix has not disappeared simply because a greater quantity of women's writing was published in the 1980s than appeared in the 1920s. Many of the writers studied in this volume clearly view the sexual problematic in very similar terms to Woolf and, in emperor's-new-clothes mode, they have pointed to patriarchy as the main obstacle getting in the way of paradise.

[12] *A Room of One's Own* (London: Hogarth, 1942), p. 71.

[13] Woolf, *A Room of One's Own*, p. 73.

[14] Woolf's point about the invisibility of women's literature is amply illustrated by Christine Blattersby who traces the 'sexual apartheid' which links genius and creativity to masculinity; see *Gender and Genius: Towards a Feminist Aesthetics* (Bloomington and Indianapolis: Indiana University Press, 1989).

[15] For further discussion of this matter, see Stephen M. Hart, *The Other Scene: Psychoanalytic Readings in Modern Spanish and Latin-American Literature* (Boulder, Colorado: Society of Spanish and Spanish American Studies, 1992), pp. 63–85.

I

THE NOVEL OF DEVELOPMENT

As Kathleen McNerney reminds us, world literature 'is replete with novels of male adolescence, *Bildungsromans*, picaresque tales, and the like. But until recently, few books have dealt with the female counterparts and even few can claim the authenticity of having being written by women'.[1] But does the female *Bildungsroman* simply exchange the sex of its protagonist while retaining the same plot structure, character motivation and life experience of the male original? The answer to this question must be no, since female development, in a structural as well as psychical sense, differs from male development. Freud's essay, 'Über die weibliche Sexualität' (1931), is helpful in this regard. Arguing that the pre-Oedipus phase experienced by women is longer than for men and overriding the objection that this undermines his theory of the universal applicability of the Oedipus complex, Freud proposes that women develop later to the Oedipus complex after passing through an earlier period governed by the negative complex ('negativen Komplex').[2] Yet Freud's text does not totally *illuminate* this issue. When describing the pre-Oedipal stage of female development, for example, Freud compares the young girl's attachment to the mother to the discovery of the Minoan-Mycean civilization *behind* the civilization of Greece ('der minoisch-mykenischen Kultur hinter der griechischen'; p. 519), which graphically suggests to what extent the female operates as a Dark Continent within his text.[3] It does not surprise us, thus, when we

[1] *On Our Own Behalf: Women's Tales from Catalonia*, edited by Kathleen McNerney, p. 3.
[2] *Sigmund Freud. Werke aus den Jahren 1925–1931* (London: Imago, 1948), p. 518.
[3] The metaphor of archeological discovery is an apt one. Freud often saw himself as a discover in archeological terms; he discovered the Unconscious in the same way that the excavations in contemporary Egypt revealed the hidden historical past of the Pharoahs. Yet Freud's metaphor also reveals, perhaps inadvertently, to what extent the discourse of psychoanalysis saw femininity as an unknown, hidden from the present because buried in the past, as a discourse which could only be known

9

find Freud concluding by giving up any hope of establishing a strict parallelism between male and female patterns of sexual development: 'Alle Erwartungen eines glatten Parallelismus zwischen männlicher und weiblicher Sexualentwicklung haben wir ja längst aufgegeben'.[4]

Since, according to the Freudian model at least, female development differs from male development, it is only to be expected that the notion of the *Bildungsroman* needs to be revised when applied to a series of formation-novels written by women in the twentieth century. The *Bildungsroman*, literally the 'self-cultivation novel', is in origin a masculinist genre which flourished in Germany from the end of the eighteenth century until the beginning of the twentieth. W. H. Bruford provides the following definition:

> In a typical *Bildungsroman* we are shown the development of an intelligent and open-minded young man in a complex, modern society without generally accepted values; he gradually comes to decide, through the influence of friends, teachers and chance acquaintances as well as the ripening of his own intellectual and perhaps artistic capacities and interests as his experience in these fields grows, what is best in life for him and how he intends to pursue it. (. . .) the hero meets well contrasted friends in different social milieux, and of course falls in love with more than one kind of girl, some appealing to his senses and some to his mind. The novel

---

fragmentarily. Freud was clearly aware that his views would not meet with universal approval. As he wrote in a footnote: 'Mann kann vorhersen, dass die Feministen unter den Männern, aber auch unsere weiblichen Analytiker mit diesen Ausführungen nicht einverstanden sein werden. Sie dürften kaum die Einwendung zurückhalten, solche Lehren stammen aus dem ''Männlichkeitskomplex'' des Mannes und sollen dazu dienen, seiner angeborenen Neigung zur Herabsetzung und Unterdrückung des Weibes eine theoretische Rechtfertigung zu schaffen. Allein eine solche psycho-analytische Argumentation mahnt in diesem Falle, wie so häufig, an den berühmten ''Stock mit zwei Enden'' Dostojewskis' (p. 523, n. 1). Freud's reference to the 'knife that cuts both ways' is intriguing since Dostoevsky's image offers little protection for Freud's own theoretical edifice. The 'knife that cuts both ways' could also be seen as the branch of feminism which has turned Freud's argument back on itself. Freud clearly did not see his rather unbalanced view of female sexuality as problematic, since he relegates discussion of this point to a footnote. It has, however, proved to be one of Freud's most contentious areas, as witnessed by recent books by, *inter alia*, Kate Millett, Juliet Mitchell, Jacqueline Rose, Hélène Cixous, and Luce Irigaray. Ernest Jones was one of the first psychoanalysts to question Freud's views of female sexuality. The Freud-Jones debate has become an apple of discord to which many feminists have returned. Among them should be mentioned Cixous's essay 'Sorties' and Michèle Montrelay's 'Inquiry into Femininity'. See English translation in, respectively, *New French Feminisms: An Anthology*, edited by Elaine Marks and Isabelle de Courtivron, pp. 90–98; and *French Feminist Thought: A Reader*, edited by Toril Moi (Oxford: Basil Blackwell, 1987), pp. 227–49.

[4] *Sigmund Freud. Werke aus den Jahren 1925–1931*, p. 519.

usually ends when he has attained to some degree of maturity, and what he does with his life later is not revealed to us.[5]

The idea of a woman being the author and creator of her own history was, in the nineteenth century at least, seen as less natural than that of a man. When she did write, she tended to see the world through masculinist spectacles, as Cecilia Böhl von Faber's pseudonym, Fernán *Caballero* (my emphasis), assertively suggests. In Germany, for example, during the period 1790–1914, women *did* write autobiographies, it is true, but as in the rest of Europe, they were constrained by the masculinist perspective of the genre. As Katherine Goodman suggests, the female autobiographer rode through history as if through an 'economically deprived village, peering into the lighted windows as she passed, encased and protected by her carriage'.[6] Thus, as Goodman continues, for the major part of the nineteenth century, 'it was only from the vantage point of a non-harmonious concept of "self" that women were able to articulate a "self" at all' (*Dis/Closures*, p. 210). Goodman's model cannot, however, be applied willy-nilly to the Hispanic context, since a comparable autobiographical tradition (whether male or female) was not then in existence in the Hispanic world; neither Spain nor Latin America, for example, produced contemporary works to match Rousseau's *Les Confessions* (1782) in France or Goethe's *Dichtung und Wahrheit* (1812) in Germany.[7] One point made by Goodman (see above), however, can be justifiably retained: the feminine text, in Spain and Latin America as elsewhere, only achieved expression through its vision of the disharmony of identity. The female version of

[5] W. H. Bruford, *The German Tradition of Self-Cultivation: 'Bildung' from Humboldt to Thomas Mann* (Cambridge: C.U.P., 1975), pp. 29–30.

[6] *Dis/Closures: Women's Autobiographies in Germany Between 1790 and 1914* (New York: Peter Lang, 1986), p. 209.

[7] Two recent studies by Biruté Ciplijauskaité and Sylvia Molloy go some way towards tracing the development of female autobiography in Spain and Latin America. The helpful first chapter of Biruté Ciplijauskaité's *La novela femenina contemporánea*, pp. 13–33, sketches out some basic guidelines, although the majority of the nineteenth-century primary texts Ciplijauskaité cites are examples of novelized autobiography rather than genuine autobiographical texts. Sylvia Molloy's excellent study, *At Face Value: Autobiographical Writing in Spanish America* (Cambridge: C.U.P., 1991), provides an insightful reading of the autobiographical tradition from the nineteenth century to the present day in Spanish America. The work of female autobiographers, such as Condesa de Merlin (pp. 85–94), Victoria Ocampo (pp. 55–75), and Norah Lange (pp. 125–36) are, however, not discussed in separation from the male autobiographers. For additional notes on female religious autobiography in Spain, see Electra Arenal and Stacey Schlau, 'Strategems of the Strong, Strategems of the Weak: Autobiographical Prose of the Seventeenth-Century Hispanic Convent', *TSWL*, 9:1 (1990), 25–42.

the *Bildungsroman*, thus, far from seeking to express a phallic self-identity, sought to embody the traces of feminine absence.

Criticism has already gone some way towards establishing the basis for looking at the modern female formation novel. Two important recent studies have underlined that the notion of development in the female *Bildungsroman* more often takes the form of accomodation to or withdrawal from the world, unlike the male model.[8] Criticism on the Spanish female *Bildungsroman* has reached similar conclusions; Emilie Bergmann, in her analysis of five Spanish novels points to how they each in different ways 'illuminate questions of femaleness, self-definition and maturity in a repressive society undergoing its own processes of change'.[9] In the present chapter I intend to draw on the valuable analysis provided by Bergmann's essay but I will be focussing on three novels, two of which appear in Bergmann's article – *Nada* and *La plaça del Diamant* – and one other, Lispector's *Perto do coração selvagem*. In each of these three novels, as we shall see, the female character experiences 'lostness' as a result of the absence of a mother-daughter relationship. Andrea in *Nada* is an orphan; Natàlia in *La plaça del Diamant* has recently lost her mother, and Joana in *Perto do coração selvagem* never knew hers. All three novels, thus, echo the archetypal framework of the novel of female growth in which, as various critics have suggested, the woman's initiation involves withdrawal rather than action in a masculinist sense (see footnote 8). This should not lead us, however, to expect these novels to be lame justifications of failed lives; they are anything but this. *Nada*, *La plaça del Diamant* and *Perto do coração selvagem* vigorously expose the masculinist lies which keep the world in place, a process which is as painful for others as it is for the protagonists, as we shall see.

[8] In their introduction to *The Voyage In*, Elizabeth Abel, Marinanne Hirsch, and Elizabeth Langland argue that novels of female development 'typically substitute inner concentration for active accommodation, rebellion, or withdrawal'; 'Introduction', *The Voyage In: Fictions of Female Development*, edited by Abel, Hirsch and Langland (Hanover and London: University Press of New England, 1983), pp. 3–19 (p. 8). Likewise Annis Pratt has underlined that in the female *Bildungsroman* the woman's initiation typically is 'less a self-determined progression *towards* maturity than a regression *from* full participation in adult life'; see her study, *Archetypal Patterns in Women's Fiction* (Brighton: The Harvester Press, 1982), p. 36.

[9] 'Reshaping the Canon: Intertextuality in Spanish Novels of Female Development', *ALEC*, 12 (1987), 141–57 (p. 142). The five novels are: *Nada* by Carmen Laforet, *Primera memoria* by Ana María Matute, *Julia* by Ana María Moix, *El cuarto de atrás* by Carmen Martín Gaite, and *La plaça del Diamant* by Mercè Rodoreda. For a discussion of *Primera memoria* and *El cuarto de atrás*, see below Chapter III.

CARMEN LAFORET: *NADA*

Critics agree that *Nada* (1944) by Carmen Laforet (1921: Spain) is a *Bildungsroman*. The protagonist of Laforet's novel, Andrea, experiences a traumatic year going to university in war-ravaged Barcelona while living with her relatives, and, as Janet Pérez points out, 'loses many adolescent illusions and matures socially and emotionally in the process'.[10] Again, like the typical *Bildungsroman*, Laforet's novel depicts the protagonist within 'a complex, modern society without generally accepted values' (see Bruford, quoted above). These two histories – the personal and the national – are closely knit throughout *Nada*, as we shall see. The most visible aspect of the 'complex, modern' society in which Andrea matures is its dire poverty; *Nada* faithfully describes the hunger which characterised the so-called 'noche negra' of the early Franco years, when Spain was without foreign exchange, aid or credit, and when dried leaves and potato-peelings took the place of tobacco, and crushed acorns were used as a substitute for coffee.[11] Andrea's own experience of life in post-war Barcelona seems to confirm this bleak picture, although it is important to bear in mind that history is reflected in *Nada* not in the grand mythical terms common in the novels of contemporary male writers, but through a personal lens.[12] Andrea describes herself as suffering from 'un hambre que a fuerza de ser crónica llegué casi a no sentirla' (p. 144).[13] As she ominously points out later on: 'Hay quien se ha vuelto loco de hambre' (p. 263), a theme evident in Rodoreda's contemporaneous *La plaça del Diamant* (see below).

The world depicted in Laforet's novel is mediated by repression and innuendo. Overt sexuality was taboo during Franco's regime, and in keeping with this, a brooding, sexual repression pervades *Nada*.[14]

---

[10] *Contemporary Women Writers of Spain*, p. 119. Roberta Johnson argues in a similar vein that the portrayal of 'the crucial stage of development in the life of the adolescent' is the lynch-pin of *Nada*; see *Carmen Laforet* (Boston: Twayne, 1981), p. 48.

[11] Edouard de Blaye, *Franco and the Politics of Spain* (Harmondsworth: Penguin, 1976), pp. 169–70.

[12] Roberta Johnson, 'Personal and Public History in Laforet's Long Novels', in *Feminine Concerns in Contemporary Spanish Fiction by Women*, pp. 43–53.

[13] Edition used throughout is *Nada* (Barcelona: Destino, 1949), 7th edition.

[14] In the early days of Franco's regime, as Blaye suggests, 'the word "leg" was forbidden, even in football matches or when discussing fractures, so as to avoid suggestiveness'. During the period 1940–45 it was not permissible to refer in the gossip columns to the honeymoons or wedding-trips of newly-married couples; see *Franco and the Politics of Spain*, p. 481.

Sexuality thereby becomes each character's unmentioned and unmentionable life; it lies submerged in the text, unable to speak its secret, like that obsession identified by Andrea as existing in the inhabitants of the Arribau household 'a la que pocas veces aludían directamente' (p. 70).[15] To underline its taboo function, sexuality is often expressed in *Nada* via the trope of incest. Román, given half the chance, would seduce his niece, Andrea. Through Gloria's conversation with the grandmother, we know that Román also once had an affair with Gloria (this when Gloria was already pregnant at the time with her husband's child); Andrea's dream provides a subconscious confirmation of this (p. 58). The relationship which most approximates the figure of incest, however, is the growing sexual attraction between Román and Ena since the former once had an affair with Ena's mother, as revealed in the *agnorisis* scene at the end of the novel (pp. 276–78).

The most grotesque sexual relationship narrated in *Nada* is between Román and Antonia, the maid. As Lucía Fox-Lockert points out, she is 'Román's woman; she adores him and he treats the dog Trueno as if it were their child'.[16] Antonia is frequently compared to the dog: 'Los ojos del animal relucían amarillos mirando a la mujer y los ojos de ella brillaban también chicos y oscuros' (p. 66). She identifies in an erotic sense with Trueno when its ears are being stroked by Román: 'Román mientras hablaba acariciaba las orejas del perro, que entornaba los ojos de placer. La criada en la puerta los acechaba; se secaba las manos en el delantal – aquellas manos aporradas, con las uñas negras – sin saber lo que hacía y miraba, segura, insistente, las manos en las orejas del perro' (p. 69). Antonia's self-projection into the figure of the dog explains why

---

[15] This sense of an obsession which the characters of the novel never allude to directly, is applicable not only to sexuality, but also to the main themes of *Nada*, such as repression, hunger, history, the Civil War. In the harbour, an image of occlusion, the destroyed hulls of sunken boats are half-visible (p. 148). There are veiled allusions to the two brothers' various activities during the war in the reported conversation between Gloria and the grandmother (pp. 46–56). While they both fought on the side of the republicans, Román was a traitor and gave secrets to the nationalists (p. 49). Likewise, Pons shows Andrea a church in Barcelona of which part was destroyed during the war (p. 158). We glimpse traces of a past narrative, but we are never privy to the whole story. In an interview with Geraldine C. Nichols, Laforet speaks of how in *Nada* she was unable for political reasons to tell the whole truth about what was going on in Barcelona in the post-war years, for this would have involved denouncing some of her *catalanista* friends; as she says, 'no se podía contar entonces'; *Escribir, espacio propio: Laforet, Matute, Moix, Tusquets, Riera y Roig por sí mismas* (Minneapolis, Minnesota: Institute for the Study of Ideologies and Literature, 1989), p. 139. This would tend to confirm the notion that Laforet's text operates obliquely, hinting at its narrative rather than unfolding it completely before the reader's eyes.

[16] *Women Novelists in Spain and Spanish America*, p. 74.

she takes it so personally when Román bites the dog's ears (p. 219). There are indications that her relationship with Román is purely sexual. When she discovers Román's dead body, for example, her first reaction is to say to the dog: 'Trueno, hijito mío, ya no tienes padre. . .' (p. 287), as if to suggest the dog is the fruit of their carnal relationship.

That incest is the novel's favoured trope to figuralize sexuality is suggested by its use in some incongruous contexts. Angustias, for example, had an affair with her boss, Jerónimo Sanz, when he was living temporarily in the Arribau household, thereby stressing the incest motif even when it would not be obviously present. The girl that Pons drops Andrea for happens to be his cousin, Nuria (p. 231). The family unit, thus, becomes the space in which sexual relations are played out. Incest is the ghost sitting in the wings of the family unit which, in turn, comes to stand as a symbol of Spain's isolationism during the 1940s, cut off from the rest of the world and thrown back on its own resources.[17]

Any empiric reading of the novel would tend to suggest that an innocent eighteen-year-old girl like Andrea is likely to be mentally unprepared for her sojourn in the Arribau household. True to the spirit of the *Bildungsroman*, Andrea is faced with deciding 'through the influence of friends [Gloria], teachers [the grandmother, Román] and chance acquaintances [Ena]' what is 'best in life' for her, to paraphrase and desexualize Bruford's definition. More particularly, she has to choose between two life-patterns which are: political and sexual conformism *versus* non-conformism. Angustias, who is based in name and character on one of the embittered sisters in Lorca's *La casa de Bernarda Alba* (1936), encapsulates the discourse of Francoist conformism; she represses her sexuality (becoming a nun when her affair with Jerónimo Sanz backfires), accepts life as punishment, and wills retributions on the head of others. Andrea, not surprisingly, finds Angustias overbearing; she is terrified by 'aquella mirada de Angustias' (p. 102). Angustias accuses Andrea of immoral Republicanism: 'Parece que hayas vivido suelta en zona roja y no en un convento de monjas durante la guerra. Aun Gloria tiene más disculpas que tú en sus ansias de emancipación y desorden' (p. 106). Emancipation (feminist or otherwise) becomes 'disorder' according to Angustias's world vision. She feels happier when

---

[17] During World War II, Spain attempted to remain uninvolved in the conflict, and gained the wrath of both the Allies and Hitler's regime because of its neutrality. The attitude of the nations of the world did not improve after the conclusion of hostilities. On 12 December 1946 the United Nations passed a resolution 'recommending that ambassadors be withdrawn from Madrid and economic sanctions applied against Spain'; see Edouard de Blaye, *Franco and the Politics of Spain*, p. 164. To make matters worse, Spain was excluded from the Marshall Plan in 1948.

Andrea is submissive (p. 32), and at one point expresses a psychotic desire to control Andrea at all costs: '¡Hubiera querido matarte cuando pequeña antes de dejarte crecer así!' (p. 107). This is clearly the discourse of Francoism – *better dead than red*. Angustias merely pays lip-service to the church; she attends mass in order to inspect the clothes of the church-goers, as Gloria suggests (p. 111), and also in order to see her secret lover, Jerónimo. Her life-style is a thinly veiled allegory of the repressive, hypocritical ideology underwriting Franco's regime. The second life-option available to Andrea, non-conformism, is epitomised by Román, a bohemian musician, and Gloria, a 'wild woman' who often spends the night out and is not averse to the idea of sleeping with her brother-in-law. Andrea clearly feels more attracted to this non-conformist style of life; she often listens to Román playing the violin, and she confides in Gloria.[18] Ena certainly sees Andrea as a non-conformist; like her uncle, Ena says, Andrea has 'un átomo de locura' (p. 170).

Thus far, Andrea's personal history can be interpreted as a female version of the male *Bildungsroman*. Yet, there are specific points in the novel when Andrea's life-path is revealed as unmistakably gendered. The illusions with which she arrives in Barcelona are seen as those typically entertained by a young girl, which are variously referred to as a 'carga de sentimentalismo' (p. 41), and 'desbocado romanticismo' (p. 117). The male members of the Arribau household see it as their duty to divest Andrea of these illusions as soon as possible. As Román says to her: 'no te forjes novelas' (p. 40).[19] Many of these expectations re-emerge when Andrea is invited to a party at Pons's house, conjuring up a fairy-tale atmosphere: 'la palabra baile evocaba un emocionante sueño de trajes de noche y suelos brillantes, que me habían dejado la primera lectura de Cenicienta' (p. 209). The story of Cinderella has a special relevance to Andrea's story. Like Cinderella, she is bullied at home; Angustias and

---

[18] It is important to point out that these two life-options are, by and large, middle-class options. Angustias's social class is suggested clearly when she tells Andrea rather haughtily that she must not wander around Barcelona as if she were a 'criada' (p. 60). Román, despite his bohemian life-style, is also middle-class, since he is attempting to eke out a living as a musician. There are two clear pointers to the social class of the calle Aribau residence; they can afford the luxury of a maid, and, unlike the inhabitants of the working-class district who speak Catalan (p. 186), the family members speak Castilian.

[19] Andrea expects to find happiness in her life but, rather like Isidora in *La desheredada*, her illusions are gradually punctured as the novel progresses. After being chided for giving away her handkerchief, Andrea remarks: 'Pensé que cualquier alegría de mi vida tenía que compensarla algo desagradable. Que quizás esto era una ley fatal' (p. 77). For a discussion of Galdós's novel, see Eamon Rodgers, 'Galdós's *La desheredada* and Naturalism', *BHS*, 45 (1968), 285–98; and Frank Durand, 'The Reality of Illusion: *La desheredada*', *MLN*, 89 (1974), 191–204.

Gloria are like the two ugly sisters (although Gloria is not in fact ugly). Her grandmother is like a fairy god-mother, although her wishes (or, in her case, her prayers during mass) never come true.[20] When Pons calls her on the morning of the party, the image of Cinderella reappears: 'El sentimiento de ser esperada y querida me hacía despertar mil instintos de mujer; una emoción como de triunfo, un deseo de ser alabada, admirada, de sentirme como la Cenicienta del cuento, princesa por unas horas, después de un largo incógnito' (p. 222). Her expectations, however, are rudely dashed when Pons eventually admits at the party that he is in love with his cousin. The fairy-tale motif is enhanced by the use of Hollywood motifs. Immediately before the break-up, Pons's cousin was seen wearing 'una sonrisa forzada de estrella de cine' (p. 230). Andrea subsequently experiences incongruence at being the protagonist 'de tan ridícula escena' (p. 230). Having left the party, she feels once more as if she has been transported into a literary world of tragic passion: 'Había algo aterrador en la magnificencia clásica de aquel cielo aplastado sobre la calle silenciosa. Algo que me hacía sentirme pequeña y apretada entre fuerzas cósmicas como el héroe de una tragedia griega' (p. 232). But Andrea feels out-of-place, thrust into a drama for which she had not learned her lines: 'Unos seres nacen para vivir, otros para trabajar, otros para mirar la vida. Yo tenía un pequeño y ruin papel de espectadora' (p. 233). By the end of the novel, true to the spirit if not the letter of the *Bildungsroman*, Andrea has achieved a deeper understanding of life, and specifically, a feminine comprehension of lack, since the life-experience of love did not happen. The rite of passage experienced by Andrea, as the use of the Cinderella motif suggests, is, thus, specifically feminine.

An 'Images-of-Woman' study of *Nada* tends to confirm that 'desengaño' is the trope governing the formation of female personality. The life-options open to women as presented by the novel involve either marriage or the convent (p. 104). Gloria's experience suggests that an attempt to escape this dual limitation is doomed from the outset; she is subject to verbal and physical abuse from her husband, and at one stage is thrown fully clothed into the shower. Even Román gangs up on her as well; he offers Juan his gun in case he ever wants to shoot her (p. 136). Women are presented as second-class citizens in the novel. One of Andrea's dates, Gerardo, for example, states baldly that he did not believe in female intelligence (p. 147). Women share this patriarchal view of their own worth. Thus, Ena's mother describes her dismay when

---

[20] For further discussion of the fairy-tale elements see David William Foster, '*Nada*, de Carmen Laforet, ejemplo de neorromance en la novela contemporánea', *RHM*, 32:1–2 (1966), 43–55.

she found out she had given birth to a daughter: 'Yo sentía
remordimientos por haberla hecho nacer de mí, por haberla condenado a
llevar mi herencia. Así, empecé a llorar con una debilitada tristeza de que
por mi culpa aquella cosa gimiente pudiese llegar a ser una mujer algún
día' (p. 248). Because of her sex, Ena's mother feels that her daughter is
like a pitiful beggar (p. 248). Andrea, though of the younger generation,
is sympathetic to these views: 'era fácil para mí entender este idioma de
sangre, dolor y creación que empieza con la misma sustancia cuando se
es mujer' (p. 249). Because of their banishment from the syntax of
civilian life, women are forced to adopt a discourse of madness. The
grandmother is mad, according to Gloria (p. 106). Gloria complains
towards the end of the novel that Juan has tried to kill her, and she tries to
enlist Andrea's help in having him confined to a mental asylum. Even the
objects within the house seem to be tinged by madness: 'La locura
sonreía en los grifos torcidos' (p. 18); 'el aire está lleno de gritos'
(p. 39). Madness was the only language available to women in post-civil-
war Spain, apart from the non-languages of silence or invisibility. As
Adrienne Rich reminds us, in a world 'where language and naming are
power, silence is oppression, violence'.[21]

The life-path open to women as presented in the course of *Nada*,
therefore, involves marriage, the convent, or madness (which is not
really a choice at all). On one level, Andrea's choice is linked to national
destiny since the house she lives in allegorizes the Spanish nation through
the motif of incest which, as we have seen, symbolizes a Spain forced to
turn back in on itself. By implication, thus, her choice echoes the national
destiny. However, in the final analysis, Andrea refuses to allow this
national allegory to become her own. While throughout the novel she
seems to waver between the two available options of conformism or non-
conformism, Andrea ultimately chooses neither, as the conclusion of the
novel demonstrates. As Celita Lamar Morris suggests, she 'prefers to
live in a world without structure, a world of nothingness, than to remain
enclosed in the prison that Spanish society is for a thinking, independent
woman'.[22] Andrea, thus, declines to immerse her feminine identity
within the master narrative of Spain's national destiny.

Nada is a curious novel in that, despite the overwhelming pessimism of
Andrea's life-experience, it has an unpredictably positive ending hinted
at by Ena's letter.[23] Like the archetypal *Bildungsroman*, *Nada* begins

[21] *On Lies, Secrets and Silence: Selected Prose. 1966–78* (New York: Norton, 1979),
p. 204.
[22] 'Carmen Laforet's *Nada* as an Expression of Woman's Self-Determination', *LF*, 1:2
(1975), 40–47 (p. 46).
[23] As Margaret Jones has pointed out, the resolution of the novel is not exactly a happy

with the main protagonist leaving the family home to seek his/her fortune elsewhere. But Andrea's experience of life is so limiting (marriage, the convent or madness) that she in effect refuses to make a commitment to follow a particular life-path, thereby deconstructing the completion element necessary in any male *Bildungsroman*. *Nada* draws attention to the fact that the male *Bildungsroman*, with its emphasis on the 'ripening' of 'intellectual and perhaps artistic capacities' (see above, Bruford) simply does not apply to the life-story of a woman in Spain in the 1940s given the limited options open to her; the only route to personal freedom for Andrea is through the deferral of her life-decision, embodied in Ena's letter. Andrea's story demonstrates that life-experience is not something to be manipulated at will by women, but something thrust upon them. A similar set of circumstances shapes the life of the protagonist of another *Bildungsroman* based in Barcelona, Rodoreda's *La plaça del Diamant*, as we shall see.

MERCE RODOREDA: *LA PLAÇA DEL DIAMANT*

La plaça del Diamant (1962) by Mercè Rodoreda (1909–1984: Spain) is, as Arthur Terry points out, 'perhaps the finest work of fiction to have appeared since the Civil War'.[24] Critics have variously praised its 'human', 'believable' and 'epic' qualities.[25] Like Laforet's *Nada*, Rodoreda's novel has a female protagonist and is set in Barcelona during the same time period (1930s–1940s). But here the similarity ends, for *Nada* concludes with the protagonist barely having left college, while the protagonist of Rodoreda's novel, Natàlia, gets married, has children, loses her husband as a result of the Civil War, remarries for the children's sake, and is middle-aged by the end of the novel. For this reason *La plaça del Diamant* is closer to the spirit of the *Bildungsroman* in that it plots the life of an individual from puberty to middle age and shows the protagonist as having achieved a deeper understanding of life's ironies by the end of the narrative. The knowledge that Natàlia has achieved, as we shall see, is quintessentially feminine in that it involves a knowledge of dispossession. Natàlia is shown to be twice removed from

---

ending since it is more 'a consecration of individuality and thus a new beginning'; 'Dialectical Movement as Feminist Technique in the Works of Carmen Laforet', *Studies in Honor of Gerald E. Wade* (Madrid: José Porrúa Turanzas, 1979), pp. 109–20 (p. 120).

[24] *Catalan Literature* (London: Benn, 1972), p. 117.

[25] Joan Fuster, *Literatura catalana contemporània* (Barcelona: Curial, 1978), pp. 378–80.

the corridors of power, first for being a woman, and second for being Catalan.

Like Andrea in *Nada*, Natàlia has lost her mother. Her reference in the opening chapter of *La plaça del Diamant* to 'La meva mare morta feia anys i sense poder-me aconsellar' (p. 20), sets the scene for Natàlia's later experience of 'lostness'.[26] As her creator said of her in the 1982 prologue to the novel, 'té de semblant a mi el fet de sentir-se perduda al mig del món' (p. 7). Natàlia is never, it seems, in control of her life; she reacts to rather than creating events. Thus, she is chosen by Quimet in the Plaça del Diamant, and she accepts his offer of marriage. She has no say in the matter of where they will live, whether they should keep the doves which proliferate in their flat, or even whether they should have children. Similarly, when Quimet dies in the Civil War, she is offered marriage by Antoni. Throughout the novel, therefore, it seems that life happens to Natàlia. When she is faced by important decisions, we are not privy as readers to the the decision-making process. Almost every decision is presented as if it were a *fait accompli*. Natàlia, it appears, is not provided with an inner arena of debate; she only exists in the public sphere, the space which belongs to everyone, the Plaça del Diamant in Barcelona which inspires the action of the novel.

The principal reason why Natàlia stands outside the corridors of power is her womanhood. Her home life had not been happy; Natàlia describes in Chapter III, for example, how her parents spent many years arguing and then just as many years without speaking a word to each other (p. 34). This life of silence leads her to compare her former life at home to that of cat: 'Vivia com deu viure un gat: amunt i avall amb la cua baixa, amb la cua dreta, ara és l'hora de la feina, ara és l'hora de la son; amb la diferència que un gat no ha de trebellar per viure' (p. 34). The use of the cat as a symbol of female identity has, of course, a long (if rather mixed) history. Here it appears that the image of a cat is used to stress Natàlia's submissiveness and her inability to communicate with her elders. It also alludes to a benchmark of Natàlia's character, namely, her uncertainty about her identity. As this passage continues: 'A casa vivíem sense paraules i les coses que jo duia per dintre em feian por perquè no sabia si eren meves' (p. 34). Her identity as a woman leads to the destruction of innerness, to the lack of an inner being, and its corollary, a silent acceptance of life as it is.

If one were to extend and define what is meant by the 'life as it is' as presented by the novel, one would need to conclude that it is patriarchal.

---

[26] All references are to the 27th edition, *La plaça del Diamant* (Barcelona: Club Editor, 1983).

The memories of her childhood at home as they appear in Chapter III are sparked off by her awareness of the way Quimet treats her. In this particular scene, Quimet and Cintet are discussing where Quimet and his future wife will be living, and where they can buy a motorcycle. Natàlia comments laconically: 'Enraonaven com si jo no hi fos' (p. 34). This is the destiny of womanhood, to be seen and not heard. Natàlia's relationship with her husband, she soon comes to realise, is a repeat version of her relationship with her father. In the scene quoted above, he completely ignores Natàlia, and when he leaves with Cintet, Natàlia overhears them laughing at her expense: 'vaig sentir que en Cintet li deia, no sé pas d'on l'has treta, tan bufona. . . I vaig sentir el riure d'en Quimet, ha, ha, ha. . .' (pp. 34–35). There is no suggestion here that Quimet is not in love with Natàlia, or indeed that Natàlia is not in love with him. Natàlia does not question Quimet's intentions after hearing his scorn. These words *do* show how love within a patriarchal society conforms to, and indeed confirms, the underlying patterns of patriarchy. As a type of displaced revenge, Natàlia throws a ball of paper at the boy next door: 'El fill dels veïns, que feia el soldat, prenia la fresca. Vaig fer una boleta de paper, vaig tirar-l'hi, i em vaig amagar' (p. 35). Even when committing an act of rebellion, Natàlia hides afterwards, thereby swapping her silence for her invisibility, an exchange which is not really an exchange at all, since both are characteristics of the female according to patriarchy. As Virginia Woolf suggests, 'the concept of absence and its related semantic notions – invisibility, silence, inaudibility, etc. – become the distinctive feature of woman's otherness, the locus of a woman's experience in a patriarchal society'.[27]

There are many indications throughout the novel that Quimet is patriarchal-minded. Not long after the marriage, for example, Natàlia is given a long sermon by him:

> em va dir que si volia ser la seva dona habia de començar per trobar bé to el que ell trovaba bé. Va fer-me un gran sermó sobre l'home i la dona i els drets de l'un i els drets de l'altre i quan el vaig poder tallar vaig preguntar-li:
> – I si una cosa no m'agrada de cap de les maneres?
> – T'ha d'agradar, perquè tu no hi entens. (p. 27)

Quimet's dominance is revealed in a grotesque way when he forces Natàlia to admit to something that she has not done – talking to her

---

[27] Nelly Furman, '*A Room of One's Own*: Reading Absence', *Woman's Language and Style*, edited by Douglas Butturff and Edmund L. Epstein (Akron, Ohio: University of Akron, 1978), pp. 99–105 (p. 103).

previous boyfriend, Pere – and then makes her kneel before him in the middle of the street, in what one critic has called a scene of 'psychological terrorism', in order to beg for forgiveness (p. 40).[28] This incisive portrayal of jealousy is all the more shocking since it shows Natàlia prepared to accept humiliation for what she has not done, setting the tone for much of her life, which will be characterised by 'systematic alienation'.[29]

Chapter VIII provides a good insight into gender relations. This chapter, as Rodoreda has pointed out, is based on Bernat Metge's 'Descripció de la donzella', itself a lengthy description of women's vices, their vanity, hypocrisy, concupiscence, avarice, ignorance, coupled with their expertise in robbing and deceiving men.[30] Rodoreda reverses the strategy of this misogynous document and provides a distinctly unflattering character-description of Quimet. Perhaps the most telling detail is his interest in making a chair, which he grandly calls a 'cadira d'home', to symbolise his authority. This chapter also provides some insight into the way Natàlia's mind works, especially her fear of the other sex:

> Les dones, deien, moren partides. . . La feina ja comença quan es casen. I si no s'han ben partit, la llevadora les acaba de partir amb ganivet o a cops de vidre d'ampolla i ja queden així per sempre, o estripades o cosides, i per aixó les casades es cansen més aviat quan han d'estar dretes. (p. 63)

This passage – in a humourous way – conjures up the atmosphere of the fairy tale as a backdrop for Natàlia's first sexual experience. The fairy-

---

[28] Kathleen McNerney, 'A Feminist Literary Renaissance in Catalonia', in *Feminine Concerns in Contemporary Spanish Fiction by Women*, pp. 124–33 (p. 128).

[29] The phrase is Joan Triadú's. He describes Colometa's relationship with her husband as 'una mena d'alienació sistemàtica'; Quimet is 'l'home, el marit i l'amo de la seva vida'; '*La plaça del Diamant*, de Mercè Rodoreda', in *Guia de literatura catalana contemporània*, edited by Jordi Castellanos (Barcelona: Edicions 62, 1973), pp. 403–07 (p. 405).

[30] See prologue, p. 6, for Rodoreda's comment. The listing of female foibles appears in Book III of Metge's *Lo somni*, which is probably Rodoreda's source. The opening sentence of Tiresias's tirade gives an indication of what is to follow: 'Ffembra és animal imperfet, de passions diverses desplasents e abhominables passionat, no amant altre cosa sinó son propri cos e delits; e si los hòmens la miraven axí com deurien, pus haguessen fet ço que a generació humana pertany, axí li fugirien com a la mort'; *Obras de Bernat Metge*, edited by Martín de Riquer (Barcelona: Universidad de Barcelona, 1959), p. 286. For the full diatribe, see pp. 286–314. Some of the details of Metge's text are echoed, in reverse, in *La plaça del Diamant*. The scene in which Quimet, for example, unjustifiably accuses Natàlia of having had an affair is sufficiently similar to a passage in *Lo somni* in which the 'shrew' accuses her man of having affairs behind her back (*Obras de Bernat Metge*, p. 300), to be seen as a source.

tale level of the story is extended imaginatively by Quimet who humours her: 'I va riure i va dir que sí, que hi havia hagut un cas, el cas de la reina Bustamante, que el seu marit, per no tenir feina, la va fer partir, per un cavall i de resultes va morir' (p. 64). But the fairy tale, like the childhood fear, elicits a Freudian parallel between sex and death. As Rodoreda suggests in her own prologue, the knife is a 'símbol sexual' (p. 8), and the midwife uses a knife likewise in the fairy tale to finish the women off. Underlying this parable is the sense of feminine lack, split in two by the man, for the woman is pierced, and ultimately killed, by the man. Women die younger, the fairy tale continues (itself not empirically true). Women are, however, vulnerable in the etymological sense of the term.[31]

The relation between the sexes in *La plaça del Diamant* are depicted as one-sided. Quimet, for example, is hostile towards his mother's friend because she is estranged from her husband (this is the only possible motive for his hostility; Chapter V, p. 45). He pushes Natàlia around when he is bad-tempered (Chapter IX, p. 67). It is not surprising, therefore, that Natàlia's experience of marriage should only confirm her sense of lostness and otherness. During her pregnancy, for example, Natàlia's body becomes Other: 'era com si m'haguessin buidat de mi per omplir-me d'una cosa molt estranya' (p. 75). In her experience of the birth of her child is likewise characterised by otherness: 'i vaig sentir una veu que deia i de tant fora de mi que estava no vaig poder saber de qui era la veu' (p. 78). The sense of her own body as Other likewise informs the references to the doves which gradually invade her household. Quimet, in a moment of insight, uses the metaphor of the body to refer to the doves in their apartment: 'i va dir que el colomar era el cor, d'on surt la sang que fa la volta al cos i torna al cor i que el coloms sortien del colomar que era el cor, donaven la volta pel pis que era el cos i tornaven al colomar que era el cor' (p. 122). The gradual growth of the dove population puts great strain on Natàlia's life; gradually her own living space begins to retreat. The birds spread from the balcony to one of the rooms. They become part of the family; as she explains to Mateu, 'el nens i els coloms eren com una família' (p. 135). As Randolph D. Pope has pointed out, Rodoreda uses the metaphor of the dove in order to reveal 'in this malevolent and uncontrolled growth of a benevolent creature, the toils and sufferings of unwanted motherhood'.[32] This leads

---

[31] A similar fable about the destructiveness of male sexuality is contained within the picture of lobsters hanging in Enriqueta's house; see Carme Arnau, *Introducció a la narrativa de Mercè Rodoreda*, pp. 163–64. For a good overview discussion of symbolism in the novel, see pp. 152–66.

[32] 'Mercè Rodoreda's Subtle Greatness', in *Women Writers of Contemporary Spain*, pp. 116–135 (p. 126).

Natàlia gradually to lose her identity, since she is already under strain because of the work she has to do to keep the family going (p. 134). Given her nickname, Colometa, which Quimet gave to her when they first met, it is clear that Natàlia is to be seen as a dove, fit only for breeding and labour. The gradual invasion of her private space by the doves is a concrete indication of how she is being swallowed up by her animal and reproductive qualities, such that she will finally only exist as a body, a procreative machine. This leads Natàlia eventually to destroy the eggs which are the source of her own oppression, by tricking the doves into pecking holes in them. This leads to guilt feelings and Natàlia returns in her dreams to a displaced 'primal scene' in which she herself is destroyed in the womb:

> I em despertava a mitjanit, com si m'estiressin els dintres amb un cordill, com si encara tingués el melic del néixer i m'estirressin tota jo pel melic i amb aquella estirada fugís tot: els ulls i les mans i les ungles i els peus i el cor amb el canal al mig amb una gleva negra de sang presa, i els dits dels peus que vivien com si fossin morts: era igual. (p. 140)

This dream, apart from confirming Natàlia's feelings of guilt, also reveals the subconscious link, which exists in her mind at least, between her own body and the doves. Both embody procreation. The desperateness of her situation is suggested by the fact that to rid herself of oppression is also, in a deeper sense, to destroy her own life-giving qualities; she is trapped within her own body, which as a symbol of oppression, she can only escape through death.

Immediately the doves recede from the picture, rather neatly, the Civil War breaks out and Natàlia's life takes a distinct turn for the worse. Her father dies as a result of the aerial bombardment of Barcelona (p. 163), and then her husband is killed on the Aragon Front (p. 171). Again reinforcing the associations between Natàlia's life and the doves, the news of Quimet's death is followed immediately by a scene in which the last dove is found dead (p. 171), a blow from which Natàlia very nearly does not recover. She is only saved from suicide by the grocer's last-minute offer of food (itself a prelude of his subsequent offer of financial stability through marriage).

As a result of hunger Natàlia begins to hallucinate; her hallucinations are similar to Andrea's in *Nada*, but Natàlia's are more vivid:

> I van venir unes mans. El sostre de l'habitació es va fer tou com si fos de núvol. Eren unes mans de cotó fluix, sense ossos. I mentre baixaven es feien transparents, com les meves mans, quan, de petita, les mirava contra sol. I aquestes mans que sortien del sostre juntes, mentre baixaven es separaven, i els nens, mentre les mans baixaven, ja no eren nens. Eren

ous. I les mans agafaven els nens tots fets de closca i amb rovell a dintre, i
els aixecaven amb molt de compte i els començaven a sacsejar. (p. 182)

This nightmarish vision presents Natàlia's hands as if they belonged to
the ceiling. Once more the imagery linking Natàlia's procreative qualities
to those of the doves is underlined, since it was by shaking the eggs that
she had previously destroyed the dove population, a trick she borrows
from her maker, Mercè Rodoreda.[33] The scream Natàlia subsequently
stifles but which rises within her is a scream against the harshness of fate,
against the injustice of hunger, but it is also a half-conscious protest
against political oppression:

> Volia cridar i la veu no em sortia. Volia cridar que vinguessin el veïns, que
> vingués la policia, que vingués algú a empaitar aquelles mans i quan ja
> tenia el crit a punt de sortir, em repensava i tancava el crit a dintre perquè
> la policia m'hauria agafat perquè en Quimet havia mort a la guerra.
> (p. 182)

Natàlia's state of mind before she buys the sulphur with which she
attempts to kill herself and the children is the apogee of otherness; 'ja no
podria mirar, no sóc jo que miro, no sóc jo que parlo, no sóc jo que veig'
(p. 191). It is at this point that Natàlia becomes dispossessed of her self.
She is only saved from death by the grocer's altruistic offer of work and
food, as already mentioned (p. 192).

In the main events of Natàlia's life so far, from courtship to the brink
of suicide, she epitomises the otherness of female identity in that she
finds herself in a world she does not comprehend and in which she feels
'lost'. Even when she marries Antoni later on, and thereby acquires
middle-class respectability (she now has a maid to do her housework),
her 'lostness' remains with her. After their marriage, she retreats into the
haven of her home (p. 217). Natàlia then begins gradually to reconstruct
her personality. But this reconstruction of inner space is a delicate
process, since Natàlia's personality is frail and liable to break down at
any moment. Despite her marriage to the grocer Natàlia is unable to
forget her past; she remembers the doves (p. 222), and she worries for a
whole three years that Quimet might come back (pp. 218–19). It is in the
final chapter of the book that these subconscious feelings come to the
surface. In a passage which has all the hallmarks of a Joycean 'stream of
consciousness' Natàlia returns to the flat where she lived with Quimet

---

[33] As a child Rodoreda felt jealous of the pigeon eggs in her house and used to shake
them in order to kill their occupants, as she suggested to Carme Arnau; see the latter's
Introducció a la narrativa de Mercè Rodoreda: el mite de la infantesa (Barcelona:
Edicions 62, 1982), p. 314.

and carves her name on the door, after vainly trying to get in. This scene
can be interpreted on one level as a *regressus ad uterum*, given the womb
symbolism of rooms in Freud's cosmology. But, more specifically,
Natàlia's return to the apartment is also motivated by a repressed sexual
desire for her former husband. By writing her name on the door with a
knife which has a sexual significance to which the author readily admits,
Natàlia is in a sense writing her sexuality on the door:

> I em vaig tornar a girar de cara a la porta i amb la punta del ganivet i amb
> lletres de diari vaig escriure Colometa, ben ratllat endintre, i, com d'esma,
> vaig posar-me a caminar i les parets em duien que no el passos, i vaig
> ficar-me a la plaça del Diamant: una capsa buida feta de casa velles amb el
> cel per tapadora. (p. 249)

With the reference to the Plaça del Diamant the novel turns full circle,
except that then it radiated life, and now it is empty. Having finally
written her name, the novel reaches its emotional climax with Natàlia's
scream which, after years of repression, finally erupts: 'vaig fer un crit
d'infern. Un crit que devia ser molts anys que duia a dintre i amb aquell
crit, tan ample que li havia costat de passar-me per coll, em va sortir de la
boca una mica de cosa de no-res, com un escarbat de saliva' (pp. 249–
50). It is at this point in the novel that the political dimension makes its
appearance; politics emerges in *La plaça del Diamant*, as Biruté
Ciplijauskaité points out, in precisely-chosen metaphors or small,
apparently irrelevant details.[34] For while Natàlia's scream is a result of
the pain of abandonment, it is also a cry of protest against the
dispossesion of Catalunya.

The Catalan question does not surface in an obvious sense in
Rodoreda's novel. It is not discussed, for example, in the context of the
Civil War, which is simply presented as a *fait accompli*. As Chapter
XXVI begins: 'I mentre em dedicava a la gran revolució amb els coloms
va venir el que va venir, com una cosa que havia de ser molt curta'
(p. 141). The effects of war are described vividly; Natàlia is dismissed
from her cleaning job because of her husband's activities; likewise the
harrowing effects of hunger during the war drive Natàlia to the point of
suicide, as we have already noted. Perhaps most distressing of all, when
Natàlia returns to the house where she was a former employee, the
welcome she receives is an apt metaphor of the soured relations between
the two Spains; he angrily throws Natàlia out, calling her a 'pobrisalla' to
her face (p. 180). Given that the political dimension of the struggle
between the Nationalists and the Republicans surfaces in this way, it is

---

[34] *La novela femenina contemporánea*, pp. 47–48.

perhaps surprising that similar allusions to the linguistic conscquences of the war (namely, that Catalan was banned from official use) are not more evident. From internal evidence it is impossible to know the precise reason for this, but omission is probably not meant to be understood as indifference. As Mercè Clarasó has suggested, Rodoreda's choice of an unsophisticated woman like Colometa as the centre of consciousness in her novel permits her, nevertheless to make 'an unvoiced comment' on the Civil War.[35] The same point can justifiably be applied to the linguistic dimension of *La plaça del Diamant*.

Certain circumstantial pieces of evidence tend to suggest that the superficial exclusion of the Catalan question from the novel does not disqualify it from being a latent issue. Firstly, one should note that Rodoreda spent much of her life after 1939 in forced exile; indeed, she wrote *La plaça del Diamant* in Geneva. Secondly, the prologue to the 1982 edition states that one of her aims in writing the novel was to promote the Catalan language: 'Em fa contenta pensar que entre tants milers de lectors com ha tingut i continua tenint n'hi ha molts que no havien llegit mai res en català i que és llegint-la que ha descobert que la nostra era una llengua civilitzada, culta, important' (prologue, p. 6). Thirdly, the circumstances of its publication confirm that this novel was an act of defiance.[36] For these reasons we may deduce that the Catalan dimension of this novel is crucial to its understanding. As Maria Aurèlia Capmany has suggested with words that are applicable to *La plaça del Diamant*: 'Pel fet de ser una llengua oprimida, no era un gran negoci escriure en català, era, doncs, una activitat de dones.'[37] Capmany's comment is intriguing since it links the political oppression of women with the political oppression of the Catalan language. Natàlia's carving of her name on the door of her former apartment is, thus, not only to be seen as an (ambiguous) sexual metaphor but also as a political allegory of the *inscription* of a subaltern, Catalan culture which only exists in terms of repression.[38] It is in this sense that Rodoreda's novel encapsulates the

[35] 'The Angle of Vision in the Novels of Mercè Rodoreda', *BHS*, 57 (1980), 143-52 (p. 150).

[36] *La plaça del Diamant* was initially rejected by the jury of the San Jordi prize, and its eventual publication in 1962 was greeted by a deafening silence in the Castilian press; Joan Salas, 'Una mica d'història de *La plaça del Diamant* amb motiu de la 26.a edició', pp. 11-18 (pp. 15-16).

[37] In conversation with Anne Charlon in 1982; quoted by Charlon, *La condició de la dona en la narrativa catalana (1900-1983)*, translated by Pilar Canal (Barcelona: Edicions 62, 1990), p. 12.

[38] There is an element of ambiguity in the use of a knife to emblematize sexuality, since the knife can only be a symbol of phallic libido. Given this reading, the conclusion of *La plaça del Diamant* could be allegorized as a celebration of the destruction of femininity

Otherness at once of the dispossessed female but also the repressed voice of Catalan culture which, like the Unconscious, sought to write its message publicly, in the civic arena of the Plaça del Diamant.

CLARICE LISPECTOR: *PERTO DO CORAÇÃO SELVAGEM*

'*A woman's destiny is to be a woman.* '[39]

Perto do coração selvagem (1941) by Clarice Lispector (1917–1977: Switzerland-Brazil), is not this Brazilian novelist's most renowned novel, although it is, in the words of her most insightful critic, 'an originary work'.[40] More importantly for our present purposes, however, it has all the ingredients of a *Bildungsroman*. As we have seen, the *Bildungsroman* normally traces the life of one (male) individual and shows that individual as achieving a deeper understanding of life by the end of the novel. *Perto do coração selvagem* can be seen as a formation-novel since it traces the main formative experiences from childhood to adulthood of a young individual who as a result achieves a degree of insight about life. Lispector's novel focusses on the life experience of Joana beginning with her childhood relationship with her father and then with her aunt, her stay at boarding school (and specifically her relationship with an unnamed teacher), her marriage to Otávio and her subsequent divorce. The last chapter of the novel shows us a Joana who has achieved a deeper knowledge of life and has her sights focussed clearly on the future: 'serei brutal e mal feita como una pedra, serei leve e vaga como o que sente e não se entende, me ultrapassarei em ondas' (p. 179).[41] Despite the fact

through the adoption of phallic power, again perhaps underlining Rodoreda's vision of power and libido as intrinsically phallic realities.

[39] *The Hour of the Star*, translated by Giovanni Pontiero (Manchester: Carcanet, 1987), p. 84.

[40] Hélène Cixous, *Reading with Clarice Lispector*, edited, translated and introduced by Verena Andermatt Conley (London: Harvester-Wheatsheaf, 1990), p. 13. Cixous argues that because of its originary status, it is important for any reader of Lispector's fiction to pay close attention to *Perto do coração selvagem* (p. 13).

[41] Joana is here imagining herself transfigured in terms which recall her earlier conversation with Otávio on the eve of his departure (p. 162), even if this transfiguration involves being transformed into something as visually unattractive as a 'misshapen stone'. Indeed the utopian vision Joana has of an ideal state of identity often involves a fusion with inorganic matter. Edition used throughout is *Perto do coração selvagem*, 2nd edition (São Paulo: Editora Paulo de Averedo Lfda., 1963). There is an excellent English version, *Near to the Wild Heart*, translated by Giovanno Pontiero (Manchester: Carcanet, 1990).

that the protagonist is female, thus, *Perto do coração selvagem* has more than a passing resemblance to the structural formula of the male formation-novel.

There are, however, many points on which *Perto do coração selvagem* expresses themes and preoccupations which are alien to the patriarchal code of the *Bildungsroman*. While the typical formation-novel depicts the character-formation of a young male asserting his identity in the face of hostile opposition from parents or society, Lispector's novel, following the archetypal pattern of the female *Bildungsroman* identified by Pratt (see above), reveals the character-dissolution of a young female. Similar points of authority are there, but the rejection of these sites of knowledge is so radical in *Perto do coração selvagem* as to cause the dissolution of the boundaries between self and other, and the dismantling of the system of logocentrism. The latter has fundamental implications for the role of language in the novel, as we shall see.

Perto do coração selvagem presents a world in which 'bonds of affection become cages and prison bars'.[42] Joana is typical of many of Lispector's protagonists who, as Gerald Martin has pointed out, 'are entrapped and isolated in a private world of helpless rage and frustration which they often conceal even from themselves'.[43] This lostness is predicated, in Joana's case, primarily on her experience of orphanhood; she had no relationship with her mother, since she disappeared before Joana knew her. The first chapter of the novel reveals that Joana was also unable as a child to communicate with her father. Her father is irritated by her constant questions, and finally resorts to telling her to bang her head against a wall ('Bata com a cabeça na parede!', p. 12), itself an early taste of her experience of patriarchy later on. Joana's relationship with her husband follows the pattern of that with her father. At one stage she describes how her thoughts open up gaps between them: 'As vêzes, no entanto, talvez pela qualidade do que dizia, nenhuma ponte se criava entre êles e, pelo contrário, nascia um intervalo' (p. 28). The reference to the 'quality' of Joana's words hints at the new mode of thought that she is struggling to bring into being, and which is lost on Otávio. On one level, Joana's problem is an ordinary one; her marriage is not working. Thus when she says, 'A culpa era dêle' (p. 96), her dilemma seems commonplace. When she asks herself, 'como ligar-se a um homem senão

---

[42] This phrase is borrowed from Marta Peixoto's essay '*Family Ties*: Female Development in Clarice Lispector', in *The Voyage In: Fictions of Female Development*, edited by Elizabeth Abel, Marianne Hirsch, and Elizabeth Langland (Hanover and London, University Press of New England, 1983), pp. 287–303 (p. 289).

[43] *Journeys Through the Labyrinth: Latin-American Fiction in the Twentieth Century* (London: Verso, 1989), p. 349.

permitindo que êle a aprisione' (p. 26), she is voicing a question which
was destined to become central to feminism.[44] But there are clearly ways
in which her struggle does not dovetail with the aims of the women's
movement in Brazil. The First Paulista Women's Congress held in 1979,
for example, demanded financed nurseries, salary equalization and
reproductive choice.[45] Joana's feminism, however, is clearly more
ontological than social.[46] Her rejection of marriage, for example, is based
on the proposition: 'O que desejo ainda não tem nome' (p. 61).

Joana sees men in terms of violence and meat-eating.[47] In the second
chapter, for example, we witness Joana's repulsion at the sight of a man
eating meat. She becomes obsessed at the sight of the man holding a fork
which is embedded in a piece of 'carne sangrenta', and the 'música do
diabo' to which his legs beat time under the table (p. 15). This sense of
horror at eating meat reoccurs in chapter 3 when Joana's father and his
friend are eating chicken. The text reads starkly: 'Na hora do jantar,
Joana viu estupefacta e contrita uma galinha nua e amarela sôbre a mesa'
(p. 20).[48] Joana's alienation from manhood is narrated obliquely through
images of men eating meat. As might be expected, Joana's abortive
relationships with men led her to seek fulfilment in relationships with
women.

But turning to women also leads to disillusionment. During the first
meeting with her aunt, for example, Joana ends up squashed between her

[44] As Kate Millett suggested in her now classic text *Sexual Politics* (1970), in past
centuries 'a woman underwent ''civil death'' upon marriage, forfeited what amounted to
every human right, as felons now do upon entering prison'; *Sexual Politics* (New York:
Doubleday and Co., 1970), p. 67. Lispector's text is an imaginative exploration of this
idea.

[45] See Sonia E. Alvarez, 'Women's Movements and Gender Politics in the Brazilian
Transition', in *The Women's Movement in Latin America: Feminism and the Transition to
Democracy*, edited by Jane S. Jaquette (Boston: Unwin Hyman, 1989), pp. 18–71 (pp.
38–39).

[46] Lispector's fiction engaged with more social themes as time went on. *Near to the
Wild Heart*, however, belongs to Lispector's early fiction which, as Salange Ribeira de
Oliveira has pointed out, is 'socially detached'; see 'The Social Aspects of Clarice
Lispector's Novels: An Ideological Reading of *A Paixão segundo G. H.*', *La Chispa '87
Selected Proceedings*, ed. Gilbert Paolini (New Orleans: Tulane University, 1987), pp.
211–20 (p. 217).

[47] For a witty discussion of the association between raw meat and virility, see Roland
Barthes, 'Le bifteck et les frites', in *Mythologies* (Paris: Seuil, 1957), pp. 77–79.

[48] The presence of the chicken in the story, as so often in Lispector's fiction, raises
ontological questions about the origins of life. As Cixous suggests: 'There is a chicken in
Coração selvagem and in many other stories by Clarice Lispector. Often her character
stories are addressed to children. These children are adults, that is to say, the readers,
who never really know whether they are the egg or the chicken'; *Reading with Clarice
Lispector*, p. 98.

breasts, 'sepultada entre aquelas duas massas de carne macia e quente que tremiam com os soluços' (p. 30). She runs outside and vomits. Since it is her aunt's bulging breasts which revolt Joana, one must assume that she feels alienated not only from masculinity but also from femininity. A similar alienation occurs later on at school when Joana asks her teacher what you get once you are happy, and the teacher is unable to respond (p. 24).

Joana's quest to find 'as mulheres apenas fêmeas' (p. 19) at one point looks promising when she meets an un-named woman simply described as a 'mulher da voz'. Since she is a widow, as Joana muses, 'ela não tinha história' (p. 66), she now has simply *herstory*. The widow no longer achieves meaning and presence via the patriarchal system: 'Ela era em si, o própio fim' (p. 67). Despite Joana's overtures, however, the woman with the voice shows Joana to the door; their meeting ends in failure on an interpersonal level. Taking some inspiration from the 'mulher da voz', however, Joana later attempts to achieve a new way of being outside the prisonhouse of patriarchy.

Joana's attempts to communicate with Otávio's lover, Lídia, also end in failure. When Joana makes the magnanimous, anti-patriarchal gesture of offering to share Otávio, Lídia recoils in disgust (pp. 137–38). It becomes clear, as the novel progreses, that Joana will not find the femininity she so desires in other women, only within herself. In the second part of the novel, Joana begins to look inward: 'Sentia o mundo palpitar docemente em seu peito, doía-lhe o corpo com se nele suportasse a feminilidade de tôdas as mulheres' (p. 120). Once Otávio leaves, Joana is free is pursue her quest for inner femininity.

Joana's quest for femininity is predicated on a rejection of all that is exterior to her being, and is body-centred: 'tenho um corpo e tudo o que eu fizer é continuação de meu começo; se a civilização dos Maias não me interessa é porque nada tenho dentro de mim que se possa unir aos seus baixos relevos' (p. 16). The mythic past of the Mayas becomes irrelevant when compared with the language of the female body in the here and now (though the Mayas are less culturally relevant to a Brazilian than they might be to a Mexican). Joana's search for an Amazonian utopia involves casting the lies of patriarchy to the winds: 'renascer sempre, cortar tudo o que aprendera, o que vira, e inaugurar-se num terreno novo onde todo pequeno ato tivesse um significado, onde o ar fôsse respirado como da primeira vez' (p. 71). The imagery associated with rebirth recurs throughout the narrative and often has baptismal connotations, as when Joana runs out of her aunt's house down to the sea (pp. 32–35), or when she has a bath and emerges from the water as a woman (pp. 56–58). It is clear that her desire to 'cut away everything she had learned' is based on a rejection of patriarchal law. We may recall that it is while Otávio is reading his law books that Joana decides to leave him (Part II, Chapter 1, 'O Casamento').

The New World which Joana seeks to create is rooted in the body and involves a return to a pre-Edenic chaos: 'uma grande vontade de se dissolver até misturar seus fins com os começos das coisas' (p. 168), that 'sublime inconsciência criadora' (p. 171) as it is later called. Her freedom from the laws of patriarchy is echoed by a perception of physical matter which is itself released from the bonds of natural law. Later on in the same passage, the sea becomes a dominant image:

> Deus, como ela afundava docemente na incompreensão de si própria. E como podia muito mais ainda, abandonar-se ao refluxo firme e macio. E voltar. Haveria de reunir-se a si mesma um dia, sem as palavras duras e solitárias. . . Haveria de se fundir e ser de novo o mar mudo brusco forte largo imóvel cego vivo. (p. 169)

The laws of patriarchy, however, threaten to disrupt this world: 'Mas a grade do portão era feita por homens; e lá estava brilhando sob o sol. Ela notou-a e no choque da súbita percepcão era de novo uma mulher' (p. 169). Patriarchy, symbolised by the iron gate in the garden, traps the protagonist in the name of 'woman'. This introduces a further dimension of the oppression which Joana experiences, which concerns the limiting power of language which devalorizes the female and the feminine.

In *Perto do coração selvagem* Lispector adopts two routes to address the issue of language and gender. On the one hand, she explores the suggestive power of neologisms (see below) and, on the other, she adopts the stream-of-consciousness technique in its Joycean form. In the last chapter of the novel Lispector uses the ebb and flow of the stream-of-consciousness in order to underline the semantic elusiveness of the new world she is bringing into being. At one point, Joana retreats from the hierarchy of language into a fluid region: 'Afastava-se aos poucos daquela zona onde as coisas têm forma fixa e arestas, onde tudo tem un nome sólido e imutável. Cada vez mais afundava na região líquida, quieta e insondável, onde pairavam névoas vagas e frescas com as da madrugada' (p. 172). As this monologue reaches its crescendo, it becomes clear that, as well as espousing the values of womenhood, Joana wants to give voice to a new consciousness which is being born within her body. As she asks, echoing the stance of the mystic waiting for revelation:

> Por que não vem o que quer falar? Estou pronta. Fechar os olhos. Cheia de flôres que se transformam em rosas à medida que o bicho treme e avança

em direção ao sol do mesmo modo que a visão é muito mais rápida que a palavra, escolho o nascimento do solo para. . . Sem sentido. (p. 175)

The text finally breaks down; at this point, thus, Joana's attempt to express the new language of womanhood is caught at the threshold of expression.[49] When reaching the confines of expression, following the familiar Romantic formula of ineffability, this feminine language evaporates. All the narrator is left with is an apparently meaningless clause: 'palco escuro abandonado, atrás de uma escada' (p. 175). But the narrator tries once more to body forth this new language:

> De profundis. Vego um sonho que tive: palco escuro abandonado, atrás de uma escada. Mas no momento em que penso 'palco escuro' em palavras, o sonho se esgota e fica o casulo vazio. A sensação murcha e é apenas mental. Até que as palavras 'palco oscuro' vivam bastante dentro de mim, na minha escuridão, no meu perfume, a ponto de se tornaren uma visão penumbrosa, esgarçada e impalpável, mas atrás da escada. Então terei de novo uma verdade, o meu sonho. (p. 175)

Of the two elements used in this metaphor, it is likely that 'palco escuro' emblematizes the dark continent of womanhood, hidden behind the stairs (with their connotations of upwardness and sky) of patriarchy. As Lispector's text suggests, immediately women-speak comes close to expression, it fades like a dream when greeted by the dawn of conscious thought.

Lispector uses another technique in her attempt to body forth the language of womanhood, as already mentioned: the neologism. Intriguingly, Joana uses a neologism to describe her inner world when confronted with her husband's pleas that she reveal its secret, almost as if to suggest that neologistic discourse is the nearest approximation to female language that patriarchal knowledge can accommodate:

> – Diga de novo o que é Lalande – implorou a Joana.
> – É como lágrimas de anjo. Sabe o que é lágrimas de anjo? Uma espécie de narcisinho, qualquer brisa inclina êle de um lado para outro. Lalande é também mar de madrugada, quando nenhum olhar ainda viu a praia, quando o sol não nasceu. Tôda a vez que eu disser: Lalande, você deve sentir a viração fresca e salgada do mar, deve andar ao longo da praia ainda escurecida, devagar, nu. Em breve você sentirá Lalande. . . (p. 150)

---

[49] For further discussion of this theme, see Stephen Hart, 'On the Threshold: Cixous, Lispector, Tusquets', in *Feminist Readings on Spanish and Latin-American Literature*, eds. L. P. Condé & S. M. Hart (Lampeter: Edwin Mellen Press, 1991), pp. 91–105.

Since Lalande, which acts as a synecdoche of the land where feminine experience lies, is inexpressible, Joana attempts to define its power with a gliding signifier which darts from 'angel's tears', to 'daffodil', and 'the sea at dawn'.[50] Lalande cannot be fixed within language, being a concrete example of one of those 'palavras não pensadas e lentas' (p. 178) which Joana dreams of expressing in the closing pages of the novel.[51] The implication at the conclusion of the novel is that the world of 'slow, unthought words' has not yet been born – it exists as a future utopia – but we leave the narrative with a sense of hope that, one day, Joana's dream will come true, and she will be able, in Christine Froula's words, to 'think the unthought world beyond the pale of masculine culture'.[52] As the novel ends, 'basta me cumprir e então nada impedirá meu caminho até a morte-sem-mêdo, de qualquer luta ou descanso me levantarei forte e bela como um cavalo novo' (p. 179).

Lispector's *Bildungsroman* is, in some senses, a more mature formation-novel than Laforet's *Nada* and Rodoreda's *La plaça del Diamant*. Unlike Laforet's protagonist who has barely emerged from

[50] 'Lalande' is a neologism in Portuguese, and there is no equivalent in English. This word is also probably a composite reference to the work of the French astronomer and the French composer, both of whom bore this word as a name (Joseph-Jérome Le Français de Lalande [1732–1807], and Michel-Richard de Lalande [1657–1726] respectively). Joseph-Jérome's expertise in planetary theory and Michel-Richard's composition of sacred music hint that Lispector may have been using this word to allude to a newly-discovered world based on musical structures; see *The New Encyclopaedia Brittanica*, 15th edition (Chicago: Encyclopaedia Inc., 1980), vol. v, p. 1001. I am grateful to Giovanni Pontiero for clarifying the hypothetical roots of this elusive word in Lispector's cosmology. In emphasising the difference between the male and female languages, Lispector is anticipating an important facet of French feminist thought, as demonstrated particularly in the work of Cixous, Irigaray and Herrmann. As the latter suggests, it is 'enriching for the two sexes to try to learn each other's language, instead of declaring one official language'; *The Tongue Snatchers*, translated by Nancy Kline (Lincoln & London: University of Nebraska Press, 1989), p. 136.

[51] It is important to bear in mind that Lispector does not fall into the trap of binarism which splits language and thought into separate categories. Language is the only root to knowledge. As Lispector explained in her essay, 'Dois modos', 'when writing I have insights that are "passive" and so intimate that they write themselves the very instant I perceive them without the intervention of any so-called thought process'; she makes a similar point in another essay 'Escrevendo': 'What comes to the surface is already expressed in words or simply fails to exist'; quoted by Earl Fitz, *Clarice Lispector* (Boston: Twayne, 1985), p. 123. Comprehension of the world, thus, in Lispector's terms, derives from language rather than thought. As she laconically pointed out in an interview with Renato Cordeiro Gomes, 'Escrever é comprender melhor'; quoted by Emir Rodríguez Monegal, 'Clarice Lispector en sus libros y en mi recuerdo', *RI*, 50 (1984), 231–38 (p. 235).

[52] 'Rewriting Genesis: Gender and Culture in Twentieth-Century Texts', *TSWL*, 7:2 (1988), 197–220 (p. 198).

university, Joana is already a mature woman, married and separated. *Perto do coração selvagem* is also a more mature novel in the sense that, unlike *La plaça del Diamant*, it explicitly deals with the issue of feminine language, and the ways in which patriarchal discourse limits the experience of women. It is in this sense, particularly, that Lispector's novel was ahead of its time, as Cixous has suggested.[53] Language, like patriarchy, as Lispector's novel suggests, can be experienced as a prison. Lispector's revolution is, thus, at once feminist and epistemological. All three novels, however, share one common feature – that of innovatively reworking the patriarchal values of the *Bildungsroman*, imploding the form from within in search of a female ontology.[54]

[53] Hélène Cixous, *Reading with Clarice Lispector*, p. 122. It was Lispector's innovative use of language that led Cixous to proclaim her writing as the epitome of 'écriture féminine'. For further discussion of the links between the two writers, see Earl Fitz, 'Hélène Cixous's Debt to Clarice Lispector: The Case of *Vivre l'Orange* and *L'Ecriture féminine*', *RLC*, 251:1 (1990), 235–49.

[54] For a discussion of women's fiction in Brazil in the 1980s, which has been heavily influenced by Lispector's work, see Novaes Coelho, 'A presença da "Nova Mulher" na ficção brasileira atual', *RI*, 50 (1984), 141–54.

II

THE PATRIARCHAL PRISON

Caridad L. Silva-Velázquez and Nora Erro-Orthman have pointed out that the image of the prison, particularly in the context of an unhappy marriage, is a recurrent leitmotif of contemporary women's writing in Latin America.[1] In this chapter the aim is to focus on three novels/short stories (*La amortajada*, 'Lección de cocina', *Los recuerdos del porvenir*) which, in different but mutually complementary ways, point to the experience of patriarchy as a prison. This image is particularly relevant to María Luisa Bombal's *La amortajada* in which the protagonist's body, for the duration of the novel, is confined within a coffin; as the novel unfolds, however, it becomes clear that far more dangerous and insidious than physical extinction of the individual is the death which patriarchy spells for women. Ana María, the heroine of Bombal's novel, thus, in an important sense, comes to stand for the violation of liberty that patriarchy visits upon the female sex. Rosario Castellanos's 'Lección de cocina' likewise focusses on the issues of gender and patriarchy. Here the emphasis is more on the everyday aspects of woman's confinement within the domestic space of the kitchen. Thoughts pass through the mind of the protagonist as she prepares a meal for the husband she has recently married. Alluding to Sor Juana's own thoughts about food and philosophy contained in her *Respuesta de la poetisa a la muy ilustre Sor Filotea de la Cruz*, Castellanos's short story is a witty jibe at the overarching forces which imprison womanhood in the kitchen. Elena Garro's *Los recuerdos del porvenir*, like the two previous texts, emphasises the discourse of patriarchy which seeks to limit women's sexuality. The only escape from the prison of patriarchy, Garro's novel suggests, is through the imagination which surfaces in *Los recuerdos del porvenir* as a power which can not only upturn the values of patriarchy, but also those of time and space as well. Each of these three novels are acutely aware of the bonds that patriarchy imposes on women, and each,

[1] *Puerta abierta: la nueva escritora latinoamericana*, p. 13.

in turn, proposes different ways of escaping its law. What they do not attempt to do, however, is to take the law to court. They ignore the court-room hearing, and flee to a world of imagination. As we shall see, as a solution, this can only be a double-edged sword.

MARIA LUISA BOMBAL: *LA AMORTAJADA*

Critics have often interpreted *La amortajada* (1938), the second novel of María Luisa Bombal (1910–1980: Chile), in terms of the Romantic archetype. Marjorie Agosín, for examples, argues that the use of the pantheism in Bombal's novel makes of it 'una novela profundamente romántica'.[2] Given its Romantic undercurrent, it is not surprising, therefore, that *La amortajada* should exemplify the image of womanhood projected by the Romantic mind, specifically, as victim of man's love. Romantic literature was obsessed by this image. Especially Victorian literature and art, for example, used the classical Perseus-Andromeda story (Perseus saves Andromeda, who is about to be devoured by a monster, releases her from her chains and then marries her), in a markedly gendered form. Since this myth appealed, during the period 1830–1895, to male rather than female artists, it can be thought of as a male myth since, as Adrienne Auslander Munich argues, it depicts 'a female with no power, seemingly no volition, opposite a male with supernatural powers'.[3] As Munich further points out, the plot typically takes the same form: 'Perseus saves Andromeda, then keeps her for sexual and dynastic purposes; obligated to her rescuer, she can neither rescue herself nor refuse his offer of marriage' (p. 14). We find a similar presentation of women in Bombal's work, and especially *La amortajada*. Bombal's novel describes the thoughts which run through the mind of a woman, Ana María, who is lying in her coffin reviewing the main events of her past life and, in particular, her frustrated attempt to find happiness through a loving relationship with a man. Bombal herself seems to have had what might best be described as a 'pre-feminist' view of the male-female relationship.[4] As she explained in an interview in 1980, only months before her death, man is the axis of a woman's life:

[2] *Las desterradas del paraíso, protagonistas en la narrativa de María Luisa Bombal* (New York: Senda Nueva Editores, 1983), p. 76. Agosín also points to the presence of the pathetic fallacy, supernatural elements, the valorization of the imagination, and obsession with death as typically Romantic elements in Bombal's novel; pp. 76–77.

[3] Adrienne Auslander Munich, *Andromeda's Chains: Gender and Interpretation in Victorian Literature and Art* (New York: Columbia University Press, 1989), pp. 13–14.

[4] Gabriela Mora has argued that Bombal's work belongs to an era when fiction linked women 'al ámbito doméstico y a la búsqueda del amor como única posibilidad de

> La mujer tiene un destino de amor. En la relación hombre-mujer hay falta
> de comunicación intelectual y sexual. La vida sentimental depende del
> hombre. Uno se enamora locamente. El es el eje de su vida. Sin ellos está
> la soledad; con ellos hay apoyo y protección ¡aunque se porten mal![5]

This, it would seem, is also the experience of the protagonists of the
novels and, in particular, Ana María, the character with whom Bombal
has admitted to have most identified with in her own work.[6]

There are a number of structurally significant points in the novel where
this notion – woman only achieves being through a man – is echoed. Ana
María experiences a rude awakening when she sees Antonio kicking her
blue slipper in disgust, unaware that he is being watched. The blue
slipper in Bombal's text is a quasi-Symbolist image of the beauty of
woman under the aegis of patriarchy (Cinderella's slipper, its blue colour
relating back to the 'blue' symbolising the ideal in Mallarmé's and Rubén
Darío's poetic systems).[7] Ana María cries and then she thinks:

> ¿Por qué, por qué la naturaleza de la mujer ha de ser tal que tenga que ser
> siempre un hombre el eje de su vida?
> Los hombres, ellos, logran poner su pasión en otras cosas. Pero el destino
> de las mujeres es remover una pena de amor en una casa ordenada, ante
> una tapicería inconclusa.[8]

A reading which privileges the interconnection of life and art would point
to the use of the same word 'axis' to refer to woman's dependence on
man in the novel as in Bombal's 1980 interview.[9] According to the

realización personal'; 'Narradoras hispanoamericanas: vieja y nueva problemática en
renovadas elaboraciones', in *Theory and Practice of Feminist Literary Criticism*, edited
by Gabriela Mora and Karen S. Van Hooft (Ypsilanti, Michigan: Bilingual Press, 1982),
pp. 156–174 (p. 157). In her essay Mora identifies the 1970s as a watershed in Latin-
American fiction when subjects considered taboo until then, such as the limitations of
marriage and female sexuality, began to be explored.
    [5] Gloria Gálvez Lira, 'Entrevista con María Luisa Bombal', in her study, *María Luisa
Bombal: realidad y fantasía* (Potomac, Maryland: Scripta Humanistica, 1986), pp. 105–
10 (p. 108).
    [6] *María Luisa Bombal: realidad y fantasía*, p. 108.
    [7] Stephen Hart, *Spanish, Catalan and Spanish-American Poetry from "modernismo"
to the Spanish Civil War* (Lampeter: Edwin Mellen Press, 1990), p. 33.
    [8] *La última niebla. La amortajada* (Barcelona: Seix Barral, 1984), p. 142. All
subsequent references will be to this edition.
    [9] It is, of course, quite possible that the plot and experiences of the heroine of *La
amortajada* are based on Bombal's first – and disastrous – marriage to the Argentine
painter, Jorge Larcos, from whom she separated after two years of marriage; see Gálvez
Lira, *María Luisa Bombal: realidad y fantasía*, p. 7. But to attempt to pin down details of
the novel to real-life events would run the same risk as Bombal's decision to make the
ending of *La última niebla* less problematic in the English version; see Gálvez, p. 7.

scheme of things, which Ana María, in a highly essentialist gesture, simply denominates 'naturaleza', women are born to be losers in love.

The designation of womanhood is implicated in the central metaphor of the novel, the shroud which figures in the title. Womanhood is explicitly linked to death at various junctures of the novel; one particularly striking passage epitomises this idea:

> Hay pobres mujeres enterradas, perdidas en cementerios inmensos como ciudades – y horror – hasta con calles asfaltadas. Y en los lechos de ciertos ríos de aguas negras las hay suicidas que las corrientes incesantemente golpean, roen, desfiguran y golpean. Y hay niñas, recién sepultadas, a quienes deudos inquietos por encontrar, a su vez, espacio libre, en una cripta estrecha y sombría, reducen y reducen deseosos casi hasta de borrarlas del mundo de los huesos. Y hay también jóvenes adúlteras que imprudentes citas atraen a barrios apartados y que un anómino hace sorprender y recostar de un balazo sobre el pecho del amante, y cuyos cuerpos, profanados por las autopsias, se abandonan, días y días, a la infamia de la Morgue. (pp. 153–54)

It is women, whether they are suicide victims, young girls, or adulteresses, whose plights are bemoaned. Men, if one follows the logic of the paragraph, are not vulnerable to the threat of death, or betrayal in love, which is exclusively reserved for women. The image of the shroud is of course crucial in this context. On a literalist level, *La amortajada* has been interpreted as occurring during a period of semi-consciousness before Ana María's death. Gálvez Lira, for example, suggests that 'la amortajada, en esa zona misteriosa de la post-vida, reconoce, recuerda y justifica a los que se inclinan sobre el ataúd'.[10] A complementary approach is to see the image of the shroud as itself a metaphor of the imprisonment of women within the prison of patriarchy. Women's existence, especially if they make a claim for subjectivity, is as superfluous as a fifth wheel on a cart.[11] An indication of the form such an approach might take is provided by Sandra Gilbert and Susan Gubar who argue that the woman writer must throw off the image of womanhood promoted by patriarchy in order to achieve autonomy. As they argue:

---

[10] *María Luisa Bombal: realidad y fantasía*, p. 80. She further compares the novel's structure to that of Fuentes's *Artemio Cruz*; both protagonists 'están en un estado de semiinconsciencia previo a la muerte definitiva en el cual se ve y se percibe todo', p. 80, n. 21. A parallel might also be drawn with Zorrilla's *Don Juan Tenorio*; see Fred Abrams, 'The Death of Zorrilla's Don Juan and the Problem of Catholic Orthodoxy', *RoN*, 6 (1964), 42–46.

[11] As Ana exclaims angrily at one point: '¡Qué se imaginan Vds. que soy yo!. . . ¿Quinta rueda de la carreta?', p. 159.

A woman writer must examine, assimilate, and transcend the extreme images of 'angel' and 'monster' which male authors have generated for her. Before we women can write, declared Virginia Woolf, we must 'kill' the 'angel in the house'. In other words, women must kill the aesthetic ideal through which they themselves have been 'killed' into art.[12]

In the excellent last chapter of her study of Bombal's fiction, Celeste Kostopulos-Cooperman quotes this passage from Gilbert and Gubar's work and argues of Bombal's protagonists that 'their creative attempts towards redefinition are entirely futile when viewed from a feminist perspective, for by frequently identifying themselves with essentially patriarchal images, Bombal's heroines cannot possibly achieve the full autonomy that they desire'.[13] There is clearly much to be said for a reading of this kind of Bombal's fiction; Kostupulos-Cooperman further points to the images of confinement in *La amortajada* ('Ana María is imprisoned within the shroud of her prior existence'; p. 74) which reinforce the appropriateness of Gilbert and Gubar's critical approach to Bombal's novel.[14] There are, however, a few points on which the Gilbert/ Gubar thesis does not mesh entirely with *La amortajada*. The most significant section of the novel in this context is the conclusion, particularly the last twelve paragraphs of the novel which describe Ana María's descent into the earth, and which begin with the deictic phrase: 'Y he aquí que, sumida en profunda oscuridad, ella se siente precipitada hacia abajo, precipitada vertiginosamente durante un tiempo ilimitado hacia abajo; como si hubieran cavado el fondo de la cripta y pretendieran sepultarla en las entrañas de la tierra' (p. 161). The conclusion of the novel is presented not simply as an acceptance of a male-imposed role, namely the woman as killed in art, but rather in terms of a joyous pantheistic rebirth. As the novel concludes: 'Lo juro. No tentó a la

---

[12] Sandra M. Gilbert and Susan Gubar, *The Madwoman in the Attic. The Woman Writer and the Nineteenth Century Literary Imagination* (New Haven: Yale University Press, 1979), p. 17.

[13] *The Lyrical Vision of María Luisa Bombal* (London: Tamesis, 1988), p. 70.

[14] Ana María's marriage to Antonio leads her to experience death, what she calls at the conclusion of the novel, 'la muerte de los vivos' (p. 162). Her death begins after she miscarries Ricardo's baby, and she takes to weaving furiously, 'tejiendo, tejiendo con furia, como si en ello me fuera la vida' (p. 111). Although the verb is used intransitively here, it refers synedochically to the shroud which will cover her during her marriage. While Penelope in *The Odyssey* weaves at her loom in order to keep suitors at bay, Ana María's marriage is experienced as a shroud. Thus, when she dies, her female body is already prepared: '¡Qué bien se amolda el cuerpo al ataúd!' (p. 119). Even her experience of love with Fernando is such that she feels trapped by his love as if it were a shroud: '¿Por qué aún amortajada le impone su amor?' (p. 119). By contrast, Ana María's experience of true love with her cousin, Ricardo, lacks any sense of spatial confinement; their love-making always takes place in the open countryside (p. 103; p. 156).

amortajada el menor deseo de incorporarse. Sola, podria, al fin, descansar, morir. Había sufrido la muerte de los vivos. Ahora anhelaba la inmersión total, la segunda muerte: la muerte de los muertos' (p. 162). Rather than an acceptance of patriarchy, Ana María's act of communion with the earth is an act of self-affirmation which unravels the chains of patriarchy.[15]

A related theme which throws some light on the role of patriarchy in the novel is silence. Silence is employed consistently by Bombal's heroines as a means of combatting patriarchy. As Kostopulos-Cooperman argues, however, it is a double-edged weapon: 'These angelic retreats into silence, however, are potentially more destructive than the despair that initially engendered them, for by outwardly perpetuating meek and powerless images of the self, they contrive to reinforce a view of their sex that has historically denied women the authority to articulate their own lives. Although we as readers can penetrate their silent worlds, their voices are destined to drown in the metaphysical vacuum of their own mute and insular monologues' (p. 77). While few would take issue with the first sentence quoted, the second is more open to discussion, since it is surely the case that the literal fact that Ana María's thoughts have reached the printed page is an indication that, despite the repression of patriarchy, the silence of womanhood's voice has been heard.

Another reading is surely necessary. If one looks at Bombal's text from a perspective which privileges female sexuality/textuality, it becomes clear that *La amortajada* disinstalls the hermeneutics of patriarchy. For Ana María, orgasm is not necessary for, or even related to, love. When with her true love, Ricardo, Ana María did not experience an orgasm: 'Tú me hallabas fría porque nunca lograste que compartiese tu frenesí, porque me colmaba el olor a oscuro clavel silvestre de tu beso' (p. 104). There is an indication that Ricardo, ironically, left her because she did not experience an orgasm during love-making.[16] On

---

[15] Lucía Guerra-Cunningham argues, however, that this return to nature is negative: 'la restitución de la armonía mujer-naturaleza no debe tomarse como un mensaje positivo de la obra con respecto a la situación de la mujer. Si la única forma de recuperar la esencia natural y cósmica se encuentra en la muerte implícitamente se ha anulado toda posibilidad de una salida en el contexto individualizado de la sociedad en un momento histórico específico'; *La narrativa de María Luisa Bombal, una visión de la existencia femenina* (Madrid: Playor, 1980), p. 105. Kostopulos-Cooperman agrees with this view; see *The Lyrical Vision of María Luisa Bombal*, p. 34, n. 34. It could be argued, however, that a reading of this kind imposes feminist expectations on a pre-feminist text. This is not to deny that Bombal's novel is unable to draw attention to the very real bonds which patriarchy places around the female body; it clearly *is* able to do this.

[16] The quotation above is followed by the narrator's statement that Ricardo left her,

the other hand, Ana María does experience orgasm with her husband, Antonio, whom she does not love. Once she has experienced orgasm, referred to euphemistically/poetically as 'un temblor', she starts to fight against it. Antonio, however, is unaware of her struggle: 'Nunca supo que noche tras noche, la enloquecida niña que estrechaba en sus brazos, apretando los dientes con ira intentaba conjurar el urgente escalofrío. Que ya no luchaba sólo contra las caricias sino contra el temblor que, noche a noche, esas caricias lograban, inexorables, hacer brotar en su carne' (p. 134). Ana María's resistance to orgasm experienced within the patriarchal structure of marrige has implications for the textuality of her memoirs. Ana María's textuality, as well as her sexuality, echo the failure of patriarchy. The use of the verb 'brotar' in the above quote exposes the extent to which the pre-nuptial and the post-nuptial experience are parallelled in Ana María's mind. Early in the text, we learn that her non-orgasmic love-making with Ricardo gave her a child; a parallel is drawn between the 'minúsculos brotes' of spring outside her window and her two breasts which 'parecían desear florecer con la primavera' (p. 106). The loss of this child, as we have noted above, is the first step in her experience of death within life. Later on, her love-making with Antonio simply makes orgasm – rather than a child – break forth in her body ('brotar en su carne').

Ana María's resistance to orgasm under the aegis of patriarchy needs to be understood in terms of textuality, for text and sex are related terms. Much critical discourse on narratology, though appearing to be gender-innocent, highlights the male orgasm as an underlying biological parameter of the novel's structure. Two critics in particular, Peter Brooks and Robert Scholes, ought to be mentioned in this context. As the latter argues:

> The archetype of all fiction is the sexual act. In saying this I do not mean merely to remind the reader of the connection between all art and the erotic in human nature. . . . For what connects fiction – and music – with sex is the fundamental orgiastic rhythm of tumescence and detumescence, of tension and resolution, of intensification to the point of climax and consummation.[17]

and she does not understand why: 'Aquel brusco, aquel cobarde abandono tuyo, ¿respondió a una orden perentoria de tus padres o a alguna rebeldía de tu impetuoso carácter? No sé'; p. 104. Her frigidity is more likely to have been the reason.

[17] Robert Scholes, *Fabulation and Metafiction* (Urbana: University of Illinois Press, 1979), p. 26. See also his essay 'Reading Like a Man', in *Men in Feminism*, edited by Alice Jardine & Paul Smith (New York and London, Methuen, 1987), pp. 204–18.

Susan Winnett quotes this passage and argues that a woman's encounter with the text is 'determined by a broad range of options for pleasure that have *nothing to do* (or can choose to have nothing to do)' with Scholes's theory of textual representability, proposing instead feminine versions, such as birth and breast feeding, which run counter to the phallocentric mastertext.[18] Ana María's life, whether judged by Scholes's masculinist criteria or Winnett's feminist criteria, fails, since her marriage is childness and she miscarries her lover's child.

While *La amortajada* can be interpreted in terms of patriarchal failure on a thematic level, a different reading suggests itself on a textual level. One point which many critics of Bombal's work have pointed to is that Ana María's text privileges narrative discontinuity and fluidity.[19] Francine Masiello, for example, has argued that Bombal's fiction is part of a feminine narrative movement (including writers such as Norah Lange and Teresa de la Parra) which sought, in the 1920s and 1930s, to undermine the masculinist thrust of such avant-garde writers as Oliverio Girondo and Vicente Huidobro. In Masiello's words:

> Endowed with few stable meanings and now replete with contradictions and echoes, the texts produced in the feminized mode announce their own ambiguity. They register plural narrative voices that challenge all linearity, they insist on a self-referential vagueness, which consumes all marks of difference. As if to challenge the authority invested in a single, hierarchical bond between father and child, the feminine mode in narrative disperses all centralized power.[20]

Thus, to give but one example of the dispersion of centralized power in Bombal's text, family members and relatives pass in and out of the room in which Ana María is lying, and they do so without that emphasis on realism and verisimilitude which, as Janet Todd suggests, is 'character-

[18] Susan Winnett, 'Coming Unstrung: Women, Men, Narrative and Principles of Pleasure', *PMLA*, 105:3 (1990), 505–18 (p. 507; p. 509).

[19] Verity Smith, for example, notes that Bombal 'writes in a discontinuous manner, leaving gaps to be filled by the reader's imagination'; see her 'Dwarfed by Snow White: Feminist Revisions of Fairy Tale Discourse in the Narrative of María Luisa Bombal and Dulce María Loynaz', in *Feminist Readings on Spanish and Latin-American Literature*, eds. L. P. Condé & S. M. Hart, pp. 137–49 (p. 143).

[20] 'Women, State, and Family in Latin American Literature', in *Women, Culture, and Politics in Latin America*, pp. 27–47 (p. 38). It is important to clarify the distinction Masiello is making here about what she calls the 'feminine narrative mode'; the last two sentences of Masiello's quotation could, indeed, be applied to a text written by a man (Rulfo's *Pedro Páramo*, for example). What Masiello identifies as intrinsic to the feminine narrative mode should not therefore be restricted to texts authored by women. I am grateful to Verity Smith for pointing this out to me.

istic of certain strands of male writing'.[21] Likewise, character fixity is disturbed. The agent of consciousness moves freely from person to person throughout the text, expressing Ana's thoughts and, then without warning, her interlocutor's.[22] In this sense, *La amortajada* deconstructs the expectations of the patriarchal text with its emphasis on linear narrative direction and fixed narrative focus.

This discontinuity is echoed on an imagistic level by the water symbolism in the novel. Ana María's (heretical) projection of heaven on earth is framed within water imagery: 'me gustaría también que mi primo Ricardo estuviera siempre conmigo, y se nos diera permiso para dormir de vez en cuando por las noches en el bosque, allí donde el césped es verdadero terciopelo, justo al borde del afluente' (p. 156). It is clear at this point in the text that liquidity is being utilised as a means of reversing the patriarchal version of love. Despite Ana María's experience of paradise on earth next to the stream, Ricardo's image is used simply to inspire the narrative; he is unaware of its power. (This is proved, for example, when he decides to leave her.) In perhaps the most important example of the use of the image of fluidity in *La amortajada*, which occurs at the conclusion of the novel, Ana María sinks into a subterranean world containing wells full of frozen devils' saliva, strange beings with viscous bodies, and dew-covered cracks. This world is also explicitly female: '¡Ah, si los hombres supieran lo que se encuentra bajo ellos, no hallarían tan simple beber el agua de las fuentes!' (p. 161). Bombal's text, thus, ends with a retreat into a dark, feminine knowledge which is unavailable to mankind. It is significant, for example, that it is men, rather than women, who are described as unable to face the reality of death and the earth. As Ana María continues: 'Porque todo duerme en la tierra y todo despierta de la tierra' (p. 161). This no doubt explains the special resonance of Ana María's words to her daughter.

> Ya ves, la muerte es también un acto de vida.
> No llores, no llores, ¡si supieras! Continuaré alentando en ti y evolucionando y cambiando como si estuviera viva; me amarás, me desecharás y volverás a quereme. (p. 149)

---

[21] *The Sign of Angellica. Women, Writing and Fiction, 1660–1800* (New York: Columbia University Press, 1989), p. 3.

[22] For a good example of Bombal's criss-crossing narrative, see the conversation between Ana María and her confessor, Father Pedro, pp. 154–61. Magali Fernández compares this change of focus to cinematographic cutting: 'Es como si el lente de una cámara, de repente, cambiase de posición de enfoque'; *El discurso narrativo en la obra de María Luisa Bombal* (Madrid: Editorial Pliegos, 1988), p. 88. For a discussion of narrative structure with special reference to flash-backs and flash-forwards, see Fernández, pp. 83–89.

Since this is the only dialogue which Ana María expresses herself so forcefully, Bombal is hinting that the mother-daughter relationship is based on a communion which transcends death. The mother-daughter relationship hollows out the 'muerte de los vivos' associated with patriarchal love, and yet is able to face 'la muerte de los muertos' without flinching. As Ana María suggests: 'Ya ves, al muerte es también un acto de vida' (p. 149). Against all the (phallocentric) odds, Bombal's *La amortajada* proclaims the victory of female bonding.

ROSARIO CASTELLANOS: 'LECCIÓN DE COCINA'

In her essay 'Woman and Her Image', Rosario Castellanos (1925–1974: Mexico) employs Simone de Beauvoir's study, *Le Deuxième Sexe*, to analyse the ways in which women have been mythified and therefore dis-abled (either through beauty or angelicness) concluding that 'woman is stripped of her spontaneity of action, forbidden the initiative of decision, taught to obey the commandments of an ethic that is completely alien to her and has no more justification or basis than that of serving the interests, goals, and end of others'.[23] In her essay Castellanos lists the means by which women are incarcerated within the phallocentric code (her most significant test-case is the male's requirement of virginity in his marriage partner), and then points to images of liberated women who range from real life, such as Sor Juana Inés de la Cruz, to the fictional such as Ana Ozores and Anna Karenina: 'Each one in her way and in her own circumstances denies the conventional, making the foundations of the establishment tremble, turning hierarchies upside down, and achieving authenticity' (p. 244). Their denial of the conventional is a knife which cuts both ways, to use Dostoevsky's phrase (see Chapter I, note 3), for the act of making the foundations of society tremble often leads to their own death. Strangely, however, few of the female characters in Castellanos's fiction ever manage to embody these feminist values; they are often depicted as trapped in a phallocratic prison.[24] An

[23] 'Woman and Her Image', *A Rosario Castellanos Reader*, edited by Maureen Ahern (Austin: University of Texas Press, 1988), pp. 236–44 (p. 240).

[24] Naomi Lindstrom discusses the ways in which Castellanos's characters are silenced; see 'Rosario Castellanos: Representing Women's Voice', *LF*, 5:2 (1979), 29–47. On the same theme, see also Lucía Fox-Lockert, *Women Novelists in Spain and Spanish America*, pp. 202–15. Castellanos has also published a number of novels, of which the best known are *Balún Canán* (1957) and *Oficio de tinieblas* (1962), but it is in her short stories that Castellanos's narrative skill achieves its cutting edge. For a discussion of Castellanos's fiction, see Jean Franco, *Plotting Women: Gender and Representation in Mexico*.

exception to the rule, however, is the narrator of her short story, 'Lección de cocina'.

'Lección de cocina', the opening short story of *Album de familia* (1971), is Castellanos's master text in the feminist mode, having become, in Seymour Menton's words, 'una especie de manifiesto de la mujer intelectual'.[25] It concentrates on the split Castellanos identified within womanhood, and which she defined (in personal terms) as 'the discrepancy between what that role imposed on me in a country like Mexico and what I wanted to and was able to accomplish in life'.[26] As Beth Miller suggests, 'Lección de cocina' is based in part on a critique of the traditional portrayal of women in ladies' magazines (such as Mexico's *Casa*) and television commercials.[27] The action of this particular short story takes place within the mind of a woman preparing a meal for her husband who will shortly be returning from work, and it enacts a type of self-discovery which has led one critic to compare 'Lección de cocina' to the work of Virginia Woolf and Simone de Beauvoir.[28] Set in the kitchen it deals specifically with feminine, domestic space; 'Lección de cocina' is therefore not only a 'cookery lesson' but also a (moralist) lesson about the social and conceptual space allotted to women by patriarchal law.

In the opening pages of the story, irony is specifically directed at the un-named narrator who is presented as a archetypal Mexican woman, inured to suffering and to whom the liberational discourse of feminism is a closed book. On the surface at least, the narrator seems to accept her appointed lot: 'Mi lugar está aquí. Desde el principio de los tiempos ha estado aquí. En el proverbio alemán la mujer es sinónimo de Küche, Kinder, Kirche' (p. 7).[29] On one level, therefore, Castellanos is, as one

---

[25] Seymour Menton, 'Las cuentistas mexicanas en la época femenista, 1970–1988', *Hispania*, 73:2 (1990), 366–70 (p. 367). For further discussion of Castellanos's work, see Beth Miller, *Uma consciência feminista: Rosario Castellanos* (São Paulo: Editora Perspectiva, 1987).

[26] Quoted in Oscar Bonifaz, *Remembering Rosario: A Personal Glimpse into the Life and Works of Rosario Castellanos*, translated by Myralyn F. Allgood (Potomac, Maryland: Scripta Humanistica, 1990), p. 43.

[27] 'Female Characterization and Contexts in Rosario Castellanos's *Album de familia*', *AmH*, 4:32–33 (1979), 26–30 (p. 26).

[28] Kathleen O'Quinn, '*Tablero de damas* and *Album de familia*: Farces on Women Writers', in *Homenjae a Rosario Castellanos*, ed. Maureen Ahern and Mary Seale Vásquez (Valencia: Albatros, 1980), pp. 99–105 (p. 104).

[29] All textual references are to 'Lección de cocina', in *Album de familia* (Mexico: Joaquin Moritz, 1985), 2nd impression of 4th edition, pp. 7–22. Raúl Ortiz y Ortiz, a good friend of Rosario Castellanos and the dedicatee of *Album de familia*, pointed out in a lecture given at University College, London in December 1990 that Castellanos was neither an enthusiastic or a very good cook, a problem which was compounded by her

critic puts it, '*parodying* an interior monologue' (my emphasis).[30] But in another sense the narrator is clearly an alter ego of the narrator since she is, like the writer Rosario Castellanos, more at home with her books and literary quotations than in the kitchen. Like Castellanos, she is a writer; as she notes later on, her finger-tips are not very sensitive 'por el prolongado contacto con las teclas de la máquina de escribir' (p. 9). Thus, she compares the discourse of advertising food in the supermarket ('¿Qué me aconseja usted para la comida de hoy, experimentada ama de casa, inspiración de las madres ausentes y presentes, voz de la tradición, secreto a voces de los supermercados?', pp. 7–8), with a scene from Cervantes's *Don Quijote*, 'La cena de don Quijote'.[31] The narrator compares the discourse of literature with that of the cookery book, and wonders why literature has such a rich metatext, while the cookery book implicitly takes for granted that its readers will immediately understand its contents: 'Si yo supiera lo que es estragón y ananá no estaría consultando este libro porque sabría muchas cosas. Si tuviera usted el mínimo sentido de la realidad debería, usted misma o cualquiera de sus colegas, tomarse el trabajo de escribir un diccionario de términos técnicos, redactar unos prolegómenos, idear una propedéutica para hacer accesible al profano el difícil arte culinario. Pero parten del supuesto que todos estamos en el ajo y se limitan a enumerar' (p. 8). The answer which the text does not provide is that literature, a male-dominated code, therefore has more importance than the female-dominated discourse of the cookery-book. The comparison between the two codes becomes playful; the narrator goes off the idea of preparing a roast because 'no representa la superación de ninguna antinomia ni el planteamiento de ninguna aporía' (p. 9). The meat will only become tasty if, like a piece of prose taken to pieces by a critic immersed in New Criticism, or like the recipes which effortlessly combine contradictory qualities such as 'la esbeltez y la gula, el aspecto vistoso y la economía' (p. 7), it expresses the transcendance of antimony.

The text continues in its playful vein when referring to the redness of the meat which reminds the narrator of the colour her back went during

clumsiness. The fact that the narrator of 'Lección de cocina' refers to how clumsy she is ('Y yo, soy muy torpe'; p. 16) reinforces the possibility that the narrator is a projection of some of the author's character traits.

[30] Phyllis Rodríguez Peralta, 'Images of Women in Rosario Castellanos's Prose', *LALR*, 6:11 (1977), 68–80 (p. 75).

[31] Castellanos is here no doubt alluding to the meal during which don Quijote gives a speech about 'las armas y las letras'; *El Ingenioso Hidalgo Don Quijote de la Mancha*, ed. John Jay Allen (Madrid: Cátedra, 1977), chapter XXXVIII, vol. I, pp. 447–51. A mock-ironic parallel is thus established between the hype of advertising and Don Quijote's fulsome speech.

her honeymoon in Acapulco. Despite her sunburnt skin she accepts her husband's advances on the wedding night: 'El podía darse el lujo de "portarse como quien es" y tenderse boca abajo para que no le rozara la piel dolorida. Pero yo, abnegada mujercita mexicana que nació como la paloma para el nido, sonreía a semejanza de Cuahtémoc en el suplicio cuando dijo "mi lecho no es de rosas y se volvió a callar"[*sic*]' (p. 9).[32] The reference to Cuauhtemoc's torture by fire at the hands of Cortés's men during the Spanish Conquest of America gives a grim poignancy to the narrator's experience of her womanly role which she accepts 'like a dove born for the nest'. The allusion to the Aztec King's fate draws a parallel between the conquest of America and the war between the sexes. For the woman, as for the Amerindian population in the sixteenth century, the odds were stacked against the subaltern.

Once her husband falls asleep the narrator initially feels as if she were reduced to exile, the excluded consciousness of womenkind in a patriarchal society. But she rejects exile, and its implication of gendered surrogacy. She is no longer simply the reflection of male consciousness: 'yo no soy el reflejo de una imagen en un cristal; a mí no me aniquila la cerrazón de una conciencia o de toda conciencia posible. Yo continúo viviendo con una vida densa, viscosa, turbia, aunque el que está a mi lado y el remoto, me ignoren, me pospongan, me abondonen, me desamen' (p. 10). This passage is the first sign of the emergence of a liberated consciousness in the narrator. She considers going to the bathroom and wiping her husband's semen away which, in this context, must be taken as a desire to abolish the presence of patriarchy, but, significantly, she does not do so, since she is joined to her husband through an ecclesiastic bond. Her statement – 'Prefiero creer que lo que me une a él es algo tan fácil de borrar como una secreción y no tan terrible como un sacramento' (p. 11) – suggests that, despite her personal preference, the bonds of patriarchy are not so easy to release. It is while the narrator is engrossed in these thoughts that the narrative cuts back to the meat which is cooking. The link term between the two levels is the reference to 'la muerte' (the narrator is prepared to retain the privilege of insomnia until death) which leads to the description of the meat as having taken on a

---

[32] This is an embellished version of what Cuauhtemoc is reputed to have said. According to Gómara's account, he said '¿Estoi yo en algun deleite, ó baño?'; quoted by W. H. Prescott, *The Conquest of Mexico* (New York: Henry Holt and Company, 1922), II, p. 445. Castellanos's source may have been Rubén Darío's poem, 'A Roosevelt', *Cantos de vida y esperanza* (1905), in which the Nicaraguan poet has Cuauhtemoc say 'Yo no estoy en un lecho de rosas'; Rubén Darío, *Poesías completas*, ed. Alfonso Méndez Plancarte (Madrid: Aguilar, 1968), p. 641. Castellanos's text curiously intercalates the expression 'y se volvió a callar', which is commentary rather than speech.

grey hue once the pepper was added ('la carne parece haber encanecido'). It is while her thoughts are on death that the most visible sign of patriarchy surfaces in the text; in marriage, the narrator lost her maiden name and acquired a new identity: 'Porque perdí mi antiguo nombre y aún no me acostumbro al nuevo, que tampoco es mío' (p. 11). She finds herself in a limbo realm; the way in which the narrator describes this no-woman's land is intriguing: 'Cuando en el vestíbulo del hotel algún empleado me reclama yo permanezco sorda, con ese vago malestar que es el preludio del reconocimiento' (p. 11). This vague sense of dis-ease, the text suggests, is the 'prelude to recognition', but this recognition is something which the text implicitly rejects since this would imply an acceptance of the alienating discourse of patriarchy. Recognition, as Castellanos's text goes on to suggest, is always misrecognition for womankind, since it is based on acceptance of phallocentric knowledge, itself closely connected with language and its identity-giving property. This insight is echoed later on when the narrator refers to her husband's body on top of her during love-making in necrological terms: 'Cuando dejas caer tu cuerpo sobre el mío siento que me cubre una lápida, llena de inscripciones, de nombres ajenos, de fechas memorables. Gimes inarticuladamente y quisiera susurrarte al oído mi nombre para que recuerdes quien es a la que posees' (p. 14). The reference to the signs of language ('inscripciones', 'nombres', 'fechas') reinforces once more how language is perceived as a discourse which alienates and marginalises the feminine consciousness.

Once more the narrative returns to the roast; she thinks it is too big, and then that it is taking too long to cook. Once more she questions the gender-coded assumption of the cookery book. When the recipe says that the meat doesn't take long to cook, she asks, how long is long? 'Naturalmente, el texto no especifica. Me supone una intuición que, según mi sexo, debo poseer' (p. 13). Her husband expects his wife to be a virgin, but the narrator's gradually questioning attitude towards this patriarchal assumption is suggested by her statement: 'Cuando la descubriste yo me sentí como el último dinosaurio en un planeta del que la especie había desaparecido' (p. 13). The metaphor of a dinosaur is intriguing, since it relegates the system of values underpinning patriarchy to a pre-human epoch. Halfway through the story the narrator begins to express rancour at her fate, since she is caught between being a housewife (for which 'no se me paga ningún sueldo', p. 15) and her professional career.

Having finished cooking the roast, the narrator is overtaken by a burst of enthusiasm; she imagines her husband and herself disappearing into a film idyll of romantic happiness, or she herself living the life of a

wealthy, single woman in New York, Paris or London, or being picked
up by a rich gentleman in a car. Unfortunately, however, the meat
continues to cook and then starts to shrink and turn black ('La carne está
encogiendo. [. . .] La estoy viendo muy pequeña [. . .] está empezando a
soltar un humo negro y horrible [. . .] se enrosca igual que una
charamusca'; pp. 17–18). The narrator's wild fantasies begin to shrink
accordingly, and she is soon left with no more than 'un miserable pedazo
de carne carbonizada' (p. 19). When recapitulating her experience, she
compares the various stages of the roast to her husband's meta-
morphoses:

> Mi marido también da la impresión de solidez y de realidad cuando
> estamos juntos, cuando lo toco, cuando lo veo. Seguramente cambia, y
> cambio yo también, aunque de manera tan lenta, tan morosa que
> ninguno de los dos lo advierte. Después se va y bruscamente se
> convierte en recuerdo y. . . Ah, no, no voy a caer en esa trampa: la del
> personaje inventado y el narrador inventado y la anécdota inventada.
> Además, no es la consecuencia que se deriva lícitamente del episodio de
> la carne. (p. 20)

The narrator resists the temptation to conclude her narrative in the self-
reflexive mode, thereby converting it into simply an exercise in writing
fiction. Rather than a metafictional direction, the story takes a feminist
turn and suggests how the burnt meat will continue to operate 'en otros
niveles. En el de mi conciencia, en el de mi memoria, en el de mi
voluntad, modificándome, determinándome, estableciendo la dirección
de mi futuro' (p. 21). At this point in the narrative, it is clear that the
narrator has gone through a metamorphosis. She is aware of the non-
feminist option, which is to declare weakness, and thereby guarantee 'el
triunfo por la sinuosa vía que recorrieron mis antepasadas, las humildes,
las que no abrían los labios sino para asentir, y lograron la obediencia
ajena hasta al mas irracional de sus caprichos' (p. 21). Declaring oneself
the weaker sex, thus, can have its advantages. But the narrator rejects
this option as hypocritical; she cannot accept an option just because it is
sanctioned by common sense. This will lead to conflict with her husband:
'Si insisto en afirmar mi versión de los hechos mi marido va a mirarme
con suspicacia, va a sentirse incómodo en mi compañía y va a vivir en la
continua expectativa de que se me declare la locura' (p. 22). It is
significant that the narrator chooses to describe her act of defiance as 'mi
versión de los hechos', which suggests that her agenda is linguistic as
well as performative. To accept her new role is to enter the space of
madness, to be declared mad by the system of patriarchy. But to sacrifice
her own being for the benefit of her marriage is no longer an option. The

narrator has been transformed from a cultural subaltern into a woman in control, intellectually and physically, of her destiny.

'Lección de cocina' ends with a recognition that her experience of burning the meat was a trivial event of everyday life: 'es algo muy insignificante, muy ridículo. Y sin embargo. . .' (p. 22). The 'and yet. . .' with which the story ends is an indication that the culinary mishap raises ideological issues which stretch beyond the trivial event itself. There are four literary/historical references in 'Lección de cocina', all of which imply how the story relates back to wider ideological issues. Two of these (Cervantes and Cuauhtemoc) have already been mentioned. The other two, Santa Teresa and Sor Juana, because they are women, act as pivotal reference points in 'Lección de cocina'. Both women appear together in what is Castellanos's perhaps most famous poem 'Meditación en el umbral'. As the poem opens:

> No, no es la solución
> tirarse bajo el tren como la Ana de Tolstoi
> ni apurar el arsénico de Madame Bovary
> ni aguardar en los páramos de Avila la visita
> del ángel con venablo
> antes de liarse el manto a la cabeza
> y comenzar a actuar.
>
> Ni concluir las leyes geométricas, contando
> las vigas de la celda de castigo
> como lo hizo Sor Juana (. . .).[33]

In her poem Castellanos ultimately rejects the life-option offered by Santa Teresa which involves waiting in the wilderness for 'la visita / del ángel con venablo', as well as Sor Juana's counting the beams in her cell. It is not that she rejects what they did, but rather the patriarchal society in which they lived which barred them from writing and knowledge (most spectacularly so in the case of Sor Juana). In 'Lección de cocina' Castellanos offers a similar view of these two mother figures. Her allusion to Santa Teresa strives to express the saint's perception in the language of the modern age: 'Yo estuve todo el tiempo pendiente de la carne, fijándome en que le sucedían una serie de cosas rarísimas. Con razón Santa Teresa decía que Dios anda en los pucheros. O la materia que es energía o como se llame ahora' (p. 20). The narrator of 'Lección de cocina' re-interprets Santa Teresa's reference to God as a reference to energy, or, more probably, electricity. The narrator concurs with Santa

---

[33] Rosario Castellanos, *Meditation on the Threshold* (New York: Bilingual Press, 1988), p. 48.

Teresa but distances herself from her belief, reinterpreting the saint's perception of God in contemporary terms. The reference in 'Lección de cocina' to Sor Juana is more pointed: 'De mí se puede decir lo que Pfandl dijo de Sor Juana: que pertenezco a la clase de neuróticos cavilosos. El diagnóstico es muy fácil ¿pero qué consecuencias acarrearía asumirlo?' (p. 22). As an essay Castellanos wrote on Sor Juana clearly shows, she saw the Mexican writer as a model to be followed.[34] Sor Juana, indeed, had used a culinary metaphor in her famous *Respuesta de la poetisa a la muy ilustre Sor Filotea de la Cruz*, in which she referred ironically to the Church authorities' argument that her intellectual energies might be better served if she were to take up cooking. Sor Juana turned this idea around, poking fun at the church dignitaries, by showing how her mind frequently became involved in the solving of intellectual problems during cooking:

> Pues ¿qué os pudiera contar, Señora, de los secretos naturales que he descubierto estando guisando? Veo que un huevo se une y fríe en la manteca o aceite y, por contrario, se despedaza en el almíbar; ver que para que el azúcar se conserve fluida basta echarle una muy mínima parte de agua en que haya estado membrillo u otra fruta agria; ver que la yema y clara de un mismo huevo son tan contrarias, que en los unos, que sirven para el azúcar, sirve cada una de por sí y juntos no. Por no cansaros con tales frialdades, que sólo refiero por daros entera noticia de mi natural y creo que os causará risa; pero, señora, ¿qué podemos saber las mujeres sino filosofías de cocina? Bien dijo Lupercio Leonardo, que bien se puede filosofar y aderezar la cena. Y yo suelo decir viendo estas cosillas: Si Aristóteles hubiera guisado, mucho más hubiera escrito.[35]

The intertextual allusion to this text turns Rosario Castellanos's 'Lección de cocina' into a barbed attack on patriarchy which confronts twentieth-century woman as it did Sor Juana in the sixteenth century. Like Sor Juana, Castellanos adopts a mock-ignorant stance in order to give more

[34] 'Once Again Sor Juana', *A Rosario Castellanos Reader*, edited by Maureen Ahern (Austin: University of Texas Press, 1988), pp. 222–25.

[35] 'Respuesta de la poetisa a la muy ilustre Sor Filotea de la Cruz', *Obras completas de Sor Juana Inés de la Cruz* (México: Fondo de Cultura Económica, 1957), vol. IV, pp. 440–75 (pp. 459–60). Sor Juana would seem to be referring here to Aristotle's discussion in *Physics*, 1, i–vi, of the relationship between substance and its attributes. Though Aristotle does not mention eggs in this section, he uses the example of 'whiteness' to illustrate his argument on various occasions, concluding that 'our principles must be contraries'; both of these ideas are echoed – tongue-in-cheek – in Sor Juana's text; see *The Basic Works of Aristotle*, edited and with an introduction by Richard McKeon (New York: Random House, 1941), pp. 213–28. The quotation may be found on p. 228. Sor Juana no doubt also uses the egg because of its feminine connotations. Castellanos's own text continues and expands Sor Juana's feminocentric dialogue with Aristotle's text.

urgency to her critique of the patriarchal institution of marriage. Though few and far between, the intertextual allusions in Castellanos's text help to create a critique of phallocentric knowledge which takes its point of departure from the space which feminism has identified as the source of female oppression, namely, the kitchen. Like Sor Juana's *Respuesta*, 'Lección de cocina', in true emperor's-new-clothes mode, is a reply to those forces within society which attempt to control women's lives.

ELENA GARRO: *LOS RECUERDOS DEL PORVENÍR*

Los recuerdos del porvenir (1963) by Elena Garro (1920: Mexico) is ostensibly a novel about the ravages caused by the Mexican Revolution; the poor are duped and eventually find themselves in a prison of their own making. The *cristero* revolution leaves everyone off as badly as before. Absolute power is held by the *caciques* who do what they want with their subalterns; General Rosas, for example, epitomises the arbitrary, cruel nature of political power. There is, however, a sub-plot operating within Garro's novel which weaves through the text, sometimes interweaving with the macro-plot, sometimes contrasting with it, and this involves the issue of gender. John S. Brushwood, for example, argues that beneath the story of the *cristero* rebellion is a story of love. The novel's major theme, he contends, is 'love – the concept of love, particularized into cases of possessiveness, frustration, fulfillment, and violence'.[36] Brushwood then points to what he sees as a failure of the novel:

> Garro employs one narrative device that does not work very well. Her town, Ixtepec, tells its own story. The immediate problem is characteriza- tion of the town clearly enough to give the narrative voice an authentic tone. The author never really achieves this desirable goal. Fortunately, other aspects of the book are interesting enough to subordinate this deficiency.[37]

This begs the inevitable question: how is a town to have a narrative voice which has 'an authentic tone'? What would this be like? As James

---

[36] *The Spanish American Novel: A Twentieth-Century Survey* (London and Austin: University of Texas Press, 1975), p. 258.

[37] Brushwood, *The Spanish American Novel*, p. 258. Luz Elenea Gutiérrez de Velasco, in contrast, finds the technique of *Los recuerdos del porvenir* 'atinada'; see 'Entre la originalidad y la persecución: la narrativa de Elena Garro', *CAm*, 183 (1991), 57–61 (p. 58).

Mandrell pertinently points out, Brushwood labels the voice as false 'rather than analyzing why it is disconcerting'.[38] Brushwood's comment implies a foreknowledge of what the narrative voice of a town would be, coupled with the contention that Garro's version does not live up to this ideal, and is redolent of the 'circular logic' identified by Dale Spender.[39] His analysis also presents *Los recuerdos del porvenir* as overshadowed by the work of a male contemporary, Julio Cortázar, since 1963 was, as we are reminded for seventeen pages, 'the year of *Rayuela*'. Elena Garro's novel is not even allowed to possess the year of its publication, since it has already been comandeered by a male writer.

Fernando Alegría's analysis of *Los recuerdos del porvenir* has some suggestive parallels with Brushwood's. In a section which is meant to be devoted to her novel, Garro agains loses out to male writers; she is dwarfed by Juan Rulfo on one side and García Márquez on the other. As Alegría suggests: 'Si no resulta obvio el por qué pongo este nombre entre los de García Márquez y Rulfo, bastará decir que Garro coincidió con ellos al descubrir las claves de un lenguaje narrativo abierto a la mitificación de la historia americana'.[40] If this were not enough, Alegría then goes on to compare Garro's novel unfavourably with García Márquez's later works. At one point in his analysis Elena Garro looks as if she is to be credited with having inspired García Márquez's *Crónica de una muerte anunciada*: 'en el caso de Felipe Hurtado dejó la pauta de una muerte anunciada'. But her momentary glimpse of fame as a precursor is dashed by Alegría's next sentence: 'Es una tentación decir que la novela de Elena Garro queda como una extraña partitura que García Márquez años después ejecutó a gran orquesta'.[41] García Márquez's novel was an orchestra; Elena Garro's no more than a strange 'partitura'.

The strangeness of Garro's novel, to adopt Alegría's adjective, has much to do with its narratological discontinuity. It seems to change place, change time, change mood, and one feels tempted to say, change gear in a way which readers will find disconcerting. As Daniel Balderston points out: 'In *Los recuerdos del porvenir* the fantastic touches the central concepts of time, the body, memory, history. All of these are rendered problematic in the course of the novel. Linear time stops, the body is petrified, memory turns from the past toward the impossible future, history is coloured with the impossible and the

[38] 'The Prophetic Voice in Garro, Morante, and Allende', *CL*, 42:3 (1990), 227–46 (p. 232).

[39] *Man Made Language* (London: Routledge and Kegan Paul, 1980), p. 7.

[40] *Nueva historia de la novela hispanoamericana* (Hanover, N.H.: Ediciones del Norte, 1986), p. 276.

[41] Fernando Alegría, *Nueva historia de la novela hispanoamericana*, p. 277.

improbable'.[47] There are many examples of disruption of the spatio-
temporal continuum in Garro's novel, but one example will suffice for
our purposes. The event concerns the point in the novel when we expect
Julia to be killed by the General when he finds out about her affair with
Hurtado. The narrative eye had been following Julia's movements, when
she walked to the house where her lover, Hurtado, lived, when she talked
to him and during her slow walk home. The text then simply states:
'Nadie oyó que Francisco Rosas y Julia Andrade entraron a su cuarto'
(p. 136). The narrative then cuts abruptly to doña Matilde's house; the
latter feels that something terrible has happened: '– ¡Joaquín, sucedió
algo terrible!' (p. 137). The whole village voice unanimously their
opinion about the relationship ('No podía acabar bien', p. 137), but, as
readers, we are none the wiser as to what actually happened in the room
after Julia returned. When we expect General Rosas to kill Julia, the
expected event never happens or, if it does, it does so behind closed
doors. The tension mounts, and the narrative begins to stretch, almost in
preparation for the news:

> – Este es un día muy largo. . .
> – No tendrá fin. Aquí nos quedaremos para siempre. . . – Y la señora se
> volvió a su hija en busca de aprobación.
> – Pues va corriendo, ya son las dos – repuso Conchita con enojo.
> – Desde la noche en que se fue Hurtado supe que algo horrible nos iba a
> suceder – agregó el viejo sin cambiar el tono de voz.
> – ¡Ojalá que todos estuviéramos tendidos! – exclamó la señora incorpo-
> rándose trágica en la cama. (p. 211)[43]

It is as if time had stopped. We have an extraordinary example of this in
the passage which concludes the first part of the novel. We see the
General cross the village and demand to see Hurtado, who is lodging in
don Joaquín's house. Francisco Rosas is waiting outside don Joaquín's
house for the stranger, Hurtado, to emerge. Then something untoward
happens. Because of its evocative power it is worth quoting the passage
in its entirety:

> El joven levantó los cerrojos, quitó las trancas, abrió el portón y salió.
> Don Joaquín iba a seguirlo, pero entonces sucedió lo que nunca antes me
> había sucedido; el tiempo se detuvo en seco. No sé si se detuvo o si se fue
> y sólo cayó el sueño: un sueño que no me había visitado nunca. También
> llegó el silencio total. No se oía siquiera el pulso de mis gentes. En verdad

[42] 'History and Fantasy in *Los recuerdos del porvenir*', *BHS*, LXVI (1989), 41–46
(p. 45).
[43] References are to *Los recuerdos del porvenir* (México: Joaquín Mortiz, 1963).

no sé lo que pasó. Quedé fuera del tiempo, suspendido en un lugar sin viento, sin murmullos, sin ruido de hojas ni suspiros. Llegué a un lugar donde los grillos están inmóviles, en actitud de cantar y sin haber cantado nunca, donde el polvo queda a la mitad de su vuelo y las rosas se paralizan en el aire bajo un cielo fijo. Allí estuve. Allí estuvimos todos: Don Joaquín junto al portón, con la mano en alto, como si estuviera haciendo para siempre aquel gesto desesperado y desafiante; sus criados cerca de él, con las lágrimas a la mitad de las mejillas; doña Matilde santiguándose; el general montando al Norteño encabritado con las patas delanteras en el aire, mirando con ojos de otro mundo lo que pasaba en éste; los tambores y cornetas en actitud de tocar alguna música; Justo Corona con el fuete en la mano y el sombrero bien ladeado; Pando en su cantina casi vacía inclinado sobre un cliente que recogía unas monedas de plata; las Montúfar espiando detrás de sus balcones con las caras pálidas de miedo; y como ellas los Moncada, los Pastrana, los Olvera, todos. No sé cuánto tiempo anduvimos perdidos en ese espacio inmóvil. (pp. 144–45)

The scene is redolent of the fairy tale *Sleeping Beauty* when the occupants of the castle fall asleep for 100 years, caught in suspended animation doing their daily tasks. Garro's novel is, however, different from the fairy tale in that while the traditional fairy tale uses the 100 years as a hiatus which subsequently ends thus allowing the narrative proper to continue, *Los recuerdos del porvenir* does not complete the scene. We are not told what happens next; we are required to deduce it. In this, Garro consciously subverts the Eurocentric version of time (what she once called in an interview 'el tiempo occidental que trajeron los españoles').[44]

The impression of the whole village held in suspended animation is confirmed by the lone carter who arrives later that day in the village: 'Contó que en el campo ya estaba amaneciendo y al llegar a las trancas de Cocula se topó con la noche cerrada. Se asustó al ver que sólo en Ixtepec seguía la noche. Nos dijo que es más negra rodeada por la mañana' (p. 145). The scene ends on a note of magical realism. The carter subsequently sees two figures riding on a horse, Hurtado and Julia, who emerge mysteriously from the darkness: 'En su miedo no sabía si cruzar aquella frontera de luz y sombra. Estaba dudando cuando vio pasar a un jinete llevando en sus brazos a una mujer vestida de color de rosa. El iba de oscuro. Con un brazo detenía a la joven y con el otro llevaba las riendas del caballo. La mujer se iba riendo. El arriero les dio los buenos días' (p. 145). After this tantalizing glimpse of the two lovers, which is

---

[44] Quoted by Anita K. Stoll, 'Introduction', in *A Different Reality: Studies on the Work of Elena Garro*, edited by Anita K. Stoll (London and Toronto: Associated University Presses, 1990), pp. 11–22 (p. 15).

redolent of the happy end of fairy tales such as *Snow White and the Seven Dwarfs*, Hurtado and Julia disappear off into the distance.

It is no doubt the fairy tale element of *Los recuerdos del porvenir* which disrupts the linear nature of time and space in the novel. Garro's novel also dislocates one other important paradigm, that of gender. On a superficial level, the boundaries between the sexes in *Los recuerdos del porvenir* seem permanently fixed. The men are all-powerful; they have a possessive attitude towards their women. The General epitomises this, in that he keeps Julia locked up for hours at a time in their hotel room (p. 97). When men go to see their beloved they go on their horses – a symbol of masculinity – even riding their horses right into the hotel to their beloved's room (p. 36). The women, by contrast, are silent and submissive. When she is beaten up by the General, Julia does not utter a sound (p. 125). Women are classed along with stray dogs and Indians, sharing with these last two the greatest chance of being on the receiving end of violence (p. 63). The military recruits who people the novel see no distinction between women and whores (p. 248). Women are renowned for being 'ladinas' (p. 176). Most grave of all, the woman's sin is inscribed in her child (p. 239). But it is not only the men who see women as inferior; women also accept this notion, which demonstrates how they have internalized the law of patriarchy. Thus, the women of the village all see Julia as the root of evil. '¡Es Julia!' as one female observer comments, speaking on behalf of the majority, 'Ella tiene la culpa de todo lo que nos pasa' (p. 81; see also p. 14, p. 24). Julia thereby re-enacts the Malinche plot, becoming blameworthy because of her gender, as Sandra Cypess has suggested.[45]

Pointing in a similar direction, women recognise, or better mis-recognise, that men are better at expressing themselves than women. As Conchita says at one stage, '¡Qué dicha ser hombre y poder decir lo que se piensa!' (p. 26). One further consequence of patriarchy, as revealed by the novel, is that women lose their identities through marriage, or through men, itself a common theme in Garro's work.[46] This is suggested obliquely in Elvira's observation to the effect that she has forgotten what she looked like during her marriage: 'Cuando se casó, Justino acaparó las palabras y los espejos y ella atravesó unos años silenciosos y borrados en los que se movió como una ciega, sin entender lo que sucedía a su

---

[45] 'The Figure La Malinche in the Texts of Elena Garro', in *A Different Reality: Studies on the Work of Elena Garro*, edited by Anita K. Stoll (London and Toronto: Associated University Presses, 1990), pp. 117–35 (esp. pp. 120–25).
[46] See Gabriela Mora, 'A Thematic Exploration of the Works of Elena Garro', in *Latin American Women Writers: Yesterday and Today*, edited by Yvette E. Miller and Charles M. Tatum (Pittsburgh, PA.: Latin American Literary Review, 1977), pp. 91–97 (p. 93).

alrededor. La única memoria que tenía de esos años era que no tenía alguna' (pp. 27–28). Mirrors function in the novel as an indication of self-identity. Elvira is now surprised by what she looks like now. '– ¡Dios mío! ¿Esa soy yo?. . . ¿Esa vieja dentro del espejo?. . . ¿Y así me ve la gente?. . . ¡No volveré a salir a la calle, no quiero inspirar lástima!' (p. 28). In a scene clearly based on the Wicked Stepmother from *Snow White and the Seven Dwarfs*, Elvira fails to recognise her new identity. Time stands in between herself and her image in the mirror. The ever-changing nature of reality cannot be frozen or contained within a mirror image.

There are, however, junctures in the story in which a desire to escape the limiting confines of patriarchy finds expression. This normally takes the form of Isabel questioning patriarchal law: 'A Isabel le disgustaba que establecieran diferencia entre ella y sus hermanos.' In this process of questioning the premises of phallocracy, the institution of marriage naturally enough comes under fire. As Isabel continues: 'Le humillaba la idea de que el único futuro para las mujeres fuera el matrimonio. Hablar del matrimonio como de una solución la dejaba reducida a una mercancía a la que había que dar salida a cualquier precio' (p. 22). But Isabel's thoughts are seen as madness by her elders. When she says, for example, in a way redolent of Virginia Woolf's desire to have a 'room of one's own', that 'tendré un cuarto así', her remark meets a sharp response: 'Cállate, muchacha, tú no estás para quedarte sola!' (p. 16). The very notion of having one's own room is seen as unthinkable.

However, the realm of the unthinkable does occasionally emerge in the course of the novel. A mundane example is the young girls' subversive desire to see the statue of the Virgin Mary in the local church without any clothes on: 'Queremos ver a la Virgen desnuda' (p. 15). The following exchange betwen Isabel and her elders is typical of the complex ideological issues involved:

> – No, no creo que yo me case. . .
> – No se imaginen cosas que no existen, que no van a acabar bien – les recomendó la vieja cuando los jóvenes se disponían a irse.
> – Dora, lo único que hay que imaginar es lo que no existe – le contestó Isabel desde el zaguán.
> – ¿Qué quieres decir con esta tontería?
> – Que hay que imaginar a los ángeles – gritó la joven y besó a la vieja que se quedó pensativa en su puerta, mirando como se alejaban, en la calle empedrada, los tres últimos amigos que le quedaban en el mundo. (p. 17)

It is intriguing that the old women should see Isabel's desire not to get married as something not just undesirable but non-existent ('cosas que no existen'). Isabel's subsequent comment that the imagination should be reserved for what does not exist epitomises the ethos of the novel as a whole, which deals in imaginary rather than empirical happenings, as, for example, a woman who captivates the entire male population of a town, lovers who disappear into the dusk, and so on.[47]

The novel is, indeed, a forceful statement of the primacy of the imagination, but it is an imagination which, though dissident, is ruled by the prisonhouse of gender and which is, ultimately, what Derrida calls an 'invagination'.[48] On a primary level, im(v)agination is presented in *Los recuerdos del porvenir* as a faculty which is able to lift people out of their brute-like existence (the play which Hurtado brings to Ixtepec being an archetypal example of this). As Doña Elvira suggests: 'no sé cómo no se nos había ocurrido organizar alguna función. Hemos vivido como caníbales' (p. 120). Art releases the inhabitants of Ixtepec from the drudgery of everyday life and also from the purely animal existence typified by the cannibal. It is intriguing that Elvira should describe the lives of the inhabitants before they experienced the magic of drama in terms of the cannibal. For this is precisely the metaphor which is most commonly used to refer to the law of men. Cruz, for example, an epitome of the 'macho' man, is described as opening wide his mouth when he laughs, thereby 'mostrando sus dientes blancos de caníbal joven' (p. 40). Elvira's metaphor is revealing therefore since it suggests that drama provides a means of escaping the dog-eat-dog laws of patriarchy. Art allows the inhabitants of Ixtepec to take their lives into their own hands. As the narrator suggests of drama: 'Era muy dulce que podíamos ser algo más que espectadores de la vida violenta de los militares' (p. 121).

The imaginative faculty, thus, seems related, as the novel suggests through an inter-related net of metaphors, to the feminine.[49] Other motifs reinforce this parallelism, and suggest how the im(v)agination is always

---

[47] For a discussion of the connection between fantasy and the female characters in Garro's novel, see Lucía Fox-Lockert, *Women Novelists in Spain and Spanish America*, pp. 228–40.

[48] Cary Nelson defines the Derridean term 'invagination' as suggesting that 'every encapsulation and formalization of an exterior reality involves a libidinal dynamic that is coded by the cultural history of the social construction of masculinity and femininity'; 'Men, Feminism: The Materiality of Discourse', in *Men in Feminism*, edited by Alice Jardine & Paul Smith (New York and London: Methuen, 1987), pp. 153–72 (p. 169).

[49] For a discussion of how Garro creates similarly positive images of womanhood in her theatre, see Sandra Messinger Cypess, 'Visual and Verbal Distances in the Mexican Theater: The Plays of Elena Garro', in *Woman as Myth and Metaphor in Latin-American Literature*, edited by Carmelo Virgilio and Naomi Lindstrom (Columbia: University of Missouri Press, 1985), pp. 44–62.

already-caught in its gendered origins. The men engage in military pursuits, (the Revolution, for example, p. 90), whereas the women do not. Im(v)agination, and its embodiment in art, is a means of escaping the male-dominated world of war, politics and tyranny. Tyranny, as *Los recuerdos del porvenir* incessantly reveals, is as much a mental as a physical oppression of others:

> En su primera noche en Ixtepec, Felipe Hurtado había dicho a sus huéspedes: 'Lo que falta aquí es la ilusión.' Sus amigos no lo entendieron pero sus palabras quedaron escritas en mi memoria con un humo incandescente que aparecía y desaparecía según mi estado de ánimo. La vida en aquellos días se empañaba y nadie vivía sino a través del general y su querida.
> Habíamos renunciado a la ilusión. (p. 116)

The essence of tyranny consists in renouncing personal illusion in order to live life vicariously through the fortunes of the subject's political masters who, in this case, are the General and Julia. The implication is that tyranny is a phallocentric force which governs thought and language. This goes some ways towards explaining the curious passage in the novel when the President explains his love of dictionaries to Hurtado:

> ¿Qué haríamos sin los diccionarios? Imposible pensarlo. Ese idioma que hablamos sería ininteligible sin ellos. Pero si consultamos el diccionario encontramos: "Ellos, tercera persona del plural." (p. 59)

The 'ellos' which the President conveniently relegates to the status of a dictionary definition are the subjects of the society which he tyrannizes. A world without dictionaries, which lay down the laws of language, would, to the President's way of thinking, be unthinkable ('Imposible pensarlo'). As an embodiment of manhood, he rejects the notion and indeed the space of the unthinkable. His power, which as this passage reveals is predicated on language as something given, leads him to reject freedom of thought. As he says to Hurtado, '¿Sabe usted lo que es un librepensador? Un hombre que ha renunciado al pensamiento' (p. 62). The President's rejection of free thought is belied, however, by the book which contains him, *Los recuerdos del porvenir*, which revels in the freedom of the mind.

Tyranny is experienced, typically, in the novel in terms of physical asphyxiation. There is an early indication of this in the novel which sets the tone for what is to come. Part V begins by describing how the population of Ixtepec used to wait eagerly for the six 'o clock train from Mexico City which brought news of current events:

Esperábamos los periódicos con las noticias de la ciudad como si de ellas pudiera surgir el milagro que rompiera el hechizo quieto en el que habíamos caído. Pero sólo veíamos las fotografías de los ajusticiados. Era el tiempo de los fusilamientos. Entonces creíamos que nada iba a salvarnos. (p. 34)

Instead of the miracle, news of the war, which we have seen to be a specifically male enterprise, leads to the experience of anguish: 'Desde su cama doña Ana oyó los rumores de la noche y se sintió asfixiada por el tiempo quieto que vigilaba las puertas y las ventanas de su casa. La voz de su hijo le llegó: "Yo no quepo en este cuerpo" ' (p. 34). This sense of physical imprisonment within the body, experienced literally by Ana's child, is an omen of Julia's entrapment within the General's room which we learn about later on in the novel. This tyranny is so pervasive, as the narrator of the novel, the consciousness of the town of Ixtepec, complains later on, that the beauty of nature is ignored:

Todo mi esplendor caía en la ignorancia, en un no querer mirarme, en un olvido voluntario. Y mientras tanto mi belleza ilusoria y cambiante se consumía y renacía como una salamandra en mitad de las llamas. En vano cruzaban los jardines nubes de mariposas repentinas. La sombra de Francisco Rosas cubría mis cielos, empañaba el brillo de mis tardes, ocupaba mis esquinas y se introducía en las conversaciones. (p. 117)

The inhabitants of Ixtepec have their eyes closed to the beauty of the world, so deadened are they by tyranny. The image used in the passage, 'a salamander amidst the flames', might well serve as a leitmotif of the novel as a whole. For it attempts to defy the law of patriarchy, and its bye-laws of war and tyranny, promoting instead the unthinkable, such as a salamander swimming not in water but in fire. We should beware perhaps of attaching too much of an aura of the unthinkable to Garro's vision. There is an extraordinary sense in which *Los recuerdos del porvenir* is able to suggest the magic underlying the most ordinary things, and what could be more mundane than the position of a house:

– ¡Yo no quepo en este cuerpo! – exclamó Nicolás vencido, y se tapó la cara con las manos como si fuera a llorar.
– Estamos cansados – dijo Felix desde su escabel.
Durante unos segundos la casa entera viajó por los cielos, se integró en la Vía Láctea y luego cayó sin ruido en el mismo punto en que se encuentra ahora. (p. 33)

Garro's novel, as this passage demonstrates, celebrates the power of the imagination which can transport a house up to the Milky Way and bring it back down to the very same spot in seconds. *Los recuerdos del porvenir* celebrates the 'sorpresa infinita de encontrarse en el mundo' (pp. 31–32) which tyranny wishes to suppress but which the imagination, like a salamander swimming in fire, strives to activate. Since, however, imagination is shown to be always already gendered in its origins in Garro's novel, it can never do anymore than replicate the social structures which it strives to transcend; it can only ever be im(v)agination.

As we have seen, Bombal's *La amortajada*, Castellanos's 'Lección de cocina' and Garro's *Los recuerdos del porvenir*, each in their individual ways, address the issue of woman's confinement within the patriarchal prison. *La amortajada* links the imprisonment of women within marriage with the Zolaesque experience of lying in a coffin able to hear what your relatives are saying, but unable to regain consciousness. 'Lección de cocina' deftly deconstructs the logic of patriarchy which would keep a woman wedded to her kitchen, while *Los recuerdos del porvenir* exposes the social consequences of the gender war in which women seem destined to be the losers. Despite the apparent pessimism of these texts, they are united in their desire to find a way out of the man-made maze of life. Castellanos's short story draws strength in sisterhood with great female minds of the past (and particularly, Sor Juana), Bombal's novel advocates escape via the emotional bonding of mother and daughter, while *Los recuerdos del porvenir* seeks escape through the power of the imagination. Each of these escape routes are, however, edged by the discourse of death (Ana María is dead, as is Sor Juana), while the escape route offered by the imagination itself merely duplicates the epistemological *status quo*. For these writers, therefore, the prison becomes the primordial metaphor through which the image of the female body is experienced.

III

FAIRY TALES

It was the flexibility of the fairy-tale narrative which no doubt attracted contemporary Spanish women writers to explore its form. In his study of the folk tale, Vladimir Propp discovered a similar structuring of events which was common to a wide variety of folk tales as well as fairy tales, even if their surface structure differed. To explain this idea, he used the term 'function' which he defined as 'an act of a character, defined from the point of view of its significance for the course of the action' (p. 21).[1] By whittling the folk tale down to its structural common denominators, Propp concludes that 'functions of characters serve as stable, constant elements in a tale, independent of how and by whom they are fulfilled', and further, that they 'constitute the fundamental components of a tale' (p. 21). As long as the function remains identical, therefore, the characters may change, thus lending variety to the basic plot.[2] It is for this reason that women writers, in Spain at least, have seen the fairy-tale structure as providing an ideal narrative structure in which the narrator is able to insert her own life. For while the identity of the narrator can neither be Snow White nor Cinderella, nevertheless her function within the narrative with regard to other characters may have some striking similarities with the life pattern of fairy-tale, or folk-tale, figures.

Fairy tales operate in post-civil-war Spanish novels written by women in much the same way that Greek myths do in the work of many male novelists of the same period. The first significant male novel of the post-civil-war period, Cela's *La familia de Pascual Duarte* (1942), for example, traces the life pattern of an individual which has has some

[1] V. Propp, *The Morphology of the Folk Tale*, revised edition (Austin & London: University of Texas Press, 1968).

[2] Propp's further points out that 2) 'the number of functions known to the fairy tale is limited', 3) 'the sequence of functions is always identical', and 4) 'all fairy tales are of one type in regard to structure', basically expanding on his original point (see pp. 21–25). Propp goes on to discuss individual examples of the folk tale. Notice that Propp often uses the terms fairy tale and folk tale alternately, and with the same basic sense.

striking parallels with that of Orestes and Oedipus. The protagonist of Luis Martín-Santos's classic novel *Tiempo de silencio* (1964), likewise, is referred to as a modern-day Oedipus.[3] Fairy tales are employed in a similar manner by post-civil-war female novelists to flesh out a 'mythic' backdrop to the lives of the characters described in their novels. This is certainly the case *prima facie* with the works of Ana María Matute, Carmen Martín Gaite and Esther Tusquets studied in this chapter. However, while the motivation behind the use of a mythic backcloth may be similar in the male novel and in the female novel, it is important to point out that there is a difference in terms of the way in which the metaphoric macro-text is used. In Martín-Santos's *Tiempo de silencio*, for example, Greek mythology is used in order to cast an *esperpentesque* light on the inhabitants of post-war Madrid; the characters, thus, fall consistently short of the regal splendour of the world of Greek myths. In the female post-civil-war novel, however, the discourse of fairy tales is implemented recuperatively; its actualization is not necessarily accompanied by irony. As we shall see, Matute, Martín Gaite and Tusquets have recourse to different fairy-tale structures in their narratives (*The Little Mermaid* appears in *Primera memoria*, *Puss in Boots* and *Alice in Wonderland* in *El cuarto de atrás*, while *Snow White* is favoured in *El mismo mar de todos los veranos*). The discourse of the fairy tales serves a double purpose in their writing; it is used, on the one hand, by the narrator as a means of achieving insight into the purposeless kaleidoscope of everyday life and, on the other, as a means of delving into the social conditioning which formed the self of the narrator as she now knows herself. The fairy tale, thus, is used in order to understand the past but also as a tool for enlightenment in the here and now.

A preliminary comparison of the return-to-reality device in each of these three novels produces some indication of the way in which the fairy-tale narrative is used in each. In her article 'Magic Abjured: Closure in Children's Fantasy Fiction', Sara Gilead distinguishes between three types of return-to-reality closure present in fairy tales. In the first, she argues, 'the return completes a history of psychic growth and interprets the fantasy narrative as a salutary exposure of forbidden

---

[3] G. G. Brown refers to the 'manifestly Oedipal-relationship' Pascual has with his mother; see *A Literary History of Spain: The Twentieth Century* (London: Ernest Benn Limited, 1972), p. 145. For a discussion of the similarities between *La familia de Pascual Duarte* and *The Oresteia*, see J. S. Bernstein, 'Pascual Duarte y Orestes', *Symposium*, 22 (1968), 301–18. For a short but concise survey of the background to the Spanish post-civil-war novel see Gonzalo Sobejano, 'Direcciones de la novela española de postguerra', in *Novelistas españoles de postguerra*, edited by Rodolfo Cardona (Madrid: Taurus, 1976), pp. 47–64. See also Barry Jordan, *Writing and Politics in Franco's Spain* (London and New York: Routledge, 1990).

wishes and emotions' (example: *The Wizard of Oz* by L. Frank Baum); in the second, the return 'simulates the closure effects of the first type but disrupts rather than smoothly concludes a linear socialization plot' (example: Lewis Carroll's *Alice* books); and in the third type, the return neither normalizes fantasy nor rejects it, thereby revealing, 'without an assuring sense of mediation, both the seductive force and the dangerous potentiality of fantasy' (example: J. M. Barrie's *Peter Pan*).[4] These three types of return-to-reality devices roughly correspond to the narrative plottings employed in the three novels studied in this chapter: Martín Gaite's *El cuarto de atrás* echoes the first type, Matute's *Primera memoria* the second type, and Tusquets's *El mismo mar de todos los veranos* the third type. The narrator of *El cuarto de atrás* returns to reality the wiser for her nocturnal experience; the narrator of *Primera memoria* has failed to harmonize the conflicting pressures of the fantasy and the real worlds (echoed in the truncated structure of the novel); and Tusquets's narrator is simultaneously seduced by the power of fantasy but, in true postmodernist fashion, is simultaneously aware of its *kitsch* status. Yet, despite their differences, all three narrators use the discourse of fairy tales to unravel the social skein which produced their female social identity. The results of this investigative enterprise can be highly critical, as will become evident.

ANA MARIA MATUTE: *PRIMERA MEMORIA*

Janet Pérez has pointed out that *Primera memoria* (1960) by Ana María Matute (1926: Spain) uses the Cain and Abel theme 'to portray symbolically and in miniature Spain's fratricidal civil conflict from the supposedly peaceful haven of the Balearic Isles'.[5] In this early novel, which is one of Matute's best according to Margaret E. W. Jones, the Civil War acts as a functional backdrop.[6] Yet the main focus of the novel is provided by the feminine protagonist, Matia, who, as often occurs in Matute's fiction, is an adolescent.[7] In some senses, *Primera memoria* is a

[4] 'Magic Abjured: Closure in Children's Fantasy Fiction', *PMLA*, 106:2 (1991), 277–93 (p. 278).

[5] 'The Fictional World of Ana María Matute: Solitude, Injustice, and Dreams', in *Women Writers of Spain*, edited by Joan L. Brown (Cranbury: Associated University Presses, 1991), pp. 93–115 (p. 107).

[6] *The Literary World of Ana María Matute* (Lexington: The University Press of Kentucky, 1970), p. 23.

[7] Janet Pérez, 'Portraits of the *Femme Seule* by Laforet, Matute, Soriano, Martín Gaite, Galvarriato, Quiroga, and Medio', in *Feminine Concerns in Contemporary Spanish Fiction by Women*, pp. 54–77 (p. 55).

Bildungsroman which, like Laforet's *Nada*, focusses on a young girl who
has been recently orphaned and is growing up in a man's world.[8] The
Civil War, which is the cause of Matia's move to Mallorca, is often
suppressed by the consciousness of the narrator, as if history were an
irritating interlude, diverting the characters from the business of growing
up. Matia is far more preoccupied with her emotional, and sexual,
awakening. Her growing awareness of herself as a woman is created by
means of her inter-relations with Borja, Lauro el Chino, Guiem, Toni
and Jorge. It is curious that Matia seems not to have formed relationships
with girls of her own age; her experience of women seems to be
restricted to the restrictive mannerisms of her aunt and the servants.
What is clear from these relationships with her male contemporaries is
that the boys have total control over her, evidenced in particular by the
scene in which Borja teases her about her supposed lovers, and threatens
her that she will be sent to a correctional centre, a threat she takes very
seriously (pp. 160–62). As she concludes rather ruefully about this
episode, 'Borja ganó y yo perdí' (p. 162).

These, then, are the basic elements of the plot which Matute's novel
has in common with other Spanish formation-novels by women written in
the post-civil-war era. Again, like *Nada*, *Primera memoria* uses fairy
tales consistently as a means of structuring female imaginative and
ontological experience. But, before discussing the role of fairy tales in
Matute's novel, a few preliminary points about its structural dynamics
will be necessary since they will help us to focus more clearly on the
fairy-tale motifs. *Primera memoria* is composed proleptically, that is,
hindsight is available to the narrator. The novel opens, for example, with
Matia leafing through a photo album, and settling on the photograph of
the grandmother. The opening paragraphs also help to illustrate the
different levels of temporal perception employed in the novel. In the
second paragraph, we hear parenthetically of the atrocities of the Civil
War, '("Dicen que en el otro lado están matando familias enteras. . .")'
(p. 10), a device which will prove to be common throughout the novel, as
if memories of the past or of past conversations simply floated of their
own accord to the surface of the text. The novel, indeed, very much
works in this way, searching for the hidden truth or cause of events. The
concluding image of the novel makes this quite clear. The mayor's cock
is heard to be 'clamando . . . por alguna misteriosa causa perdida'

---

[8] The protagonist of *Primera memoria* is not in fact an orphan; her mother had died
four years previous to her move to Mallorca, which occurred when she was 12 years old,
while her father had effectively disowned her, leaving her in the care of others; *Primera
memoria*, in *Colección Premio Nadal*, vol. VI (Barcelona: Destino, 1971), pp. 10–169
(p. 12). All subsequent page references are to this edition.

(p. 169). This Lost Cause is the lost generation of the Civil War whose lives were literally destroyed by the Nationalist offensive. This Lost Cause is also to be understood, however, on a metaphorical level as, in Janet Díaz's words, 'lost innocence, lost idealism, lost hope, lost Republic'.[9] As Matute suggested in an interview about her own experience of the Civil War:

> Nos encontramos a un lado o a otro, éramos parte de esa guerra, queríamos o no, con todas sus consecuencias. Luego, con la adolescencia, empiezas a preguntarte por qué has tenido que estar en un lugar o en otro, si a ti no te han dado opción. Entonces, uno tiene la sensación de autotraición muy extraña, por eso la traición en casi todos mis libros tiene importancia. Entonces tenemos el recuerdo de algo más limpio, más puro, que no está mezclado con los horrores de un exilio, o de un país donde se están matando los hermanos. Y siempre añoramos un mundo en que esas cosas no ocurrían.[10]

It is this obscurely-felt sensation of self-betrayal which becomes Matia's motivating force to know ontologically the reasons for her experience. This may not at first seem the case, since she seems to experience the events which happen to her in an alienated fashion, as if they occurred to someone else. *Primera memoria*, thus, embodies a discontinuity between the protagonist who experiences and the narrator who writes, and this slippage between the two levels is nowhere more apparent than in the parentheses which introduce information only available after the event in question has taken place. When Matia sees el Chino in church, for example, we read:

> Y me dije: "Acaso le matarán en el frente, quizá en el frente, quizá una bala le atravesará así, tal como ahora está, por la espalda".
> (Y así fue, pues un mes más tarde lo mataron. . .). (p. 163)

Knowledge, as this parenthesis demonstrates, works proleptically in *Primera memoria*. The same is true of the discourse of fairy tales in the novel, a knowledge which Matute has treasured since childhood.[11]

The story of *The Little Mermaid* and *St George and the Dragon*, among others, punctuate Matute's text at semantically crucial moments. *The*

---

[9] *Ana María Matute* (Boston: Twayne, 1971), p. 133.

[10] Geraldine C. Nichols, *Escribir, espacio propio: Laforet, Matute, Moix, Tusquets, Riera y Roig por sí mismas*, p. 42.

[11] As Matute suggests in her essay, 'Diciembre y Andersen', fairy tales were a formative influence on her childhood; see Christopher L. Anderson and Lynne Vespe Sheay, 'Ana María Matute's *Primera memoria*: A Fairy Tale Gone Awry', *RCEH*, 14 (1989), 1–14 (p. 2).

Little Mermaid, in particular, as Suzanne Gross Reed points out, 'is at once the model of [Matia's] change from child to woman and of her relationship with Manuel Taronjí'.[12] *The Little Mermaid* works on a primary level for Matia as an escape valve from the unpleasant realities of everyday life, just like the map which is full of exotic names that Matia used to dream about (again, note, parenthetically):

> (Y me acuerdo de cuando metía medio cuerpo en el armario, con el Atlas abierto en la penumbra, y miraba el Archipiélago y me paraba extasiada en cada nombre: Lemnos, Chío, Andros, Serphos . . . Karo, Mykono, Polykandros. . . Naxos, Anaphi, Psara. . . Ah, sí, nombres y nombres como viento y sueños. Soñando yo también, mi dedo recorría en una comba, sobre el azul satinado, desde Corfú a Mytilene. Y las palabras, como una música: *él iba en el* Delfín, *vivía en él, y no pisaba tierra apenas: se iba hasta el Asia Menor. . .*) (p. 136)

Fairy tales are thus seen as inhabiting the same world as the dream-world the atlas offers. Though initially associated with escapism, fairy tales come, however, to fulfil the function of refracting a specific meaning onto the events described. Guiem at one point, for example, is described as Captain Hook from *Peter Pan*:

> Tiznado y oscuro, Guiem salió del bosque. Bajó la manga de su jersey hasta cubrirse los dedos, de forma que surgía el gancho, retorcido y siniestro. (*El Capitán Garfio luchó con Peter Pan en los acantilados de la Isla de Nunca Jamás.* Borja, desterrado Peter Pan, como yo misma, *el niño que no quiso crecer volvió de noche a su casa y encontró la ventana cerrada.* Nunca me pareció Borja tan menudo como en aquel momento. *Hizo la limpieza de primavera, cuando la recogida de las hojas, en los bosques de los Niños Perdidos.* Y los mismos Niños Perdidos, todos demasiados crecidos, de pronto, para jugar; demasiado niños, de pronto, para entrar en la vida, en el mundo que no queríamos – ¿no queríamos? – conocer). (p. 112).

The reference to childhood, introduced as a question in the last sentence of the quotation, makes it quite clear that fairy tales are to be seen as the childhood world which Matia does not wish to leave; the '¿no queríamos?' is simply rhetorical. Borja, for his part, epitomises Peter Pan: 'Borja estaba solo, de pie (*adiós, Peter Pan, adiós, ya no pediré ir contigo la próxima Limpieza de Primavera. . .*)' (p. 113). Yet, despite the fact that the male participants of the intrigue are clearly part of this

---

[12] 'Notes on Hans Christian Andersen Fairy Tales in Ana María Matute's *Primera memoria*', in *Continental, Latin-American and Francophone Women Writers*, pp. 177–82 (p. 181). See also Michael D. Thomas, 'The Rite of Initiation in Matute's *Primera memoria*', *KRQ*, 25 (1978), 153–64.

fairy-tale world, they are, curiously enough, alienated from its logic. The
fairy-tale world is one which is purposefully projected on the men by the
female protagonist, as if to reverse the unspoken rule of fiction whereby
women are objects created by male vision. Manuel, for example, inhabits
a world which is very different from Matia's, as evident from the
following quotation.

> Recuerdo que le dije, frotándome las rodillas:
> – Me gustaría que nevase. ¿Has visto la nieve alguna vez?
> – No. Nunca la he visto.
> El agua golpeaba las rocas, y la *Joven Simón* aparecía negruzca, casi
> siniestra. Teníamos la cara enrojecida de frío y los ojos lacrimosos. El
> viento zarandeó mi cabello, como una bandera negra. (. . .)
> Pero Manuel no mostró demasiado interés por aquello. Al hablarle o
> mostrarle algo, sólo decía:
> Sí, sí – distraídamente. (p. 153)

Matia's daydreams, and her playing with the realm of the fairy tale, is
presented as specifically feminine, as if it were outside the ken of
mankind.

The fairy tale, thus, normally acts recuperatively in the text; it is
inserted into the text, thereby existing as a metaphorical level to the text,
in which symbol and image are predominant. The two levels of fairy tale
and realist text are consistently brought together through image –
specifically the sea which surrounds Mallorca and the sea from which the
Little Mermaid emerged – and through event. Thus, the experience of
emotional isolation and lack of communication between the sexes during
the Civil War runs parallel to the story of *The Little Mermaid*. The two
stories are, at first sight, brought triumphantly together at the end of the
novel. As we read:

> Y de pronto estaba allí el amanecer, como una realidad terrible,
> abominable. Y yo con los ojos abiertos, como un castigo. (No existió la
> Isla de Nunca Jamás y la Joven Sirena no consiguió un alma inmortal,
> porque los hombres y las mujeres no aman, y se quedó con un par de
> inútiles piernas, y se convirtió en espuma.) Eran horribles los cuentos.
> (p. 169)

However, there is a discontinuity between the two levels since, while *The
Little Mermaid* has a clear and definite conclusion, Matute's novel does
not. As Christopher L. Andersen and Lynne Vespe Sheay point out,
Matia's ultimate betrayal of Manuel, her 'refusal to experience pain for
the sake of another person' indicates that she is not worthy of advancing
to the 'reward/salvation stage' common in the traditional fairy-tale

structure.[13] If anything, *Primera memoria* ends on a note of non-completion. Clearly this has something to do with the fact that *Primera memoria* is the opening novel of a trilogy entitled *Los mercaderes*. However, the subtext of the fairytale is brought to a conclusion, even if the novel is not. Unlike the mermaid, the protagonist of Matute's novel does not disappear into a cloud of foam; her life, evidently, carries on.

What is intriguing about the novel is the fact that, although the discourse of the fairy tale is presented as non-salvific since illusion and everyday life are shown finally to be at odds with one another, fairy tales possess a significant function in the novel as a discourse which allows female life to centre itself. Throughout the novel, the protagonist is described as alienated from the masculinist equivalent of fairy tales, namely, the doctrines of the Church. Mosén Mayol, for example, in the eyes of most of the inhabitants of the village, is a quasi-divine figure, dignified, cultured, highly refined (pp. 49–50). But Matia is not as overwhelmed as her peers and friends are by his aura of sanctity. During the mass which she, el Chino and Borja attend, Matia's thoughts wander off to thoughts of the Little Mermaid during the religious chants:

> *"¿Por qué no tenemos las sirenas un alma inmortal?"* No la tuvo, no la tuvo, y se convirtió en espuma. *"Y cada vez que con sus pies desnudos pisaba la tierra sentía como si se le clavesen cuchillas afiladas y agujas. . ."*
> – . . . *quos pre-ti-o-sa sanguine redi-mis-ti.* . . . La Joven Sirena quería que la amasen, pero nunca la amó nadie. ¡Pobre sirena! (p. 59)

A distinction is thus being drawn between the immortality implicit in Christ's sacrifice for mankind and the inconstancy and perishability which characterise the Little Mermaid's life. Matia's alienation from the discourse of the Christian world is further suggested when Borja asks her if she goes to confession, to which she replies: 'No tengo pecados' (p. 164). Matia finally reveals herself as a liminal figure, standing on the outer limits of the society in which she lives, no closer now than she was before to the roots of her being.

In more ways than one, *Primera memoria* is a truncated text; rather than offering a tale of 'linear socialization', Matute's novel is characterized by disruption and psychic inconclusion (thereby echoing the second type of fairy tale as defined by Sara Gilead; see above). Though ultimately unable to provide a finality to Matia's life which is anything but proleptic, the discourse of the fairy tale is nevertheless promoted as the only hermeneutic strategy truly available to womankind.

[13] 'Ana María Matute's *Primera memoria*: A Fairy tale Gone Awry', p. 11.

CARMEN MARTIN GAITE: *EL CUARTO DE ATRÁS*

The publication in 1978 of *El cuarto de atrás* established Carmen Martín Gaite (1925: Spain) as one of the major Spanish female novelists of the contemporary era. It has attracted a great deal of critical attention; in bibliometric terms, as Joan L. Brown has pointed out, it is 'the most frequently examined novel by a contemporary Spanish woman author over the past decade'.[14] *El cuarto de atrás*, which is dedicated to Lewis Carroll, opens with the protagonist (who is clearly a projection of the author herself) falling asleep while reading Tzvetan Todorov's work on the literature of the fantastic, follows with a description of her being woken up by a mysterious stranger dressed in black who gives her a searching interview during the night, and concludes when her daughter wakes her up early next morning; as a result the reader is led to question the boundaries between the real and the imaginary. As Marie Murphy has suggested, this particular novel's 'playfulness, humor and technical virtuosity make it the author's most intriguing and open work to date', seeming to enchant Martín Gaite's readers to the exclusion of all else.[15] Despite its apparent uniqueness in Martín Gaite's canon, though, *El cuarto de atrás* is essentially a re-casting of *Entre visillos* (1957), the main difference between the two texts being that the publication of *El cuarto de atrás* after Franco's death meant that the author was no longer hampered by censorship.[16] Just as important as the relaxation of censorship, however, is the status that *El cuarto de atrás* has as a *re-written* text, and therefore more a scriptural exercise than a documentary. In this reading of Martín Gaite's novel I shall be concentrating on

[14] 'Carmen Martín Gaite: Reaffirming the Pact Between Reader and Writer', in *Women Writers of Contemporary Spain*, pp. 72–92 (p. 86).

[15] *An Encyclopedia of Continental Women Writers*, ed. Katharina M. Wilson, Vol. II, p. 793.

[16] See J. L. Brown, 'One Autobiography Twice Told: Martín Gaite's *Entre visillos* and *El cuarto de atrás*', *HJ*, 7 (1986), 37–47. See also J. L. Brown and E. M. Smith, '*El cuarto de atrás*: Metafiction and the Actualization of Literary Theory', *Hispanófila*, 90 (1987), 63–70. There are also a number of good essays on *El cuarto de atrás* in Mirella d'Ambrosio Servodidio and Marcia L. Welles (eds.), *From Fiction to Metafiction: Essays in Honour of Carmen Martín Gaite* (Lincoln: Society of Spanish and Spanish American Studies, 1983); Manuel Durán, '*El cuarto de atrás*: imaginación, fantasía, misterio: Todorov y algo más' (129–37); Kathleen M. Glenn, '*El cuarto de atrás*: Literature as *juego* and the Self-Reflexive Text' (149–59); Linda Gould Levine, 'Carmen Martín Gaite's *El cuarto de atrás*: A Portrait of the Artist as a Woman' (161–72); Elizabeth J. Ordóñez, 'Reading, Telling and the Text of Carmen Martín Gaite's *El cuarto de atrás*' (173–84); and Robert C. Spires, 'Intertextuality in *El cuarto de atrás*' (139–48).

the use of fairy tales and populist literature motifs, as well as their integration into the 'novel-as-self-reflexive' device.

El cuarto de atrás is predicated on the escapism characteristic of children's fantasy literature, as Martín Gaite would be the first to point out. As she notes in an interview: 'When one experiences the dazzling impact of reading at an early age, the effect is akin to that of an arrow wound. Reading provides insight into a secret world that liberates one from the hostile pressures of the environment, from the routines and deception that the confrontation with reality produces'.[17] In line with the thrust of Martín Gaite's observation, *El cuarto de atrás* consistently draws attention to the haven provided by the world of fantasy, romantic fiction and the fairy tale in the narrator's mind. Intriguingly, however, the worlds of fantasy and reality are never presented in the novel as separate worlds; there is, indeed, often an uncanny interrelation, and even identity, between them. The novel opens, for example, *in medias res* with the narrator trying to establish the identity of the man who has sent her a love letter, and noting that his hand-writing seems vaguely familiar. The scene suddenly changes and the beautiful girl on the cover of a magazine sitting on the table is now looking at the narrator: 'Ahora la niña provinciana que no logra dormirse me está mirando a la luz de la lamparita amarilla, cuyo resplandor ha atenuado, poniéndole encima un pañuelo: ve este cuarto dibujado por Emilio Freixas sobre una página satinada de tonos ocres, la gran cama deshecha y la mujer en pijama, leyendo una carta de amor sobre la alfombra, le brillan los ojos, idealiza mi malestar' (p. 23).[18] The world behind the glossy magazine has come alive, rather like the world behind the mirror in Lewis Carroll's *Alice in Wonderland*. The woman behind the mirror lives in a world of love and romance: 'estaban de moda los nombres con E. largos y exóticos, el mío no sorprendía a nadie, empezaba con la C. de cuarto, de casa, de cama y de aquel corazón que dibujaba con tiza ante la mirada aburrida del profesor, el que se me aceleraba cuando Norma Shearer besaba a Leslie Howard, el que grababan los novios, atravesado por una flecha, en los árboles de la Alamedilla' (p. 25). She is the embodiment of the pot-boiler novel in which people do not eat or go to work, they simply fall in love. As the first chapter of *El cuarto de atrás* make clear, the narrative consciousness moves freely between different levels, from the narrator to the glossy face in the magazine, from this side of the looking-glass to the other.

---

[17] 'The Virtues of Reading', *PMLA*, 104:3 (1989), 348–53 (p. 348).
[18] All references are to *El cuarto de atrás* (Madrid: Destino, 1978).

The 'novela rosa' (especially in its Elizabeth Mulder form), itself a grown-up version of the fairy tale, is the hermeneutic sub-structure underpinning the novel. This is so for sociological reasons; as the narrator suggests: 'es muy importante el papel que jugaron las novelas rosa en la formación de las chicas de los años cuarenta' (p. 138). The 'novela rosa', thus, has its documentary aspect, but also operates as a running commentary on the fiction/life interface. This becomes evident when the 'novela rosa' bursts into the interview between the narrator and her interviewer, the mysterious man in black. The man in black appears concerned and suddenly we read: ' "Oh Raimundo – exclamó Esperanza, mientras brotaban las lágrimas de sus párpados cerrados –, contigo nunca tengo miedo. No te vuelvas a ir nunca." Era de una novela que venía en "Lecturas". Estaba escrita la frase, según era estilo entonces, al pie de una de las ilustraciones, donde se veía a una mujer con la cabeza apoyada en el respaldo del sofá y a un hombre inclinándose solícito sobre ella' (p. 38). We later find out that this scene is one from a novel written in her youth by the narrator-protagonist (p. 140). At this juncture the narrator expects her guest to reveal his identity: 'aquel momento en que estaba a punto de ser pronunciado el famoso "¿no te acuerdas?" ' (pp. 140–41). No revelation is in fact forthcoming but the expectation created by the 'novela rosa' hovers in the background. Later on, the man in black lights two cigarettes in his mouth and passes one to her. The narrator notes: 'Muy de novela rosa este detalle' (p. 190).

Throughout the novel, the narrator-protagonist seems to live certain parts of her life according to the happy ending concept of Hollywood films in the 1950s. But she is choosy. She describes a novel she read in her childhood, for example, about a young girl who went to college and married her Latin professor, and remarks 'para ese viaje no necesitábamos alforjas . . . tanto ilusionarse con los estudios y desafiar a la sociedad que le impedía a una mujer realizarlos, para luego salir por ahí, en plan happy end, que a saber si sería o no tan happy, porque aquella chica se tuvo que sentir decepcionada tarde o temprano; además, ¿por qué tenían que acabar todas las novelas cuando se casa la gente?' (p. 92). Though absorbed by the dream world of film, the narrator simultaneously remembers the point at which she began to doubt the authenticity of the Hollywood dream.

The romantic novels which interrupt the present tense of the narrative at various points are not simply an example of socially-produced wish-fulfilment; the narrator herself created some of the fictions in her childhood. The protagonist mentions that in the past she was involved with one of her friends in writing a 'novela rosa' who had a protagonist called Esmeralda: 'también debe haber trozos de una novela rosa que fuimos escribiendo entre las dos, aunque no llegamos a terminarla, la protagonista se llamaba Esmeralda, se escapó de su casa una noche porque sus padres eran demasiado ricos y ella quería conocer la aventura de vivir al raso, se encontró, junto a un acantilado, con un desconocido vestido de negro que estaba de espaldas, mirando el mar' (p. 58). The present scene in which the narrator is being interviewed by a mysterious stranger is thus a duplication of a novel written by the narrator in the past. Time itself adds another dimension to the Heidenberg principle of uncertainty which already seems to be prime mover of the novel.

The 'novela rosa' is not introduced in a random, innocent way in *El cuarto de atrás*; it is often linked to the self-reflexivity technique. As Biruté Ciplijauskaité has pointed out, the narrative of *El cuarto de atrás* is characterized by both confession and self-analysis, themselves part of the self-reflexive stance adopted by the narrator.[19] The second page of the text provides an early example of this: 'He dicho ''anhelo y temor'' por decir algo, tanteando a ciegas, y cuando se dispara así, nunca se da en el blanco; las palabras son para la luz, de noche se fugan, aunque el ardor de la persecución sea más febril y compulsivo a oscuras, pero también, por eso, más baldío' (p. 10). This sets the tone for most of the book which is set during the night, the subconscious, where the world takes on an uncanny appearance. At the beginning of Chapter IV, for example, the narrator returns to the back room to find that the intruder dressed in black has been looking at her papers:

> – ¿Por qué ha entrado en mi dormitorio? – le pregunto desabridamente.
> Se echa a reír y mi rabia crece.
> – No le veo la gracia.
> – Perdone, es que parece una frase de folletín. (p. 99)

As we can see from this scene, the man in black and the narrator are both conscious of the way in which their meeting each other echoes the plot of a romantic novel; they suddenly become like characters from an Unamuno novel (*Niebla*) or a Pirandello play (*Sei personaggi in cerca d'autore*). As this scene makes clear, the fairy-tale level of the novel is inseparable from the theme of self-reflexivity. The fairy tale, like the 'novela rosa', is simultaneously used as an escapist space within the text to which the narrator can retreat (the 'back room'), but also fulfills a *kitsch* function within *El cuarto de atrás*; the narrator adopts an ironizing, metafictional stance towards the Never Never world of fantasy, underlining the fictionality of fiction.

---

[19] *La novela femenina contemporánea*, p. 111.

The metafictional element is emphasized by the various allusions to Todorov's work; thus the narrator mentions coming across a copy of Todorov's *Introduction à la littérature fantastique* (p. 19). She swears that she will write a novel following Todorov's advice; and although the narrator never makes this explicit, it is clear that this is an accurate description of the book we are holding in our hands.[20] *El cuarto de atrás*, therefore, is a book which is aware of its own gestation, rather like the French Nouveau Roman in which the creative enterprise is a part of the work's message. The book being written is a concrete praxis of Todorov's theory of mystery enunciated in his *Introduction à la littérature fantastique*. One of the important characteristics of the mystery novel as identified by Todorov is its ambiguity: 'La ambigüedad es la clave de la literatura de misterio' (p. 53). Likewise there are many mysteries in *El cuarto de atrás*: among the more prominent are i) who is the man in black? and ii) how is the novel writing itself?[21] *El cuarto de atrás*, thus, effectively echoes Todorov's prescription.[22]

Throughout the novel, the work is being written mysteriously in the pile of papers which are being typewritten whenever the narrator leaves the room. At one point the narrator almost glimpses the novel being born: 'He bajado los ojos, y en el espacio que separa sus botas negras y deslucidas de los dedos que asoman por mis sandalias, me parece ver alzarse un castillo de paredes de papel, mejor dicho de papeles pegados unos a otros, a modo de ladrillos, y plagados de palabras y tachaduras de mi puño y letra, crece, sube, se va a desmoronar con el menor crujido, y

[20] Todorov defines the fantastic as 'that hesitation experienced by a person who knows only the laws of nature, confronting an apparently supernatural event'; *The Fantastic: A Structural Approach to a Literary Genre*, translated from the French by Richard Howard (Cleveland: The Press of Case Western Reserve University, 1973), p. 25. This definition aptly epitomises the reaction of the protagonist of *El cuarto de atrás* when faced with the stranger dressed in black. Of interest also is the fact that the example Todorov adduces to illustrate his theory of the fantastic, Jan Potocki's *Saragossa Manuscript*, deals, like Martín Gaite's novel, with uncanny events taking place during the night yet leaving a trace of their 'reality' the next morning; see Todorov, pp. 27–31.

[21] The man in black has been identified, as Debra A. Castillo points out, 'as a Todorovian theorist, the ideal interlocutor, the hero of a *novela rosa*, a character from the imaginary isle of Bergai, a detective, the correspondent of the author's sewing-basket love letter, a (hermeneutic) literary critic, the reader's ideal textual representation, a Jungian alter ego, a Lacanian Other, a figure from the engraver *Luther's Discussion with the Devil* brought to life, a Kafkaesque creature, the narrator's muse, her guide into the underworld (a modern role-reversal Beatrice to the narrator's Dante), a psychopomp, the devil, or simply the interviewer he announces himself to be'; 'Never-ending story: Carmen Martín Gaite's *The Back Room*', *PMLA*, 102:5 (1987), 814–28 (p. 819).

[22] For further discussion of the Todorov connection, see Aleida Anselma Rodríguez, 'Todorov en *El cuarto de atrás*', *Prismal/Cabral*, 11 (1983), 76–90.

yo me guarezco en el interior, con la cabeza escondida entre los brazos, no me atrevo a asomar' (p. 57). Their growth is a mystery: 'Pero, bueno, estos setenta y nueve folios, ¿de dónde salen?, ¿a qué se refieren? El montón de los que quedaron debajo del sombrero también parece haber engrosado, aunque no me atrevo a comprobarlo' (p. 101).

Populist fiction and the fairy-tale happy-ending of a romantic liaison are, as we have seen, actively brought to the surface of the text in *El cuarto de atrás*. Both are used as hermeneutic devices to understand and structure feminine experience. However, as the novel makes clear, there is a type of fairy-tale discourse which is actively rejected, and this concerns the discourse of Francoism. At one stage in the novel, the narrator says that she believes in fairy tales but not in Isabel la Católica: 'Que sí creo en el diablo y en San Cristóbal gigante y en Santa Bárbara bendita, en todos los seres misteriosos, vamos. En Isabel la Católica, no' (p. 105). Isabel I was the model which Francoism promoted as the feminine ideal, as the narrator points out: 'Se nos ponía bajo su advocación, se nos hablaba de su voluntad férrea y de su espíritu de sacrificio, había reprimido la ambición y el despotismo de los nobles, había creado la Santa Hermandad, expulsando a los judíos traicioneros, se había desprendido de sus joyas para financiar la empresa más gloriosa de nuestra historia, y aún había quien la difamara por la fidelidad de sus ideales, quien llamara crueldad a su abnegación' (p. 95). Based on Isabel la Católica, the two virtues which were promoted for women were hard work and happiness (p. 94). But the narrator is unconvinced; her rejection of Isabel I is in effect to offer a 'resisting reading' of her (and indeed, Spain's) past, a new feminist version of past events. Instead the narrator turns to traditional fairy-tale figures, such as Tom Thumb and Hansel and Gretel. The latter story, unlike the myth of Isabel I, is recuperated in *El cuarto de atrás*: the trail of breadcrumbs Hansel and Gretel left in the forest becomes a metaphor of white written memories we leave behind in our lives, and which are reconstructed in the novelistic process: 'Cuando dejó un reguero de migas de pan para hallar el camino de vuelta, se las comieron los pájaros. A la vez siguiente, ya resabiado, dejó piedrecitas blancas, y así no se extravió, vamos, es lo que creyó Perrault, que no se extraviaba, pero yo no estoy seguro, ¿me comprende?' (p. 105). Authentic, rather than man-imposed, fairy tales are allowed to function in the text as recuperative devices: the narrator is happy to record without comment the idea suggested to her by the woman who telephones her that the man in black is really Blue Beard (p. 157).

The rationale behind the narrator's rejection of man-made fairy tales becomes clear in her references to Franco's daughter who, by chance, has the same name as the narrator (Carmen): 'pensaba en la niña de

Franco como en un ser prisionero y sujeto a maleficio, y me inspiraba
tanta compasión que hasta hubiera querido conocerla para poderla
consolar, se me venían a la mente los versos de Rubén Darío que aprendí
de memoria: "La princesa está triste, / ¿qué tendrá la princesa?" '
(p. 64). The narrator's allusion to Darío's poem 'Sonatina', *Prosas
profanas* (1896), is apposite. Though she lives in a world of romantic,
exotic dreams the princess of Darío's poem is caged in luxury ('Está
presa en sus oros, está presa en sus tules, / en la jaula de mármol del
palacio real'), which establishes a telling parallel with the *trappings* of
Francoism.[23] Carmencita is thus an emblem of femininity trapped within
the paternalist cage of Franco's regime and, by extension, a concrete
emblem of the disempowerment of women when they are subsumed
within the narrative of the patriarchal fairy tale. Given Franco's ruling of
Spain virtually as a monarch for 35 years, his daughter becomes a
proverbial princess, but she is no more than a male-created princess: 'allí
sola, sin hermanos, entre los tapices de su jaula de oro' (p. 65).

A distinction is thus clearly made in the novel between the
feminocentric fairy tale and its populist adult version, the 'novela rosa',
and the patrocentric discourse focussing on figures such as the chaste,
industrious Isabel I or the obedient princess. The metafictional element in
the novel tends to draw attention not only to the fictionality of the fiction,
but also that of patrocentric fairy tales. Feminism also operates within *El
cuarto de atrás* as a site of knowledge from which patriarchal narratives
are criticised. Halfway through the novel, for example, we find a
discussion of feminism, and, in particular, how Franco turned the clock
back on the changes brought about by the Second Republic (1931–1936):
'La retórica de la postguerra se aplicaba a desprestigiar los conatos de
feminismo que tomaron auge en los años de la República y volvía a poner
el acento en el heroísmo abnegado de madres y esposas, en la
importancia de su silenciosa y oscura labor como pilares del hogar
cristiano' (p. 93). Franco's rhetoric was geared towards the domestica-
tion of women: 'a que aceptásemos con alegría y orgullo, con una
constancia a prueba de desalientos, mediante una conducta sobria que ni
la más mínima sombra de maldicencia fuera capaz de enturbiar, nuestra
condición de mujeres fuertes, complemento y espejo del varón' (p. 94).
The mirror metaphor the narrator employs here is crucial: according to
the discourse of Francoism, women become the mirror which comple-
ments the identity of men; mirrors on their own have no identity, and
simply reflect the identity of others (like women, according to

---

[23] Rubén Darío, *Poesías completas*, ed. Alfonso Méndez Plancarte (Madrid: Aguilar,
1968), p. 557.

patriarchy). But at the same time, men need women in order to constitute their identity, by projecting a reflection of their identity in the Other.

El cuarto de atrás sets out to cloud over that mirror and send back a *distorted* image to mankind, thereby initiating a two-way channelling of images which disrupts the transmitter-receiver situation. Martín Gaite's use of motifs derived from the 'novela rosa', therefore, has the specific purpose of overturning the patrocentric fallacy. *El cuarto de atrás*, like the discourse of feminism, refuses simply to reflect passively the patriarchal myth and thereby produces a text which is at once metafictional and feminist. *El cuarto de atrás*, thus, narrates the history of a 'psychic growth' characteristic of the first type of fairy tales as identified by Sara Gilead (see above). When the novel concludes, as Ruth El Saffar notes, the reader is reassured that the association between dreaming and 'madness and danger' has been dispelled; the narrator 'has transformed her tossing and turning, through the recording of a mysterious dialogue born out of insomnia, into a virtue'.[24] Metatextuality, the 'novela rosa' and the fairy tale have, thus, been triumphantly woven into a new syntax designed to liberate womanhood from the law of the patriarchal *master* text and produce a new *mater* text.

ESTHER TUSQUETS: *EL MISMO MAR DE TODOS LOS VERANOS*

El mismo mar de todos los veranos (1978), the first novel of Esther Tusquets (1936: Spain) is, as Mirella d'Ambrosio Servodidio has suggested, 'the progenitor of all her works to come', since her subsequent novels proved to be 'no more than the diverse intonations of an artistic universe that is already developed and in place'.[25] Tusquets's first novel has a narrative which is, indeed, echoed by her later novels, *El amor es un juego solitario* (1979) and *Varada tras el último naufragio* (1980); it traces the life experience of a middle-aged female university professor called E., beginning with her lonely childhood, the suicide of her lover,' her meaningless marriage and inability to find emotional fulfilment through children, followed by her intense, but short-lived, lesbian relationship with a student, Clara. In the following discussion, I shall be concentrating on the role played by fairy tales in *El mismo mar de todos los veranos*, and the ways in which they are used by the female characters to shun and/or subvert the laws of patriarchy. But, before

[24] 'Redeeming Loss: Reflections on Carmen Martín Gaite's *The Back Room*', *REH*, 20 (1986), 1–14 (p. 11).
[25] 'Esther Tusquets's Fiction: The Spinning of a Narrative Web', in *Women Writers of Contemporary Spain*, pp. 159–78 (p. 161).

undertaking a study proper of the fairy-tale motif in Tusquets's novel, I intend to make some preliminary comments about the links between patriarchy, language and knowledge which will help to elucidate the subsequent discussion.

I have argued elsewhere that Tusquets's writing is characterised by excess.[26] In this essay I hope to demonstrate that, in *El mismo mar de todos los veranos*, fairy tales are presented as epitomising what Jacques Derrida in another context has called the 'dangerous supplement of language'. According to Derrida, writing itself is 'at once the source of all cultural activity and the dangerous knowledge of its own constitution which culture must always repress'.[27] In *De la grammatologie* (1967), for example, Derrida analysed the subversive nature of writing as evident in two classic essays (Rousseau's *Essai sur l'origine des langues* and Lévi-Strauss's *Tristes tropiques*), demonstrating that the unspoken metaphysics underlying these two works is based on the idea that writing (which is linked to absence) is dependent on speech (which is linked to self-presence) and arguing that this idea is a fallacy. Derrida then focussed his attention on the ambiguous value attached to the word 'supplement' in their writings. Often the word and the concept on which it is based has a contradictory meaning. This is most evident in Rousseau's work. On the one hand, language is seen as acting as a supplement to the presence of nature: 'Le supplément s'ajoute, il est un surplus, une plénitude enrichissant une autre plénitude, le comble de la présence. Il cumule et accumule la présence. C'est ainsi que l'art, la technè, l'image, la représentation, la convention, etc., viennent en supplément de la nature et sont riches de toute cette fonction de cumul'.[28] Yet, the supplement fulfills the opposite function in Rousseau's work, since it is – paradoxically enough – also identified with absence. As Derrida goes on to argue: 'Mais le supplément supplée. Il ne s'ajoute que pour remplacer. Il intervient ou s'insinue à-la-place-de; s'il comble, c'est comme on comble un vide. S'il représente et fait image, c'est par le défaut antérieur d'une présence' (p. 208). Derrida goes on to identify the shifting semantic value attached to the concept of supplement in relation to language in Rousseau's essay and carries out a similar critique of Lévi-Strauss's essay.

In a strikingly similar way, language plays a double function in Tusquets's novels. On the one hand, it acts as a supplement to the natural

---

[26] See 'Esther Tusquets: Sex, Excess and the Dangerous Supplement of Language', *Antípodas*, 3 (1991), 85–98.

[27] Christopher Norris, *Deconstruction: Theory and Practice* (London: Methuen, 1982), p. 32.

[28] *De la grammatologie* (Paris: Minuit, 1967), p. 208.

and physical acts of love (specifically in terms of the sexual scenes), but on the other hand it simultaneously acts as a barrier between the two lovers. The duplicity underlying the use of language is most clearly evident in the context of one of the most important connections explored within the novel, namely, that between sex and the text.

Fairy tales play a major 'broker's' role within the sex/text relationship in *El mismo mar de todos los veranos*. Along with the references to Greek mythology, and in particular the Theseus-Ariadne story, fairy tales form the main metaphorical and symbolic framework to the novel. Hardly a page goes by without a reference to a character or an event from a fairy tale. Most of the fairy-tale references are to traditional texts; the two main exceptions are the allusion to the evil Snow Queen and her six white reindeer from C. S. Lewis's *Tales of Narnia* (p. 81, p. 136), and the reference to the men from Lilliput which derives from Swift's novel (p. 93).[29] The most significant set of references are drawn from the archetypal story of the princess who, after a series of trials, finally marries her Prince Charming. This heterosexual fairy tale, however, is disrupted at various crucial points in the novel by the story of The Little Mermaid which introduces a note of sexual ambiguity into the heterosexual pattern of life to which the young girls of the story seemed pre-destined.

Fairy tales operate in two main ways in the novel. On a more obvious level they act as a kind of metaphorical backdrop against which the characters measure the silhouette of their own emotional lives. This first type of allusion functions as a short-hand. Thus, Julio is referred to as a 'grotesco capitán de algún yate fantasma' (p. 16), the attendant who works in the university at which the narrator teaches is imagined as saying 'Off with their heads' about some lackadaisical students (p. 51), the narrator dreams of a passionate wedding-night with an Oriental prince from the *Thousand and One Nights* 'de ojos de azabache, labios glotones, pelo negro' (p. 20), the narrator's mother's hands were like 'manos de hada' (p. 74), the refrain 'Rapunzel, let down your hair' is repeated three times in the text (p. 25, p. 60, p. 93), Peter Pan rubs shoulders with Homer and Shakespeare (p. 61, p. 70, pp. 152–53), the narrator's return to university calls to mind a visit to the Enchanted Forest after a slumber of 100 years (pp. 54–55), girls dressing up for a party are like Cinderellas (p. 129), and so on. References of this kind never tend to go further than a brief allusion to a world of mystery which

---

[29] Page references are to *El mismo mar de todos los veranos* (Barcelona: Lumen, 1978). There is an excellent English version: *The Same Sea as Every Summer*, translated by Margaret E. W. Jones (Lincoln: University of Nebraska Press, 1990).

is seen as informing the everyday world, although they do possess what Nina L. Molinaro calls a 'transformative quality'.[30]

A more sophisticated level of allusion to the world of fairy tale occurs when the narrator begins to explore the implications of the fairy tale, and in a sense recreate its evocative power. This may be either ironic, in the sense of distorting the original meaning of the fairy tale, or recuperative, in the sense of extending its significance. It is clear from the narrator's words that the world of fairy tale is a world which matters more to her than the political or empirical world. As she says at one point, 'lo único que irremisiblemente habrá de hacerme llorar no son las catástrofes que ocurren en la India ni las atrocidades del Vietnam, no es siquiera lo absurdo de la condición humana, ni los abandonos de Julio ni mi propia irremediable soledad, ni este vacío sin fondo en el que ha naufragado mi vida, sino los tontos cuentos para niños con princesas infelices y muchachas abandonadas, las historias de patitos feos, de panteras que mueren en la nieve, de sirenas convertidas en espuma' (p. 133). The fairy tale is seen as being able to unlock the secret of human relationships. The narrator sees her relationship with her mother as that of Snow White *vis-à-vis* the wicked step-mother:

> Porque la madre de inconformismo fácil y de risa insolente, nos atacó durante años con su furia renovadora y terrible, con su racionalismo olímpico, con su esteticismo cuadriculado y perfecto, arremetió de frente, y sus ojos – tan pavorosamente azules, tan despiadamente claros – me dejaban, al traspasarme, desarmada y desnuda, y sus manos tan blancas parecían capaces de dar nueva forma, de dar simplemente una forma al universo, y era, oh espejito mágico, la más bella y la más inteligente entre todas las mujeres del reino – ahí estaban mi padre y todos sus amigos para atestiguarlo. (. . .) (p. 24)

Likewise her (failed) relationship with her husband, Julio, becomes a story of the princess who was seduced by a handsome prince and then abandoned (pp. 132–33). When the narrator comes to describe her lesbian relationship with Clara (for which the novel is now famous), the terms of reference become more complex because more fluid.[31] At first the narrator sees Clara as an Aztec princess (p. 59); this metaphor then disappears to give way to a second metaphor which is to prove more

---

[30] *Foucault, Feminism, and Power: Reading Esther Tusquets* (London and Toronto: Associated University Presses, 1991), p. 36.

[31] Biruté Ciplijauskaité, *La novela femenina contemporánea*, p. 174. Ciplijauskaité argues that Tusquets's view of lesbian love is more subtle than that of Wittig, Reinig or Stefan. For further discussion of Tusquets's vision of love, see Janet L. Gold, 'Reading the Love Myth: Tusquets with the Help of Barthes', *HR*, 55 (1987), 337–46.

sustainable, the mermaid. This metaphoric vision of Clara first emerges in the café scene, where the narrator addresses Clara as 'tiernísima sirena de senos adolescentes y hermosa cola casi piernas' (p. 66). It is at this juncture in the novel that, as Kathleen M. Glenn points out, we are left with a 'composite image, an artful construct', while the real Clara 'vanishes from sight'.[32] Clara, as this particular passage makes clear, is being created by the narrator and this may explain the ambiguity of the latter's emotions towards Clara, which vary from physical violence to romantic idealization. At one point, the narrator, for example, imagines cutting Clara's head off slowly, and then raping her if given the opportunity (pp. 67–68), thereby desecrating the mermaid statue image superimposed on her earlier. She then imagines the two of them on a journey in an imaginary subterranean world where they are directed by the pedantic White Rabbit and the Snow Queen (p. 81). From this point onwards, as their relationship develops, a split seems to emerge between them, and it is now Clara who becomes the Beauty while the narrator plays the role of onlooker: 'Y Clara es sin lugar a dudas la Bella de mi historia, y yo soy apenas un espectador' (p. 84). As the novel progresses, however, the narrator loses her supposed neutrality, and she refers to herself explicitly as a witch: 'pronta (. . .) a encaramar a Clara al palo de mi escoba, porque entre las brujas quizá puedo ser yo todavía, a mis casi cincuenta años, la más bella y la más joven' (p. 114). The loving relationship is addled by the time we get to the middle of the novel, since the narrator now begins to sound suspiciously like the wicked step-mother:

> la grácil princesa que avanza – siguiendo algún extraño hechizo que he olvidado – a lomos de una tortuga gigante, la mirada ensoñada y la oscura trenza cayéndole a lo largo de la espalda hasta el caparazón del animal lentísimo en su marcha, se parece mucho a Clara, y yo debo de ser una de estas altivas reinas ya maduras, con rígidos vestidos de tejidos pesados y suntuosos, una enorme corona en la cabeza, todavía hermosas sin embargo, aunque tal vez un poquito acartonadas y duras, haciendo tontas preguntas a unos espejos que no pueden ser a un tiempo aduladores y veraces, o pinchándose las yemas de los dedos con cuchillitos de sangre maternal y protectora en leves pañuelitos de encaje. (pp. 150–51)

Towards the end of the novel, the narrator begins to suspect that Clara will betray her for a heterosexual relationship, and to express her anger at Clara's folly she alludes to the Little Mermaid. She sees in Clara's eyes:

---

[32] '*El mismo mar de todos los veranos* and the Prism of Art', in *The Sea of Becoming: Approaches to the Fiction of Esther Tusquets*, ed. Mary S. Vásquez (New York: Greenwood Press, 1991), pp. 29–43 (p. 35).

la mirada de los hermosos adolescentes orientales que aman a los viajeros perdidos, sobrevivientes para su mal de mil naufragios, viajeros que han arribado a la isla y han roto el sello de la gruta y habrán de asesinarlos el mismo día de su quince o diecisiete cumpleaños, tiene la mirada de las sirenas enamoradas que avanzan impávidas sobre las hojas aceradas y cortantes de infinitos cuchillos para lograr a cambio un alma de mujer – alma que ninguna falta les hace, y que para nada habría de servirles, pues los príncipes encantadores que pueblan la tierra no suelen entender nunca nada, ignoran a las sirenas románticas y locas, puestos los ojos desde un principio en princesas bobaliconas. (p. 163)

The narrator's worst fears are confirmed later on when she learns that Clara has indeed betrayed her and run off (although not for love) with a Prince Charming (pp. 226–27), epitomised by her last words: 'Y Wendy creció' (p. 229).

The motive behind the use of fairy-tale motifs of this kind is to illustrate the gradual divestment of illusions which the characters, and particularly the narrator, experience. As the narrator points out: 'lo peor y más triste es descubrir que el príncipe encantador es también, como su princesa, el más vulgar de los príncipes, que todo ha sucedido en definitiva para nada' (p. 170). When the characters fall from their grand status as royal participants in the narrative of life, they are typically reduced to pygmies, or dwarfs. When Clara goes back to the world of conventionality, for example, the narrator describes her as returning to her island of dwarfs (p. 226). The narrator cannot bring herself to return to the everyday world; she wishes to remain safely imprisoned 'en el acuario de mi tiempo ido, siguiendo en la bola hechizada del adivino o en la mágica pantalla donde se reflejan las futuras edades una peripecia a la que pienso no he de incorporarme' (p. 84). There is no sense in which the narrator's penchant for reading life in terms of fairy tales and vice-versa is castigated because unrealistic. This is suggested by the fact that the apogee of love experienced by the narrator is accompanied by a surplus of metaphorical images which draw upon the world of make-believe. When the narrator and Clara first make love in the Opera House, an act which is simultaneously an 'affirmation of authenticity' as well a 'deliberate defiance' of moral conventions,[33] the description is couched in a fairy tale about some gnomes stealing a diamond. The narrator describes Clara's hand as follows: 'se sumerge y pierde bajo la ropa y va rodando cauteloso mi pecho hacia su centro, como un gnomo curioso y travieso aunque asustado que pretendiera robar el diamante que fulgura

---

[33] Margaret E. W. Jones, 'Barcelona's Restrictive Space in *El mismo mar de todos los veranos*', *Ideas '92*, 7 (1990), 95–101 (p. 99).

en la cumbre (. . .) rodea el gnomo una y otra vez la colina, siempre un
poco más arriba, pero no mucho, sólo un poquito más alto (. . .)'. Then
she feels that a crowd of gnomes 'ahora me están besando además con
cuidadito el cuello, las orejas, las sienes, me mordisquean el cuello' (p.
136), and later on, 'el gnomo ha llegado por fin a la cima y olvida toda
cautela – ya innecesaria – y aferra feroz el diamante con su mano tan dura
y tan pequeña y hunde en la cumbre algo – seguramente una bandera'
(p. 137). When the narrator returns Clara's caresses, the metaphor
switches from itinerant gnomes to a sea grotto:

> Acaricio sin prisas las piernas de seda, me demoro en la parte tiernísima,
> turbadora, del interior de los muslos, para buscar al fin el hueco tibio
> donde anidan las algas, y, aunque la ondina ha salido hace ya mucho del
> estanque, el rincón de la gruta está extrañadamente húmedo, y la gruta es
> de repente un ser vivo, raro monstruo voraz de las profundidades, que se
> repliega y se distiende y se contrae contra estos organismos mitad
> vegetales, mitad animales, que pueblan los abismos del océano, y después
> cede blandamente, y desparecen los gnomos y las ninfas, y yo no siento ya
> dolor, ni oigo ningún ruido, porque he llegado al fondo mismo de los
> mares, y todo es aquí silencio, y todo es azul, y me adentro despacio,
> apartando las algas con cuidado, por la húmeda boca de la gruta.
> (pp. 138–39)[34]

At this point in the narrative it would appear that the empiric event has
been swallowed up by the metaphor; the gnomes and the sea grotto are
more prominent than the description of the sexual act itself. The
crescendo of sexual and textual excitement described in this scene is
never to return. The description of the next love scene is almost devoid of
metaphoric images (pp. 154–55). The one striking metaphor of the piece
refers to Clara's moan as like 'el aullido de una loba blanca degollada o
violada con las primeras luces del alba' (p. 155), a shocking, violent
image which contrasts sharply with the *soft* images of the previous
passage.

Tusquets's use of fairy tales in *El mismo mar de todos los veranos* has a
precise aim. On the one hand they act, as we have already noted, as a
type of narrative backdrop against which the lives of the characters are

---

[34] Tusquets's recourse to explicit sexual scenes has a counterpart in the work of a
writer herself launched by Tusquets's publishing company named after her, Almudena
Grande. As one of the characters from her second novel *Te llamaré viernes* (1991)
suggests, with words which are appropriate to Tusquets's own fiction: 'la verdadera
conquista es el impudor de las palabras, el lenguaje es el último campo de batalla'; see
Fernando Valls, 'El eterno juego del sueño y de la vida', *La Vanguardia* (1 March
1991).

measured.[35] At times this leads to strains between the macro- and micro-text. During the costume party, for example, the narrator suddenly realises that they are all 'actores de segunda' in a pitiful play (p. 99). Despite the pitfalls, people, Tusquets suggests, like to dress up, divesting themselves of one identity and clothing themselves in another more glamorous role. When first opening up the clothes trunk, for example, the narrator muses '¿no es acaso un hermoso, un perverso juego de suplantaciones y disfraces?' (p. 90). But this pleasure is wont to turn sour. There are, therefore, differences between the use of fairy tales in Tusquets's novel and the use of Greek mythology in post-civil-war male fiction (see above). Whereas Martín-Santos's allusion to Greek myth-ology in *Tiempo de silencio* is bitterly ironic, Tusquets explores the suggestiveness of the fairy-tale narrative, manipulating its evocative power in order to cast an unorthodox light on the characters who people her world.

One other point needs to be made about Tusquets's use of fairy tales in her novels; they are seen as quintessentially feminine texts. They are able, like no other text, to express the feminine consciousness as distinct from the phallic knowledge contained in Greek myths, an example being the Theseus story, which speak of adventure, wars and physical conquest. Fairy tales allow the narrator to assert an unbroken line of emotional continuity between herself, her mother, her grandmother, and so on and so forth. They are the verbal embodiment of feminine culture, 'una tradición ancestral sabiamente acumulada de hembra en hembra' (p. 46), related to the genealogical line referred to, rather mockingly, at one stage as 'una larga serie de mujeres correctamente alimentadas' (p. 36).[36] Finally, and just as importantly, fairy tales offer a way back to the paradise of childhood, to 'este mundo mágico del cuento donde aprendí a elegir palabras y a enamorarme de los sueños' (p. 68).

The fairy tales are the narrative equivalent of that particularly feminine voice which surfaces at various junctures of the novel. When the narrator

[35] For further discussion of the role of fairy tales in Tusquets's work, see the excellent essay by Geraldine Cleary Nichols, 'The Prison House (and Beyond): *El mismo mar de todos los veranos*', *RR*, 75 (1984), 366–85.

[36] One might speculate that the sense of a genealogical chain would extend to the relationship between the narrator and her daughter. But Guiomar is a shadowy figure, characterised by 'remoteness and frigidity' as one critic observes; Lucy Lee-Bonanno, 'The Renewal of the Quest in Esther Tusquets' *El mismo mar de todos los veranos*', in *Feminine Concerns in Contemporary Spanish Fiction by Women*, pp. 134–51 (p. 142). Guiomar is reminiscent in more ways than one of the absent lover of Antonio Machado's poetry, on whom she seems (at least in name) to be based. Guiomar's presence is undermined by the more vibrant presence of Clara who fulfills a displaced lover-daughter relationship with the narrator.

opens the door, for example, to a un-named woman, she is struck by the latter's speech: 'Me pregunto de dónde procederá este hablar lento y atropellado, gracioso y torpe, incorrecto y distante, de las mujeres de mi clase' (p. 36). Since the speaker of the voice is un-named, the voice seems to take on a life of its own, almost asserting itself as a body within the text. Later on, during one of the love-making scenes, the participants begin to speak a new language. Clara 'ronronea palabras sin sentido – tal vez sea el idioma de las hadas o de los gatos'; the narrator likewise begins to whisper 'palabras muy extrañas, palabras que tampoco tienen sentido y que pertenecen a un idioma no aprendido' (p. 157). As the narrator subsequently suggests, when describing this voice, 'este lenguaje no nace en el pensamiento y pasa desde allí hasta la voz hecho sonido: nace hecho ya voz de las entrañas' (p. 158). The words belong to an unlearned language in the sense of being part of a feminine syntax unadulterated by the language of men; it is a language which is 'already a voice' in the sense that it springs immediately from 'deep inside' the body, a Spanish version, perhaps, of Luce Irigaray's 'parler-femme'.[37] Fairy tales, like the 'unlearned language' of lesbian love, speak of a world which stands outside the patriarchal structures of our society, a utopian realm which the narrator struggles to recreate.[38] The conclusion of the novel, by quoting the return-to-reality phrase of Barrie's *Peter Pan* 'Y Wendy creció' tends to reinforce the notion that this dream of a truly feminine discourse is as real as the Never Never land of *Peter Pan*, namely, subject to the apartheid of the imagination.

As we have seen, Matute's *Primera memoria*, Martín Gaite's *El cuarto de atrás*, and Tusquets's *El mismo mar de todos los veranos* each have recourse to fairy tales (and, in the case of *El cuarto de atrás*, popular fiction as well), in order to explore the justification for the roles that

---

[37] See especially the section 'Quand nos lèvres se parlent', in *Ce Sexe qui n'en est pas un* (Paris: Minuit, 1977), pp. 205–17. Tusquets's and indeed Irigaray's promotion of 'woman talk' subverts the patriarchal law which requires female silence; for a spirited account, see Dale Spender, *Man Made Language* (London: Routledge and Kegan Paul, 1980), pp. 106–37. For the repercussions of this concept in Hispanic literary circles, see Marta Traba, 'Hipótesis sobre una escritura diferente', *Quimera*, 13 (September 1981), 9–11; Carme Riera, 'Literatura femenina: ¿Un lenguaje prestado?', *Quimera*, 18 (April 1982), 9–12; and Evelynne García, 'Lectura: N. Fem. Sing. ¿Lee y escribe la mujer en forma diferente al hombre?', *Quimera*, 23 (September 1982), 54–57.

[38] This idea of a feminine language *within* language might lead us to think of the comparable situation of Catalan *within* Castilian. While this is certainly a viable concept in the work of some Catalan female writers, such as Carme Riera and Montserrat Roig, it is not applicable to Tusquets for whom Castilian is the only language in which she feels 'comfortable'; see Geraldine C. Nichols, *Escribir, espacio propio: Laforet, Matute, Moix, Tusquets, Riera y Roig por sí mismas*, pp. 74–77. The Catalan language cannot therefore exist as a linguistic Unconscious within her work.

patriarchal society expects of women. Both *Primera memoria* and *El mismo mar de todos los veranos* effect a recuperative move with regard to the discourse of the fairy tale, and re-actualize its force in the lives of the characters who people these two novels. Tusquets's novel adopts a more sophisticated stance by equating the fairy tale not simply with a world of childhood now lost (as occurs in *Primera memoria*) but by drawing parallels between its suggestive aura and the discourse of human sexuality. *El cuarto de atrás*, for its part, takes up at times an almost Brechtian distance with regard to the fairy-tale motif, reworking its power of attraction (along with that of the 'novela rosa') in order to voice a feminist critique of Franco's Spain. In the case of all three novels, however, the fairy tale becomes a primary tool in the painful task of unravelling the skein of identity which the syntax of patriarchy has woven into the lives of the female protagonists.

IV

SEXUAL POLITICS

Kate Millett's *Sexual Politics* (1970) drew attention primarily to the cultural oppression which women have suffered and still suffer in male-orientated society. She argued that our society is a patriarchy, since 'the military, industry, technology, universities, science, political office, and finance – in short, every avenue of power within the society, including the coercive force of the police, is entirely in male hands'.[1] In her study of ideology, biology, class, education, myth and religion, Millett identified the various ideological ways in which woman is rendered subservient to man in patriarchal society. Her work called firstly for a sexual revolution which 'would bring the institution of patriarchy to an end, abolishing both the ideology of male supremacy and the traditional socialization by which it is upheld in matters of status, role and temperament' (p. 62).

The basic premise behind Millett's trail-blazing book was to reveal the presence of patriarchy where, hitherto, it remained invisible. *Sexual Politics* was also important in that it strove to unmask patriarchy not only in life but also in art. Her essay on D. H. Lawrence, for example, exposed the deeply phallocentric bias of the latter's creative work, a technique which was to become the blueprint of a specific type of feminist reading of a male writer's work.[2] The textual reading and the social reading were seen by Millett as part and parcel of the same process

[1] *Sexual Politics*, p. 25.
[2] For the original essay, see *Sexual Politics*, pp. 237–93. As Sydney Janet Kaplan suggests: 'Who can forget how powerfully Kate Millett's *Sexual Politics* (1970) acted as a catalyst for the subsequent explosion of reaction against misogyny in the works of male writers?'; see her essay 'Varieties of feminist criticism', *Making a Difference: Feminist Literary Criticism*, edited by Gayle Greene and Coppélia Kahn (London: Methuen, 1985), pp. 37–58 (p. 53). For discussion of Millett's study as a 'mother-text', see Cora Kaplan, 'Radical Feminism and Literature: Rethinking Millett's *Sexual Politics*', in *Sea Changes: Essays on Culture and Feminism*, pp. 15–30, and chapter one of *Feminist Readings/Feminists Reading* (New York-London: Harvester Wheatsheaf, 1989), pp. 16–49; and Toril Moi's *Sexual/Textual Politics* (London: Methuen, 1983).

of cognition, or X-ray to use K. K. Ruthven's term, whereby the hidden agenda of patriarchy would be mercilessly exposed.[3]

The process whereby the female writer exposes the patriarchal agenda is, however, not a straightforward ideological process. For while the work of the three novelists (Isabel Allende, Marta Traba and Montserrat Roig) studied in this section can be seen, on a straightforward level, as women unmasking the 'maleness' of the society in which they live, and therefore adopting a conflictive stance, on a societal level their work may be interpreted as a means whereby patriarchal ideology achieves self-consciousness. Louis Althusser, in his essay 'Marxisme et Humanisme' offers some clarification of the concept of ideology which is relevant to the present discussion. In his essay Althusser draws attention at one stage to the inevitably unconscious nature of ideology:

> L'idéologie est bien un système de représentations: mais ces représen-tations n'ont la plupart du temps rien à voir avec la "conscience": elles sont la plupart du temps des images, parfois des concepts, mais c'est avant tout comme structures qu'elles s'imposent à l'immense majorité des hommes, sans passer par leur "conscience".[4]

Althusser is, no doubt, using the word 'hommes' as a generic term to signify the whole of mankind, but it seems appropriate in this context to interpret his use of the term to refer to the ideology which 'men' specifically are unconscious of, and to propose patriarchy as a typical example of such an ideological system. The question which now arises, however, is the degree to which the work of a female novelist can be seen as reflecting the ideology of a society whose patriarchy she clearly feels alienated from. The question might be expressed as follows: is the anti-patriarchal female writer necessarily in conflict with the society in which she lives, or is she participating in and reflecting a new ideological sea-change occurring within society?

---

[3] As K. K. Ruthven suggested: 'Every critical method is a scanning device for picking up particular points of information, which it logs by means of a technical vocabulary specially invented for that purpose. The point of inventing a new device is to reveal what was previously invisible, and in that way to articulate a new kind of knowledge. An X-ray photograph is totally different from a snapshot of the same object, and different again from an ultraviolet photograph. All three photographs represent different kinds of knowledge, and each is produced by a different method. Feminist criticism is a scanning device in this sense: it operates in the service of a new knowledge which is constructed by rendering visible the hitherto invisible component of "gender" in all discourses produced by the humanities and social sciences.' See K. K. Ruthven, *Feminist Literary Studies: an Introduction* (Cambridge: C.U.P., 1984), p. 24.

[4] 'Marxisme et Humanisme', *Pour Marx* (Paris: Maspéro, 1966), pp. 225–49 (pp. 239–40).

In an essay 'Sur le Jeune Marx', originally published in 1961, Althusser offers some clarification of the relationship between societal and individual ideology which helps to put this clouded issue into some perspective. In his essay, Althusser takes to task a number of Marxist critics, such as Schaff, Lapine and Jahn, among others, for their betrayal of the materialist philosophy and their use of what he called an 'analytic-teleological method' based on methodologically suspect Hegelian principles. Instead he proposes a more self-reflexive type of approach. He shifts emphasis away from a universalist notion of truth towards a closer emphasis on the relationship between the thought of an individual and the existing 'ideological field' in which it operates. To quote Althusser's words: 'le sens de ce tout, d'une idéologie singulière (ici la pensée d'un individu) dépend, non de son rapport à une vérité différente d'elle, mais de son rapport au champ idéologique existant, et aux problèmes et à la structure sociaux qui le soutiennent et s'y réflé-chissent'.[5] The important verb in this definition, for our purposes, is 's'y réfléchissent' for it makes clear how social problems and structures are reflected in the ideological field in which, one may surmise, the ideology of an individual writer is, in turn, reflected. As Althusser further states, the author will be seen 'comme individu concret, et l'histoire effective, qui se réfléchit dans ce développement individuel selon les liens complexes de l'individu à cette histoire' (p. 59). It is for this reason that the ideological principles proposed by Althusser can be 'la théorie qui permet l'intelligence de sa propre genèse, comme de tout autre processus historique' (p. 60). It is this self-reflexivity identified by Althusser which offers a striking parallel with the ideological strategy at work in the work of the three female writers studied in this chapter.

All three writers are immersed in the discourse of Marxism and, as is evident particularly in the case of Marta Traba, use its critique of bourgeois society as a means of unlocking the ideological chains not only of the proletariat, but also of women. For these writers woman is subject to a double oppression since she is the proletariat *within* the proletariat. A crucial issue in this context is how the unmasking of patriarchy is performed in their texts. As Althusser has pointed out, the written word brings with it a degree of absence of the concrete individual, the author, who gave birth to the work:

A ce niveau d'échanges et de contestations, qui font la matière même des textes, où nous sont données ses pensées vivantes, tout se passe comme si

---

[5] 'Sur le Jeune Marx', reprinted in *Pour Marx*, pp. 45–83 (p. 59). Subsequent references to this essay will be embedded in the text.

les auteurs mêmes de ces pensées étaient absents. Absent, l'individu concret qui s'exprime dans ses pensées et dans ses textes, absente, l'histoire effective qui s'exprime dans le champ idéologique existant. Comme l'auteur s'efface devant ses pensées publiées pour n'être que leur rigueur, l'histoire concrète s'efface elle aussi devant ses thèmes idéologiques pour n'être que leur système. (p. 61)

These words might serve as a leitmotiv to the three authors studied in this section. Each author does indeed disappear in her text in order to become what Althusser calls the 'rigour' of her 'published thoughts', and history likewise gives way to the expression of the system underlying (patriarchal) ideology.

ISABEL ALLENDE: *LA CASA DE LOS ESPÍRITUS*

Isabel Allende (1942: Chile), as the niece of Salvador Allende, the democratically-elected President of Chile removed from office and life on September 11, 1973 by a right-wing coup which ushered in an era of repression and economic hardship for the working classes, has, at first sight, a political pedigree bolstered by genealogy.[6] It has been argued that Allende's popularity was already assured by who she was, both by being the heir of a repressed democratic tradition and by being female. For a variety of reasons, therefore, Allende was co-opted into the 'boom', or more correctly the 'postboom' (the 'boom' was by then well past its prime). Allende, however, not only had a political father through whom she derived a political pedigree; she had an artistic father, García Márquez, who was instrumental in the launching of her first novel, *La casa de los espíritus*, in 1982, and whose magical-realist manner she consciously imitated. Both 'fathers' have acted in a complementary manner in Allende's fiction, creating and sustaining the myth of her socialist credentials. Of the two 'fathers', García Márquez is the more significant. Allende's fiction, judging by the number of copies sold in recent years (27 editions from October 1982 until July 1988, for example), is as popular as García Márquez's. Like García Márquez, Allende is famous for her left-wing views. Her novels, however, especially in their treatment of Marxism and feminism, reveal a world-vision which is ideologically static.

La casa de los espíritus is a feminocentric narration which focusses on the main events of the three generations of the Trueba family, including

---

[6] See Thomas E. Skidmore and Peter H. Smith, *Modern Latin America* (Oxford: Oxford University Press, 1989), p. 135, for an account of the events leading up to Salvador Allende's death.

the grandmother, Clara, the mother, Blanca, and the grand-daughter, Alba, who is involved in collating the family memoirs. The narrative is punctured by the description of political struggles between the various revolutionary figures (Pedro García, Pedro Tercero García) and the conservative figures (most notably, Esteban Trueba). The historical backdrop of the novel is recognisably Chilean, and is also autobiographically-based. As Allende has herself pointed out, the house of the Trueba family is based on the house in which she spent her childhood:

> Dicen que toda primera novela es autobiográfica, sobre todo las que escriben las mujeres. En mi caso no es exactamente así, porque no figuro en ella, no soy ninguno de los personajes, pero no niego que a varios de ellos los conocí y que sus pasiones y dolores me tocaron de cerca. Algunas anécdotas de esas páginas las escuché de labios de mi madre y mi abuelo o las leí en los cuadernos de anotar de mi abuela.[7]

Other events in the novel are explicitly clearly based on historical events.[8] Superficially, therefore, Allende's novel appears to reflect the Marxist thesis that art grows out of historical reality.

There are other events which tend, however, to mark the novel as anti-historical, the most important of which being the novel's awareness of its own genesis. Some of these observations take the form of characters being aware of the 'literary' nature of their own lives. When forced to marry Blanca, for example, the Marquis is described as at a loss to understand 'cómo había ido a parar en ese folletín' (p. 191).[9] Blanca strives desperately to convert her passion into 'un amor de novela'

---

[7] 'Los libros tienen sus propios espíritus', in *Los libros tienen sus propios espíritus: Estudios sobre Isabel Allende*, ed. Marcelo Coddou (México: Universidad Veracruzana, 1986), pp. 15–20 (p. 15).

[8] For a discussion of the novel's realism, see Philip Swanson, 'After the Boom', in *Landmarks in Modern Latin American Fiction*, ed. Philip Swanson (London and New York: Routledge, 1990), pp. 222–45 (pp. 239–40). The military coup described at the beginning of chapter XIII, though narrated with anonymous characters, for example, is based on the military coup of September 11, 1973 when Pinochet ousted Salvador Allende from the Presidential Palace. It follows the historical narrative right down to the smallest details, such as the President's realization that crisis point had been reached once the Navy rebelled; the historical mystery as to whether Salvador Allende committed suicide or whether he was killed by the invading troops is retained in *La casa de los espíritus*. Other events, such as the cortège for the anonymous El Poeta described on pages 341–42, is based on the funeral of Pablo Neruda, which Allende described in a letter to her mother, and which she subsequently transcribed *verbatim* in her novel; see Marcelo Coddou, *Para leer a Isabel Allende* (Concepción, Chile: Ediciones LAR, 1988), p. 30.

[9] Edition of the text quoted throughout is *La casa de los espíritus* (Barcelona: Plaza y Janés, 1988), 27th edition.

(p. 276). Other techniques have a metatextual basis; thus the novel has many narrators and this fact deconstructs the sense of the novel as simply reflecting an empirically verifiable reality. In the final chapter, for example, the 'I' at this point is Alba, who states she writes her memoirs with the help of three manuscript sources: her grandfather Esteban Trueba who wrote 'varias páginas' (p. 378), the 'cuadernos de Clara', and 'las cartas de mi madre' (p. 379). The novel itself had used the technique of changing from third-person to first-person narrative, and these changes of perspective can now be retrospectively interpreted as intrusions into the main body of the narrative of the memoirs of Alba's ancestors (Esteban, Clara).[10] There are, however, very few references in the narrative to the characters as being aware of their narrator-status. One rare example is the early reference by Alba to her reorganization of the past: 'yo ordené y leí con recogimiento para reconstruir esta historia' (p. 263). However, Alba is far from being a univocal centre of awareness within the text. In the epilogue there is a sense in which Alba is alienated from her own words: 'En algunos momentos tengo la sensación de que esto ya lo he vivido y que he escrito estas mismas palabras, pero comprendo que no soy yo, sino otra mujer, que anotó en sus cuadernos para que yo me sirviera de ellos' (p. 379). A split emerges between the experiencing 'I' of the narrative and the writer who reconstructs the story.

Other techniques within Allende's fiction tend to imbue it with an anti-historical feel, especially through a relaxation of the laws of causality. This has inevitable consequences for the role of Marxist ideology within *La casa de los espíritus*. In a world without respect for the laws of cause and effect, the Marxist thesis is effectively undone. Various arguments on behalf of the 'justness' of Marxism surface in the text of *La casa de los espíritus*, but since they appear in a world which is not causally effective, they can have no more (or less) credence than a belief in spiritualism, telepathy or ghosts. An example of this occurs when Blanca remembers Pedro García's explanation as to why thieves do not wear clothes: 'entonces se acordó que Pedro García, el viejo, le había dicho que los ladrones andan desnudos, para que no los ataquen los perros' (p. 141). An orthodox Marxist viewpoint would suggest that thieves have no clothes because they have been banished from the bourgeois system

---

[10] For a good discussion of the interaction of narrative voices in *La casa de los espíritus*, see James Mandrell, 'The Prophetic Vision in Garro, Morante, and Allende', *CL*, 42:3 (1990), 227–46 (pp. 239–41). Doris Meyer argues for her part that since Alba incorporates both her paternal and maternal precursors, she therefore creates a truly 'parented' text; see ' "Parenting the Text": Female Creativity and Dialogic Relationships in Isabel Allende's *La casa de los espíritus*', *Hispania*, 73:2 (1990), 360–65.

which governs the distribution of wealth. To argue that the poor do not
have clothes *in order to* avoid dogs attacking them involves a metalepsis.
The laws of causality are undone, and Marxism, which is an exclusively
causalistic creed, in effect has the carpet pulled from beneath its feet.
What is ironic here is that this idea comes from Pedro García the elder,
supposedly an authority on socialism.

This rhetorical move is very common in Allende's text. As a general
rule, references to philosophies which contradict the premises of
phallogocentrism – Marxism, feminism, spiritualism – are all presented
as 'mad' discourses. Esteban Trueba, for example, the *paterfamilias* in
whose person societal, cultural and financial power resides, treats the
Marxist concept of justice as if it were a fairy tale (in much the same way
that the average reader might treat Allende's text as itself a fairy tale). As
he tells Clara:

> ¡Justicia! ¿Es justo que todos tengan lo mismo? ¿Los flojos lo mismo que
> los trabajadores? ¿Los tontos lo mismo que los inteligentes? ¡Eso no pasa
> ni con los animales! No es cuestión de ricos y pobres, sino de fuertes y
> débiles. (p. 125)

One important connection established in the course of the narrative which
tends to substantiate this idea is the link between Marxism and fantasy
made consistently by the right-wing elements of Latin-American society.
As Esteban Trueba's friends assure him: 'El marxismo no tiene ni la
menor oportunidad en América Latina. No ves que no contempla el lado
mágico de las cosas? Es una doctrina atea, práctica y funcional. ¡Aquí no
puede tener éxito!' (p. 272; see also further reference to this idea,
p. 337). This idea is shared by other characters who equate political
conservatism with common sense:

> – Van a ganar los socialistas – había dicho Jaime, que de tanto convivir
> con el proletariado en el hospital, andaba alucinado. No, hijo, van a ganar
> los de siempre – había replicado Clara, que lo vio en las barajas y se lo
> confirmó su sentido común. (p. 193)

Marxism is associated with fortune-telling and the discourse of the
supernatural, as this passage suggests. It is ironic that Clara, however,
should use both her Tarot cards and her common sense to predict the
triumph of the Conservatives, without being aware of the internal
contradiction of her forecasts. What makes the issue more problematic is
that Latin American reality – as a historical given – is associated *a priori*
throughout the text with the fantastic. This cultural characteristic is seen
even to reside in the language of the sub Continent. Whereas English, as
Esteban Trueba believes, is adequate for science and technology, Spanish

is 'un idioma de segundo orden, apropiado para los asuntos domésticos y la magia, para las pasiones incontrolables y las empresas inútiles' (p. 267). The metaphors of the text, therefore, despite their humour, reinforce the notion that Marxism is a fantastic creed.

It is in Pedro García's grandson, Pedro Tercero García, that a left-wing consciousness is fully actualized. He embodies political opposition to Esteban Trueba's phallocratic power, as Trueba clearly realizes in the passage quoted above. But, for all his democratic socialist credentials, he is not taken any more seriously than his political enemy. As we read in the following paragraph: 'El día que Esteban Trueba descubrió que el hijo de su administrador estaba introduciendo literatura subversiva entre los inquilinos, lo llamó a su despacho y delante de su padre le dio una tunda de azotes con su fusta de cuero de palabra' (p. 125). When Marxism, and its proponents, are taken seriously, its creed emerges in a displaced form in the guise of Pedro García's parable of the fox and the hens:

> Un día el viejo Pedro García les contó a Blanca y a Pedro Tercero el cuento de las gallinas que se pusieron de acuerdo para enfrentar a un zorro que se metía todas las noches en el gallinero para robar los huevos y devorarse los pollitos. Las gallinas decidieron que ya estaban hartas de aguantar la prepotencia del zorro, lo esperaron organizadas y cuando entró al gallinero, le cerraron el paso, lo rodearon y se le fueron encima a picotazos hasta que lo dejaron más muerto que vivo. (p. 128)

The story is a parable of the revolution of the proletariat in its act of self-justification, and union against its capitalist aggressor. The story has two levels, one comic, the other serious, one non-political, one political, which are evident in the different reactions to the same story. For, while Blanca laughs, Pedro Tercero takes its message seriously. The question which inevitably poses itself is the extent to which the parable itself can be applied to the text which encloses it, that is, *La casa de los espíritus* itself, or, put in another way: does Allende's text contain a political, political edge despite its superficial comic level? There is, perhaps, one way in which this possibilty might be upheld with regard to *La casa de los espíritus*. As opposed to nineteenth-century realism, which is rigidly phallocratic and which often depicts women from the viewpoint of a male author (as in *Clarín*'s *La Regenta*, for example, and Galdós's *Fortunta y Jacinta*), Allende's novel focusses on a man (Esteban Trueba) represented from the viewpoint of women, ranging from Clara to Blanca to Alba.[11] It ought to be said, however, that there is minimal concrete

---

[11] For a discussion of the phallocratic mind-set underlying Realism, see Susan

evidence to support a liberationist-feminist reading of this kind of Allende's novel.

Before examining the problematic of ideology in Allende's novel, it is important to survey in greater detail the role played by ideologies other than Marxism in Allende's text, such as feminism and spiritualism. The paradigmatic bearer of the knowledge of feminism is Nívea who in her youth was involved in suffragette activities. She campaigns for women to have the same rights as men, and to have the option to vote and go to college. Esteban Trueba's attitude to her is emblematic: 'Su función es la maternidad, el hogar. Al paso que van, cualquier día van a querer ser diputados, jueces ¡hasta Presidente de la República!' (p. 65). Clara, however, is undeterred and carries on her mother's activities:

> Clara esperaba que su cuñada terminara las místicas letanías de padrenuestros y avemarías y aprovechaba la reunión para repetir las consignas que había oído a su madre cuando se encadenaba en las rejas del Congreso en su presencia. Las mujeres la escuchaba risueñas y avergonzadas, por la misma razón con la cual rezaban con Férula: para no disgustar a la patrona. (pp. 99–100)

Feminism has little effect on Clara's female companions; as the above-quoted passage suggests, they accept the moral and intellectual superiority of their husbands, and their right to beat them if they wish. Clara's activities eventually lead to a confrontation with her husband, Esteban, the bearer of the values of phallogocentrism:

> Esteban gritaba como un enajenado, paseándose por la sala a grandes trancos y dando puñetazos a los muebles, argumentando que si Clara pensaba seguir los pasos de su madre, se iba a encontrar con un macho bien plantado que le bajaría los calzones y le daría una azotaina para que se le quitaran las malditas ganas de andar arengando a la gente, que le prohibía terminantemente las reuniones para rezar o para cualquier otro fin y que él no era ningún pelele a quien su mujer pudiera poner en ridículo. Clara lo dejó chillar y darle golpes a los muebles hasta que se cansó y después, distraída como siempre estaba, le preguntó si sabía mover las orejas. (p. 100)

Kirkpatrick, *"Las Románticas"*: *Women Writers and Subjectivity in Spain, 1835–1850*, pp. 293–94; and Paul Julian Smith, *The Body Hispanic: Gender and Sexuality in Spanish and Spanish American Literature* (Oxford: Clarendon Press, 1989), pp. 69–104. Allende, however, sees no difference between women's and men's writing; 'creo que la literatura no tiene sexo y que no hay que ponerse en el plan de escribir como mujer porque es una forma de autosegregación que me parece torpe'; Magdalena García Pinto, *Historias íntimas: conversaciones con diez escritoras latinoamericanas* (Hanover: Ediciones del Norte, 1988), p. 13.

But the opportunity for political confrontation is muted to produce a humorous *non sequitur*. Clara's question as to whether Esteban can wiggle his ears is bathetic. The unstated assumption is that feminism is an activity defined exclusively by gender to which men are barred because of their sex. Allende's text implies, thus, that feminism is natural for women, but unnatural for men. Indeed, many of the events of the plot present Esteben Trueba's violent assertion of his dominance as part and parcel of his sex, rather than as cultural constructs. According to the rhetorical world-vision which emerges through the events of the novel, it seems that the sexes are imprisoned in the oppositeness of their respective genders.

This tends to clarify the references throughout the novel to history as a series of repetitions. As Clara explains, 'los nombres repetidos crean confusión en los cuadernos de anotar la vida' (p. 107), a feature of Allende's fiction which conjures up an inevitable intertextual link with García Márquez's *Cien años de soledad*.[12]

Working in a similar direction – that of desexualizing gender – is the treatment of spiritualism, which, like feminism and indeed the discourse of the fairy tale, is restricted to the female sex.[13] Spiritualism initiates women into a sisterhood which transcends origin and family. The three Mora sisters, for example, 'se enteraron, por conductos misteriosos al alcance de los iniciados, de la existencia de Clara, se pusieron en contacto con ella y de inmediato comprendieron que eran hermanas astrales'. Although, as Patricia Hart has argued, Allende presents this episode 'with tongue firmly in cheek', it nevertheless tends to mute the political confrontation by transforming it into a (universalist) struggle

---

[12] See Marcelo Coddou, *Para leer a Isabel Allende*, p. 44. Predestation fulfils a similar purpose in *La casa de los espíritus* as in García Márquez's *Cien años de soledad*. Allende's text often concludes a particular episode by looking forward to the future completion of that particular narratological unit. An example of this occurs in chapter VIII: 'Amanda los estrechó contra su pecho frenéticamente y en una inspiración del momento le dijo: "daría la vida por ti, Miguelito". No sabía que algún día tendría que hacerlo' (p. 199). The emphasis on predestination, itself again reminiscent of *Cien años de soledad*, is predicated on a non-dialectical view of the flow of history. Patricia Hart, in a review of *The Stories of Eva Luna*, argues of *La casa de los espíritus*, however, that 'most of the superficial similarities to *One Hundred Years of Solitude* were ironic, even parodic', 'Boom Times-II', *The Nation* (11 March 1991), 314–16 (p. 314). For further discussion of the Allende-García Márquez interface, see Juan Manuel Marcos, *De García Márquez al postboom* (Madrid: Orígenes, 1986), pp. 99–101; and Gerald Martin, *Journeys Through the Labyrinth*, pp. 351–52.

[13] For a discussion of the links between femininity and the fairy tale in the novel, see Sandra M. Boschetto, 'Threads, Connections, and the Fairy Tale: Reading the Writing in Isabel Allende's *La casa de los espíritus*', in *Continental, Latin-American and Francophile Women Writers*, Vol. II, pp. 51–63.

between man and woman.[14] Esteban Trueba is, after all, the paradigm of
the phallocratic man and he tends to group together indiscriminately
feminism, spiritualism and Marxism. Thus he reacts to the workers'
insurrection (p. 63) with the same outrage as when he discovers his
wife's lesbian tendencies (p. 121). For Esteban, thus, feminism,
Marxism, spiritualism and lesbianism all amount to much the same thing.
Allende's text seems, almost in spite of itself, to echo this cast of thought.
An example of this occurs at the structurally significant conclusion of
Chapter 2 which had focussed on some of these political issues. The
world of politics gives way to the world of the supernatural, as Esteban
has a premoniton about the contents of a letter he has just received: 'La
carta de Férula era igual a todas las que había recibido de ella, pero al
tenerla en la mano, supo, aun antes de abrirla, que su contenido le
cambiaría la vida' (p. 69). This emasculation of Marxist ideology tends
to deconstruct the metaphors on which the novel is apparently built.

Given Allende's clear critique of phallogocentrism in the person of
Esteban Trueba, one might have thought that she would also have
presented a less clichéd view of femininity. But the women are as
stereotypical as the men. They are intuitive (telepathic), weak (they put
up with a thrashing from their husbands), procreative and passive,
although Allende herself states that her female characters are 'seres bien
plantados en sus pies, altivos, generosos, fuertes, jamás derrotados,
plenos de ternura y coraje'.[15] They are epitomes of the female stereotype
(woman as unintelligent, passive and submissive) against which feminists
such as Kate Millett have struggled.[16] Political struggle is neutered by
being at once expressed in universalist terms as a struggle between the
archetypes of male and female. Perhaps the best example of sexual
antagonism is the passionate love affair between Blanca and Pedro
Tercero who make love every night from dusk to dawn in a river nearby:
'Pasaban la noche en el río, inmunes al frío o el cansancio, retozando con
la fuerza de la desesperación, y sólo al vislumbrar los primeros rasgos
del amanecer, Blanca regresaba a la casa y entraba por la ventana a su
cuarto, donde llegaba justo a tiempo para oír cantar a los gallos' (p. 143).
It is also hardly coincidental that Clara's realization about her daughter's
love affair should take place at precisely the same moment that an
earthquake begins (the 'earth shaking' being a popular metaphor for the
sexual act).

[14] *Narrative Magic in the Fiction of Isabel Allende* (London and Ontario: Associated
University Presses, 1989), p. 116.
[15] In an interview quoted by Marcelo Coddou, *Para leer a Isabel Allende*, p. 58.
[16] *Sexual Politics*, p. 28.

Also indicative of the translation of political conflict into gender-specific conflicts is the fact that the student revolution described in chapter XI misfires because Alba suddenly has her period. Soon after she is taken away, the strike collapses. A political struggle is shrouded, thus, within a feminine mystique. By consistently translating political conflict into universalist sexual archetypes in *La casa de los espíritus*, as well as depicting relationships in terms of the natural world, Allende turns what might have been a political allegory into a naturalist symbol. Allende's metaphors, therefore, deconstruct the conspicuous level of political commitment which hovers on the surface of the text. The text's metaphors refer back to a biologically sexualized universe which effectively mutes any putative political message.

MARTA TRABA: *CONVERSACIÓN AL SUR*

The work of Marta Traba (1930–1983: Argentina) focusses on sexual politics in a way which has some striking similarities with that of a fellow woman writer from the Southern Cone, Cristina Peri Rossi. Both writers, as Elia Kantaris has pointed out, 'attempt to work through to the root mechanisms underlying the phenomenon of dictatorship, seen as a particularly crude expression of a more insidious, generalized oppression'. For both Traba and Peri Rossi, as Kantaris goes on to argue, 'the struggle against a seemingly all-pervasive alienating hegemony must be linked to the exposure of the role played within that hegemony of a patriarchal *sexual* economy in which (male) desire is construed as the desire to possess and in particular to monopolise the means of (re)production'.[17] Crucial in this context is the notion of 'subaltern'.

In her essay 'Subaltern Studies: Deconstructing Historiography', Gayatri Spivak explores the link between the notions of the subaltern, insurgency and consciousness, arguing that the notion of consciousness is problematic since it is inescapably dependent on the agency of the élite culture.[18] In her analysis of the work of the Subaltern Studies group Spivak identifies, despite their professed aim to express empirical historical facts, a suggestion that 'subaltern consciousness is subject to the cathexis of the élite, that it is never fully recoverable, that it is always askew from its received signifiers, indeed that it is effaced even as it is disclosed, that it is irreducibly discursive' (p. 203). In order to

[17] 'The Politics of Desire: Alienation and Identity in the Work of Marta Traba and Cristina Peri Rossi', *FMLS*, 25 (1989), 248–64 (p. 248).
[18] *In Other Worlds: Essays in Cultural Politics* (New York and London: Methuen, 1987), pp. 197–221.

circumvent this blindspot within our knowledge of the subaltern, Spivak proposes a re-inscription of the positive subject-position for the subaltern as a 'strategy for our times'. As she goes on to argue, re-inscription of this kind 'acknowledges that the arena of the subaltern's persistent emergence into hegemony must always and by definition remain heterogeneous to the efforts of the disciplinary historian. The historian must persist in *his* efforts in this awareness, that the subaltern is necessarily the absolute limit of the place where history is narrativized into logic' (p. 207). The space occupied by the subaltern in the historian's text will thus always be elusive, 'effaced even as it is disclosed', to quote Spivak's words. Spivak concludes her essay by pointing to the importance of the 'subject-constitution of the subaltern-female' in this context (p. 219), arguing that 'the figure of the woman, moving from clan to clan, and family to family as daughter/sister and wife/mother, syntaxes patriarchal continuity even as she is herself drained of proper identity' (p. 220). Woman is the chain on which the continuity of society depends, and any trace of which patriarchy systematically hides.

A remarkably similar sexual system emerges in Traba's *Conversación al sur* (1981), where the space of subaltern consciousness is occupied simultaneously by the political insurgent and the female. Traba's novel centres on the memories of two women, Dolores and Irene, who were involved in the Revolutionary Movement in Uruguay, Argentina and Chile in the 1970s; as a result, both suffer mental and physical torture and lose their loved ones. Traba's presentation of the political conflict, as we shall see, is gendered in that it projects femaleness and political insurgency as indivisible notions.

Sex and politics are intimately linked in *Conversación al sur*, but not in an obvious sense. Indeed, in one important way, sex and politics are seen as antagonistic elements in Traba's novel. Towards the end of the novel, for example, Dolores is attracted by the reassuring warmth of a house she sees, noting 'fragmentos de piezas iluminadas, paredes, bibliotecas, plantas, lámparas encendidas' (p. 161).[19] But she senses that a desire for these things is dangerous:

> Desear esto era desear otras felicidades que se encadenaban unas con otras; la luz a las piezas, las piezas a la vida familiar. De ahí podía saltarse con facilidad a la pérdida del miedo; y en ese punto, haciendo maravillosas acrobacias, se saltaba a las voluptuosidades, a la pasión y al reposo, a todo

[19] All references are to *Conversación al sur*, third edition (México: Siglo Veintiuno Editores, 1988). For an excellent translation of the work, see *Mothers and Shadows*, translated by Jo Labanyi (London: Readers' International, 1989).

aquello que fuera capaz de establecer las debidas distancias con la muerte. ¡Ah, no!, debía defenderse de estas locas aspiraciones a la felicidad, como se defendían los demás cerrando las casas a cal y canto y cayendo en sueños como pozos. A conciencia o sin saberlo todos lo hacían, así que no era el caso de dar un paso en falso. (p. 161).

A clear distinction is being drawn between the non-domestic life of the revolutionary and the sensual pleasures of domesticity. Sex and revolution, in Dolores's mind, are clearly ill-suited. A similar parallel is drawn in the description of the life-style of the Head of the Revolutionary Movement in Argentina, Andrés. After visiting Victoria, Andrés is overcome with a brief moment of gay abandon:

Por primera vez en muchos años le dieron ganas de entrar a un bar y emborracharse. Calculó que en el bar de enfrente no había nadie a esa hora, que la barra estaría oscura y propicia y que con cuatro tragos, en el estado de abstinencia en que vivía, todo iba a ser posible y las cosas perdidas volverían a su encuentro. Sexo y amor, felicidad, lascivia, ¡Oh, Dios! qué clase de tipo sin vida, de impotente, de monstruo se había vuelto. (p. 110)

Rather like the protagonist in John Dos Passos's monumental *U.S.A.*, Andrés is too busy with his revolutionary activities to bother about sex. So, on one level, the term sexual politics – if understood in terms of the constituent parts of the phrase – is not relevant in a primary sense to *Conversación al sur*.

There is, however, a more complex way in which sex and politics are linked in Traba's novel, and this concerns the ways in which the political reality (and specifically oppression) is experienced by one sex in particular (women).[20] This point becomes clear when we focus on how women, as opposed to men, experience the political Real. With a striking gender bias, men are depicted in *Conversación al sur* with few exceptions as associated with the Right or, if they happen to be left-wing revolutionaries, they are portrayed as ineffectual. Even Andrés soon disappears (i.e. halfway through the narrative), murdered like many of the other male revolutionaries in the novel (the archetypal case being Dolores's lover, Enrique). The male revolutionaries, thus, are presented as lacking generational continuity, as if they were isolated events of spontaneous revolution; this is in direct contrast to the women, such as

[20] This would tend to suggest that, as far as its rhetorical ideology is concerned, *Conversación al sur* is a feminist novel; Marta Traba's connections with the women's liberation movement, however, have been tangential, as she suggests in an interview; Magdalena García Pinto, *Historias íntimas: conversaciones con diez escritoras latinoamericanas*, p. 210.

Dolores, Irene, and the 'mad women' of the Plaza de Mayo, who demonstrate a more sustained form of political commitment. Other men on the revolutionary side are given ineffectual roles.[21]

As we can see, the men on the revolutionary side are either ineffectual, or they end up murdered. This provides a noticeable imbalance and gives rise to a situation in which it is the revolutionary women who are seen as the standard-bearers of the revolutionary spirit in its more enduring qualities. As Marta Traba pointed out in an interview with regard to *Conversación al sur*, 'women are the real heroines of this drama'.[22] There is a particularly good example of this type of sexual politics in the scene in which the Police Commissioner arrests Luisa and her revolutionary comrades at a party she is throwing. The episode focusses on the reaction of the women: Luisa, Dolores, Irene. The revolutionary, Juan, has a minor role during this crucial scene. We simply see him come into the room, 'pálido' (p. 144). This tends to suggest that the revolutionary movement is being carried out in the main by women, and also, that the enemy, as in this particular scene in the figure of the Commissioner of Police, is male. The war which occurred in the Southern Cone in the 1970s was, thus, for Marta Traba not only a war about political policies – Left versus Right – but also a war of the sexes. Traba personally believed that communication *between* the sexes is impossible: 'men and women can never communicate with each other completely because their experiences are so very different. Sometimes it's useless to even talk because understanding one another is futile.'[23] *Conversación al sur* seems to bear out this remark; the sexual war is the underbelly of the taxonomy of power that Traba's text unfolds.

The political ideas for which the revolutionaries are fighting are, if anything, vague, or rather they are expressed in a fragmented form throughout the narrative. Marxist dogma is almost non-existent in this novel. The only criterion which Andrés takes into account, for example, when recruiting new members is the candidate's 'fuerza ideológica' (p. 106), although no other details of what this might entail are given.[24]

---

[21] An example is the tragic/pathetic figure of Andrés's father who clearly idolises his son and thereby acts as a foil enhancing his son's revolutionary commitment, as well as, through his grief, embodying the senselessness of Andrés's death.

[22] Evelyn Picon Garfield, *Women's Voices from Latin America: Interviews with Six Contemporary Authors* (Detroit: Wayne State University Press, 1985), p. 140.

[23] Evelyn Picon Garfield, *Women's Voices from Latin America: Interviews with Six Contemporary Authors*, p. 135.

[24] In an interview given shortly before her death, Marta Traba listed the various political injustices she found most abhorrent and she included political oppression originating from the Left (human rights violations in the Soviet Union) as well as the Right (U.S. foreign policy in Central America). In the list there was only one type of

When Dolores is musing about the generational conflict, she sees the older generation as guided by the 'sentimientos netamente posesivos' (p. 99). Dolores takes this idea further when she interprets her parents' rejection of her and her contemporaries' way of life as boiling down ultimately to 'un problema de propiedad privada' (p. 100). Dolores's political views, given her rejection of private property, can thus be broadly identified as left-wing, but the novel offers no more details than this. This is a deliberate stratagem since the novel is thus able to present the revolutionary struggle not as an argument about political alternatives but as a struggle against evil, death and oppression, that is, something outside the arena of party politics. This fact provides a clue about the rhetorical strategy used in *Conversación al sur*: synecdoche. The visible reality drawn in Traba's text alludes to the invisible reality which the reader is forced to reconstruct. The unseen reality is the systematic abduction and torture of political subversives by the Argentinian Armed Forces, and worse, because more cynical, the adoption by high-ranking military officials of the offspring of murdered revolutionaries. *Conversación al sur* does not provide empiric information of this kind in the manner of a documentary; instead it transmits, rather like an echo chamber, the experience of individuals who lost next-of-kin during the 'guerra sucia', the dirty war between the military and terrorist groups which shook Argentina, Uruguay and Chile during the late 1970s and early 1980s. The objective facts are reduced to tantalizing allusions, the metaphor shorn from its concrete referent.

Synecdoche, thus, is the rhetorical strategy underlying the most significant scenes in the novel. When Dolores finally relates the scene in which she lost her child as a result of police brutality, her account is impersonal to the point of being almost inhuman:

> Fue en ese momento que la tiraron al suelo y volvieron a ponerle un pie sobre el pecho. No apretaba; desde abajo veía la bota muy cerca de la cara y calculaba en qué parte del cuerpo empezaría a saltar. ¡Ah, sobre el vientre no se atrevería! Pensó con terror lo frágil que era el pecho, el esternón, las costillas. Sin embargo el tipo desvió la bota y la montó sobre la barriga. Fue apretando, saltó. Ella quería gritar pero no tenía aire alguno, de la boca salían sollozos y aullidos inhumanos. Ahora se arrastraba como un caracol; iba dejando una baba brillante y sangrienta. (p. 159)

injustice which was not tied to a specific historical occurrence: 'las torturas dondequiera que se denuncien'; Elena Poniatowska, 'Marta Traba o el salto al vacío', *RI*, 132–33 (1985), 883–97 (p. 895). This would tend to suggest where her 'human' allegiance largely lies.

The account of the event which has clearly unhinged Dolores's mind, a fact to which the previous 150 or so pages amply testify, reads almost like a legal report. It is a good example of the 'contrapuntal style' consistently employed in Traba's novel which, as Evelyn Picon Garfield points out, 'serves to actualize past horrors while simultaneously relating the incidents at arm's length, in a dispassionate tone'.[25] In this way the reader is drawn into an interpretative process which supplements the (unexpressed) emotional intensity of the event. Subaltern knowledge cannot appear without the consent of the oppressor; the knowledge of the subaltern is, thus, by definition, incomplete, non-originary. Significant in this context is the fact that the unborn child as the nurse later told Dolores, was a baby girl (p. 156). This tends once more to reinforce the notion of 'Us against Them' framed in terms of Woman against Man. When the men become victims, they disappear from the semantic space of the novel, seemingly without trace. It is the woman, as this passage shows vividly, who suffer oppression in the flesh. As Dolores reflects: 'De nuevo crecía, macabra, la persecución de los cuerpos' (p. 156). The process whereby the reader is drawn, through the synedoche, to re-create the discourse of the subaltern is particularly evident in the last paragraph of the novel. Here Dolores and Irene are pictured huddling together, terrified by the sound of the door being broken down:

> Los brutales golpes contra la puerta de calle las despertaron a las dos al tiempo. Dolores se levantó de un salto y se puso a gritar sin control. (. . .) Después el ruido se acercó y les pareció un raro estruendo, un trueno que retumbaba. (. . .) En ese silencio absoluto, el otro ruido, nítido, despiadado, fue creciendo y, finalmente, las cercó. (p. 170)

Like the rest of the novel, this passage, which is unsurpassed in its suspenseful dramaticism, operates synecdochially, the unexpressed tenor of the synecdoche being supplied by the reader's imagination.

Leaving the bulk of the novel to the reader's imagination is of course a deliberate ploy since it echoes the means identified by Traba whereby authority exerts control over the civilian population. In the case of Argentina during the 1970s this was by refusing to return the bodies of subversives to their families, by keeping the society around them in the dark, a form of psychological torture inducing a fear of the unknown. As Dolores says to Victoria at one stage: 'Peor es imaginarse las cosas' (p. 123). Victoria can only agree; she simply repeats Dolores's words. As Dolores muses to herself later on: 'Policía y ejército, verdugos y

---

[25] *Women's Voices from Latin America: Interviews with Six Contemporary Authors*, p. 122.

torturadores iban a sacar, indudablemente, ventaja; cualquier locura paramilitar quedaba justificada por la sucia guerra' (p. 124). The powers of authority use the people's fear of the unknown to justify atrocities. This passage suggests how Traba sees imagination, akin to other theoreticians of power, as a means of controlling the thoughts of others and thereby exerting control over them.

Not surprisingly perhaps, fear pervades Dolores's whole existence. She becomes paranoiac, at one stage, suspecting the bus-driver of considering informing on her:

> Nada era más redituable que denunciar a alguien, y todos lo sabían. Pensó que el hombre la miraba con la misma expresión codiciosa de sus vecinos, del lechero, del chico de la pensión, del vendedor de diarios. Una expresión donde siempre se leía la misma pregunta: ¿qué tajada podré sacar de ella? (p. 155)

It is significant that the various hypothetical enemies listed here are all men (the milkman, the son of the family in the boarding house, etc.). The political war between Right and Left is once more gendered.

Dolores's imagination, for example, is apt to run riot. She becomes obsessed with death. Thus, when her mother tells her how her father died, she cannot resist imagining other scenarios: 'Trató de revivir el momento en que la cabeza del viejo iba cayendo sobre el plato de sopa. No, no podía ser, debió inventarlo la maldita harpía' (p. 155). Dolores's imagination renders the image of her father's death all the more grotesque.

A good example of the use of (imaginative) power in the interests of political oppression occurs during the scene when the coffin, in which Enrique's body (supposedly) lies, is returned to Dolores:

> Nos metimos en el furgón militar con el cajón. En realidad, una caja no muy larga de madera sin pintar. Enrique no era grande, apenas más alto que yo; pero imposible que cupiera en esa caja; ese pensamiento fijo me martirizaba. (p. 117)

Dolores's dilemma, which is focussed on what Traba has elsewhere called the 'interstitial' detail, also becomes the reader's.[26] The text cannot reveal who, or what, was contained in the coffin. As she asks herself

---

[26] Evelyn Picon Garfield, *Women's Voices from Latin America*, p. 126. Traba also mentions the importance of detail in another interview in which she defines what she sees as the specificness of women's writing: 'es una narración directa, reiterativa, emotiva, más semejante a la tradición oral que al texto masculino'; Magdalena García Pinto, *Historias íntimas: conversaciones con diez escritoras latinoamericanas*, p. 211.

later on: '¿Fue el cuerpo de Enrique el que metieron bajo tierra y Luisa señalizó con una piedra? ¿O un perro callejero?' (p. 156).

Throughout the novel it is the women who are cast in the role of victims. This emerges during a tearful exchange between Victoria and Dolores: '– Y si salimos con vida – oigo que me dice Victoria al oído – nos vamos a hundir en la tristeza, porque de todos modos fuimos los perdedores' (p. 132). Irene voices a similar sentiment. The female revolutionaries are unable to break out of their role as perpetual victims:

> Ahora el misterio es por qué quedamos vos y yo del lado de las víctimas, cuando tampoco somos capaces de matar una mosca; (. . .) yo imagino muchas veces a un tipo dando la orden de fusilamiento, o a otro enchufando la picana eléctrica o metiéndole la cabeza a una chica en un balde lleno de mierda y quedo paralizada del horror, pero no se me ocurre que la situación se invierta y que sea yo la que enchufe la picana para aplicársela a los testículos del monstruo. (p. 166)

The suggestion is that the monster is always male and the female is always victim; the subaltern, Traba's text suggests, is always gendered. Yet it is in this forced identity of victim that the women are collectively able to draw strenth. This is particularly evident in the so-called 'madwomen' who congregate every Thursday in the Plaza de Mayo to protest the disappearance of loved ones. This sense of solidarity reaches a crescendo when the 'locas' begin repeating their collective chant:

> Yo hacía lo mismo que las locas, y no te puedo decir lo que sentía; como si me estuvieran por arrancar las entrañas y me las agarrara con una fuerza demencial para salvarlas. (. . .) Oí un amenazador rumor sobre mi cabeza y la bajé instintivamente; al momento comprendí que lo hacían las palomas, planeando despavoridas sin encontrar lugar donde posarse. (. . .) Estaba en la mitad de un círculo que coreaba al unísono, y ahí sí pude entender claramente 'dónde están', 'dónde están'. (pp. 89–90)

The repeated chant of the women becomes almost non-human, a 'womenspeak' which defies the phallocentric parameters of language; it is at first identified with the 'threatening noise' made by the pigeons. The words they use 'estaban como tajeadas por sollozos y aullidos' (p. 89). Although greeted by indifference by the occupants of the Casa Rosada, their question 'Where are they?' returns to haunt the authority figures. Although *Conversación al sur* has a pessimistic level, since it seems to accept defeat as inevitable and ends with a scene in which Irene and

Dolores are about to meet their doom, it also has a positive message in that the sense of solidarity shared by the women points the way forward to the path of social justice.[27]

MONTSERRAT ROIG: *L'HORA VIOLETA*

L'hora violeta (1980) by Montserrat Roig (1946–1992: Spain) is a novel that 'openly reflects a number of feminist issues' and which is characterized by its 'political thrust' and 'satirical tone'.[28] It is structured around three basic conflicts. The first two are political and involve, on the one hand, the destruction of Catalan soldiers at the hands of the S.S. in German concentration camps during World War II, and, on the other, the destruction of the Republican cause by Francisco Franco during the Spanish Civil War. Both of these conflicts have a Catalan dimension, the first obviously so, and the second because the onslaught of the Nationalist forces is seen from the point of view of the inhabitants of Barcelona, and particularly the female inhabitants. By implication, since one story is woven on top of the other, the respective enemies in each case, Franco and Hitler, are seen as one. These two conflicts act as a backdrop to the third basic conflict, the one which the novel concentrates on, that is the battle between the sexes. All of these three stories are linked by the story told to her son by Norma which appears towards the end of the novel about the salmon which swim against the current: 'Fill, diuen que cada primavera els salmons surten del mar on han viscut a l'hivern, remunten els rius, xoquen contra la rocalla, alguns s'hi estavellen, d'altres se'n surten i moren tot sovint allà on han nascut' (p. 210).[29] The reference immediately afterwards to the planting of pine trees in memory of those Catalan soldiers who died in German concentration camps makes the metaphor transparent (p. 211). The act of writing in Catalan is by extension promoted as itself an act of liberation against political tyranny.[30]

---

[27] María Sola argues that the creation of identity in solidarity and living for others are themes which emerge forcefully in Traba's novel; '*Conversación al sur*: Novela para no olvidar', *SiN*, 12:4 (1982), 64–71 (p. 67).

[28] Katharina M. Wilson (ed.), *An Encyclopedia of Continental Women Writers*, Vol. II, p. 1057.

[29] *L'hora violeta*, 6th edition (Barcelona: Edicions 62, 1981). All references are to this edition.

[30] In an interview with Geraldine G. Nichols, Roig identifies Castilian with Franco as politically oppressive; see *Escribir, espacio propio: Laforet, Matute, Moix, Tusquets, Riera y Roig por sí mismas*, pp. 147–49.

The pattern of the lives of the women narrated in *L'hora violeta*, characters from the Miralpeix and the Ventura-Claret families who appeared in Roig's earlier novels, *Ramona, adéu* (1972), *El temps de les cireres* (1977), has a disturbing similarity with the life of the doomed salmon. Each of the four main protagonists, Norma, Natàlia, Judith and Kati attempt to find happiness in a relationship with a man and in each case this leads to disaster. Norma, 'a mask of the author', as Janet Pérez points out,[31] has fallen out of love with Ferran and is in love with Alfred who, however, refuses to leave his wife for her. Natàlia's story is almost identical; despite seeming to rebel against the values of the older generation, she repeats the cycle of male betrayal; she falls in love and has an affair with a married man, Jordi, who simply strings her along since he never intends to leave his wife, Agnès. The loves of Judith's life are likewise doomed to failure. She loves her mongoloid son, Pere, desperately, and seems towards the end of her life to fall in love with Kati; lesbian love, like her love of her mongoloid son, shows Judith in love with pariah figures, images which do not fit within social norms. Kati's love for Patrick, the Irishman who fought during the Spanish Civil War for the International Brigades, likewise ends in loss when he is killed in action. Kati subsequently commits suicide. Each of these different stories seems to emphasise the same sense of woman's betrayal at the hands of men. Either the man they are in love with is married and will not leave his wife (Natàlia) or he is in love with another woman (Kati). It is important to emphasise that these various narratives are gynocentric, thereby reversing the patriarchal strategy of casting woman as admired object. As Roig pointed out in an interview: 'El homes han explicat el món de les dones a través de la seva pròpia visió. Jo el que intento és explicar com veig els homes a través de la meva visió'.[32] The plight of the various women in Roig's fiction is emblematized by the image of her mother that Norma recalls, when she begged her husband not to leave her: 'Com la mare, que s'havia agenollat davant de la porta del rebedor tot demanant al pare que no la deixés. Havia passat molt de temps, d'això, però sempre tenia la mateixa imatge de la mare: agenollada davant de la porta del rebedor, arrapada als forrellats, fent un crit llarg i discontinu' (p. 32). This image of female servitude is repeated in the narrative of women's lives. Judith gave up her ambition to become a

---

[31] Janet Pérez, *Contemporary Women Writers of Spain*, p. 191.

[32] Interview with Francesc Navarro, in *L'Hora* (January 1981), quoted by Anne Charlon, *La condició de la dona en la narrativa femenina (1900–1983)*, p. 14. For a discussion of Roig's gynocentrism, see Joan L. Brown, 'Montserrat Roig and the Creation of a Gynocentric Reality', in *Women Writers of Contemporary Spain*, pp. 217–39 (pp. 229–33).

concert pianist for her husband, Joan (see Patrícia's version, pp. 113–15). History, or perhaps better 'herstory', repeats itself in the next generation. Judith's son, Lluís, forces the woman he loves to give up her promising career as a ballerina which she is studying at the Liceu. Lluís does this in order to take revenge on his mother: 'li deia, ho veus?, jo també he aconseguit una dona que deixa la dansa per mi, pel matrimoni' (p. 107). As this particular relationship suggests, the sexes do not live in harmony; they are at war with each other. This separateness between man and woman is mirrored in the language they respectively speak. Natàlia puts this most eloquently:

> Fa temps que sento les mateixes paraules, surten de les nostres boques, descruien cercles com en una sínia i tornen al mateix punt de partida. Les paraules neixen i moren en un sentit de circumval.lació. Les paraules ens allunyen, Jordi. Es com si visquéssim en dues galàxies diferents. Com si cada cervell hagués estar estructurat de manera diversa i no hi hagués manera de lligar un llenguatge comú. (pp. 47–48)

Language thus becomes a sign as well as an agent of the separateness of the male and female 'galaxies', to use Natàlia's expression. The desire to find a common language between the two sexes is, Natàlia's words suggest, doomed to failure. If one considers the eventual fate of the protagonists of *L'hora violeta* this would seem to be true. This is the reason why lesbianism surfaces sporadically in the novel as a means of achieving sexual harmony. Norma envies lesbians' emotional self-sufficiency, which struck her when she met an (un-named) French writer (p. 202); however, her experience of lesbian sex ends in a fit of vomiting (p. 206). The very close relationship between Kati and Judith, hinted at in the diary which Judith writes in the section 'La novel.la de l'hora violeta' (pp. 95–109), remains Platonic, but might have taken a different direction, if one reads between the lines of Kati's suggestion to Judith that they should run away together before Barcelona falls to the Nationalist forces (p. 105). The intensity of the relationship between Kati and Judith during the war years is suggested by Patrícia's bitter jealousy of the happiness they share in each other's company (pp. 113–14).

One particularly bitter lesson that each of these narratives of love suggests is that discourses which are intended to liberate the individual through knowledge, such as Marxism and feminism, run counter to the individual experience of each woman. Natàlia, for example, idolises Jordi because of his devotion to the ideal of communism. While on the one hand she argues bitterly with Norma about feminine passivity ('No suporto les dones-víctimes. Part de l'opressió que pateix la dona és per culpa de les dones'; p. 84), Natàlia feels that, through Jordi, 'el món recobrava l'harmonia trencada'. By sharing his communist love for all mankind 'sortia, per fi, de la meva lluita individual' (p. 84). But her faith in Jordi is ill-founded. Later on in the novel he argues that romantic love is based on 'mauvaise foi' created by literature: 'ens hem inventat l'amor' (p. 90). Natàlia's love-affair with a communist seems, if anything, to underline that women invariably play second fiddle to the patriarchal world of politics. Germinal, a young star of the communist movement, finds no difficulty in harmonizing his enthusiasm for communism with his frankly *machista* attitude towards Helena:

> L'Helena no m'obligava a res, se'm lliurava tota, m'agradava acariciar-li les cuixes tèbies, la seva escalfor. Però ella demanava més amb els ulls i jo no volia continuar. Només volia el seu silenci i potser la seva submissió. D'alguna manera, era meva. No, era meva del tot. Sempre la tenia a mà, disposada a escalfar-me amb el cos petit i rodó, d'adolescent. (p. 151)

Germinal, in a truly patriarchal gesture, wishes to reduce his female companion to silence, ignore the desire expressed in her eyes, and turn her into 'el cos petit i rodó'. Communism, as these two examples suggest, despite its liberational rhetoric, offers little escape for women. Even feminism seems to offer little possibility of providing a solution to the female predicament. Norma, for example, is aware as a feminist that her love for Arthur is leading to her own oppression, but this knowledge seems useless: 'Sóc una bleda, va dir-se. De què serveixen tantes conferències de feminisme si no trobo raons per un amor tan il.logic? Per què em tanco en un amor tan inútil?, es feia, per qué no ho acabo?' (p. 173). As Norma complains later on: 'El feminisme no havia previst la passió amorosa, intensa, total, entre un home i una dona' (p. 214). Feminism, like Marxism, seems not to offer a way out.[33]

As these narratives of their lives suggest, the women in *L'hora violeta* are in a Catch-22 situation. Their experience of everyday life is nightmarish. As Norma muses to herself, History is a bad dream best forgotten: 'La Història és un malson, pensava, i me n'he d'alliberar' (p. 199). The only way of escaping the nightmare of life, which is

---

[33] Catherine Davies has noted that the protagonists of *L'hora violeta* 'find themselves in limbo as the feminist strategy, unable to account for heterosexual desire or animosity among women, proves insufficient'; see 'The Sexual Representation of Politics in Contemporary Hispanic Feminist Narrative', in *Feminist Readings on Spanish and Latin-American Literature*, eds. L. P. Condé & S. M. Hart, pp. 107–19 (p. 110). It is no doubt because of her portrayal of the failure of feminism that Lidia Falcón has accused Roig's fiction of being anti-feminist; Roig, however, has argued that she is not tied to any sect in her writing, and is simply relating her personal experience; see Geraldine C. Nichols, *Escribir, espacio propio: Laforet, Matute, Moix, Tusquets, Riera y Roig por sí mismas*, pp. 157–58.

epitomised by the Nazi concentration camps which punctuate the narrative at various junctures, is to fall in love. Norma needs love in order to forget about the past: 'Volia fugir-ne. Que no en quedés ni la memòria. Esborrar. . . potser les paraules? La Norma pensava en el seu àngel, més tangible, més real dins del somni, desitjava besar-lo i ésser besada fins l'agonia. La Norma volia oblidar' (p. 213). But, as the various narratives of women's lives suggest, love only leads to frustration. Norma's desire for love, thus, has some of the tragic irony of the desire experienced by salmon to undertake a hazardous journey in order to return to their place of birth. Like the salmon which 'han xocat contra les roques' (p. 213), women die when they bang against the rock of patriarchy. Yet, *L'hora violeta* suggests that there is another culprit at work, namely, time. One of the distinctive features of bliss when achieved (momentarily) is its ability to stop the ebb and flow of time. While listening to Mozart, Norma is overcome by a sense of time's passing:

> Silenci. Només Mozart, música nostàlgica d'un pasat que enyoro i que mai no he conegut. El temps s'esfilagarsa. Intento de pensar alguna cosa de coherent. Com retenir la fugacitat? (. . .) Com expressar l'instant que se'n va? (. . .) Per què ve la nit? Voldria que el capvespre s'aturés. Com retenir-lo. (p. 179)

The desire to hold onto the past, capture the passing of time, hence the allusion to Virginia Woolf's 'The weather, perpetually changing' (p. 177), is a central motif in the novel and is the principle animating the reference to photographs throughout the novel. Desire is mobile, or polymorphous to use Freud's term, while the photograph can give a sense of permanence to images of a changing world, changing desire into memory, what Judith calls, recalling her first sexual experience 'un desig fet record' (p. 105). It is significant that the different narrators often have recourse to the same technique; they are leafing through photo-albums, their memory is jogged by certain snaps and the narrative begins. Natàlia epitomises this idea since she is a professional photographer. She explains the motive behind her love of photography:

> La meva història no és exemplar. Es ensopida. I, tot fotografiant els rostres del altres, s'obliden del meu. Les monges del col.legi em dirien, de ben segur, que peco de supèrbia.
> Però ningú no em robarà aquests moments, preciosos dins l'espai i el temps. Quan el records tornen. I és que el records només existeixen quan no ets feliç. (. . .) De vegades em sembla que em refugio en el record perquè ja no sóc capaç de viure. Com si hagués tancat la barraqueta. Però el record és literatura, recreació. (pp. 30–31)

Memories of the past, around which the different narratives of the female
protagonists are built, can thus become a safe haven in the protean and
unpredictable nature of everyday life in which 'el temps no s'atura'
(p. 89). Literature, as the above passage quoted makes clear, is also a
type of memory since, like the latter, it involves an active recreation of
the past. Love is the third element in the triangle of memory and
literature, for love is described as able (briefly) to stem the flow of time.
Norma recalls towards the end of the novel a time when her relationship
with Arthur led time to stand still: 'Recordà una de les vegades que van
ser més feliços. Havien anat de vacances, tenien una setmana per estar-se
junts. No hi havia pressa ni clandestinitat. Les hores no existien'
(p. 208). Natàlia also experiences a timelessness, but it is not through
love but through a pantheistic fusion with the natural world:

> El sol em besa l'espinada. S'hi endinsa. Els meus porus, agraïts, el xuclen.
> M'agradaria d'enclotar-me a l'arena. Sentir-me besada per l'aire – ventet
> de garbí –, per la llum, per l'aigua. Els elements em perdonen el cos
> degradat. Cos de dona que ja no recordo quan va començar a envellir. Els
> elements ni m'admiren ni em jutgen. M'hi deixen estar. Jo no sóc com la
> Norma, no. No busco l'amor dels altres. Jo només demano als elements
> que em deixin formar part de la naturalesa que m'envolta. Ser-ne una peça
> més. Oblidar les paraules i els pensaments. Roca i sorra. Llum i aigua.
> (p. 93)

The loss of identity described here has an almost mystical feel about it.
Natàlia seems to have reached a time of the body, in which memory plays
no part, and in which nature is not judgmental. In its celebration of being
unfettered by the accoutrements of patriarchal civilisation, and in
particular its water symbolism, this passage has suggestive parallels with
a similar passage in Clarice Lispector's *Perto do coração selvagem* when
the protagonist, Joana, describes her experience of 'Lalande' (see above
Chapter I, p. 34). The last two sentences of this passage, by being
verbless and therefore echoing the quietude of this experience, celebrate
a stage of being which transcends language and even thought, suggesting
that Roig is here echoing the language of mysticism. A similar mystical
presence is expressed when Judith plays the piano and refers to her
intuition of a silent music: 'amb el silenci de la nit és quan sento la
música, com una música callada. (. . .) Una música silenciosa, que em
venia de dins i que en paraules no ho sabia interpretar' (p. 107), an
allusion to St John of the Cross's description of the mystical experience
as 'música callada'.

   L'hora violeta makes few allusions to other works of literature. We
find brief allusions to the poetry of St John of the Cross (as referred to

above), reference to Vicente Aleixandre's poetry (p. 33), Thomas Mann's *Death in Venice* (p. 33), Margall's poetry (p. 70), Louis Aragon's poetry (p. 90), a reference to Virginia Woolf's *The Waves* (p. 177), Françoise Sagan's *Bonjour, tristesse* (p. 172), Bécquer's 'la poesía escrita puede desaparecer, pero mientras un hombre y una mujer se amen siempre habrá poesía' (p. 194), allusions to Dante's vision of hell when referring to the Nazi concentration camps (p. 191), Shakespeare's view of love (p. 216), to give a few examples. In the main these references are sporadic rather than sustained.

There is one sustained web of intertextual reference in Roig's novel, however, and this concerns the allusions to the *Iliad*. Verses from Homer's epic poem are quoted in sections which appear towards the beginning and the end of the novel, and which are both entitled 'La Natàlia llegeix l'Odisea en una illa del mediterrani'. Quotations are from Carles Riba's translation of Homer's epic, which is universally regarded as the best translation from the Greek into any of the Romance languages.[34] Two lines are worth quoting since they epitomise the dilemma of the protagonists in Roig's novel: 's'hi ajuntà d'amor, una cosa que a totes les dones, / pobres!, els gira el cervell, per més honestes que siguin' (p. 27). All of the women described in *L'hora violeta* exemplify to the letter Homer's insight into the desperateness of female love. What is particularly intriguing is that only one particular line from Homer's *Iliad* is quoted twice (at p. 24, and p. 225), the verse being 'Sou implacables, déus, i més que altra cosa gelosos!'. The gods referred to in Homer's epic are not to be taken literally as participants in Roig's novel about a group of women living in Spain in the twentieth century. For the modern equivalent of the gods who are railed in Homer is the social system of patriarchy which bars women from enjoying pleasure and love. The fact that the sections appear at the beginning and end of the novel is no doubt to emphasise the vicious circle and inescapability characterising the female plight. Roig's feminizing reading of the *Iliad* centres not on Odysseus but on two female figures, Penelope and Circe. These two women, Penelope waiting at home for her husband to return, Circe attempting to persuade Odysseus's men to stay on the island of Circe, are equated with the competitive figures of the wife and the mistress. The protagonists of Roig's novel invariably fall into the role of mistress trying in vain to capture the husband. As Natàlia thinks to herself ruefully: 'Es clar, Ulises vol tornar a casa. A casa, Jordi (. . .) I a la fi va vèncer

---

[34] See E. Valentí i Fiol, 'Carles Riba i la seva traducció de l'*Odisea*', *ER*, IX (1961), 127–37; and Stephen M. Hart, *The Hispanic Connection: Spanish, Catalan and Spanish-American Poetry from "modernismo" to the Spanish Civil War*, p. 107.

Penèlope. I és que era una dona sàvia' (p. 24). Their situation thus
becomes similar to that of Circe; Natàlia, like Circe, lives on an island;
but, like Circe, she will lose in the end: 'Calipso i Circe, per bé que
immortals, sabien que, a la llarga, l'haurien de perdre' (p. 25). Homer's
words by the end of the novel are proved to have been uncannily
prophetic; Natàlia is reduced to the passive role of waiting: 'Ara hauria
d'esperar, i no sabia què. Esperar, destí passiu de les dones (no li servien
de res, hauria volgut dir a la Norma, tots el mítings i llibres sobre
feminisme. Ara l'única diferència és que ho sabia, que no li servien de
res)' (p. 225). Natàlia's life has come to echo that of Norma; in both
cases the liberationist rhetoric of feminism seems not to apply. Both
Natàlia and Norma are sexually liberated, and see liberation in terms of a
rejection of the passive stance of the previous generation.[35] This is most
clearly spelled out in the case of Natàlia: 'En Jordi i la porta del rebedor
es convertien en una sola cosa i ara recorda la violència que sentí a les
mans quan buscá el sexe d'en Jordi per a xuclar-lo fins a l'enteniment.
Volgué empassar-se el seu penis, succionar-lo fins a la darrera gota de
líquid, que no en quedés res, com si d'aquesta manera engolís per sempre
la imatge de la mare agenollada davant de la porta del rebedor' (p. 32).
Feminine sexuality, which is treated in Roig's work with a frankness
which distinguishes her from other writers of her generation as critics
have noted, becomes a means by which Natàlia seeks to erase the image
of her mother's subservience to patriarchy.[36] Norma's own liberated
sexual practices are cast in a similar vein, but are given a mythic flavour:
she becomes Circe who keeps her man in her bed:

> La Norma desitjava que en Ferran hi entrés del tot, com una criatura que
> volgués recuperar el ventre de la mare. I el forat esdevenia una cova
> humida, oberta per a arrecerar-lo, o bé un gorg que l'engoliria per a
> protegir-lo de totos el perills de fora. La Norma el colgava amb les cames,
> només n'emergia el cap. I hauria volgut estallar-se, desaparèixer, ser
> destruïda. Li venien tot de sensacions contràries, recomençar i morir.
> Ferir-se, esquinçar-se. Veia el ulls d'en Ferran, lluents pel desig, i ella
> n'estrenyia amb força el cap. Com Circe, l'hauria volgut encantar i
> emportar-se'l i emportar-se'l ben endins. (p. 208)

This passage fuses a Freudian desire for *regressus ad uterum* with
Homer's description of the melodic charms used by Circe to enchant and

---

[35] Biruté Ciplijauskaité suggests that the most significant theme of Roig's novel is that
of the liberated woman; *La novela femenina contemporánea*, p. 71.

[36] Catherine G. Bellver, 'Montserrat Roig: A Feminine Perspective and a Journalistic
Slant', in *Feminine Concerns in Contemporary Spanish Fiction by Women*, pp. 152–68
(p. 159).

entrap Ulysses' sailors. The point of connection between the two levels is the 'cova humida' which simultaneously refers to the cove on the coast line and the female sex. This passage, striking in its use of maritime imagery in the context of love-making, is redolent of a similar passage in *El mismo mar de todos los veranos* in which Tusquets describes a love scene based on the image of a sea grotto.[37]

L'hora violeta casts a harsh light on the sexual and political systems which disadvantage womankind in contemporary society. In love, as Roig's novel suggests, women are always the losers. The oppression of women is linked to the destruction of the Republicans during the Spanish Civil War and the death of millions of innocent people at the hands of the Nazis during World War II. Any hope for a brighter future (Kati, for example, believes that the Republicans will change the world for the better and particularly that they will improve the lot of women; p. 122) proves to be illusory. Roig's novel stands as a indictment of patriarchy but the narrative of the lives of its main characters tends to suggest that any attempt to change that system is likely to share the fate of the salmon whose bodies, during their journey upstream, are destroyed when they crash against the rocks.

Allende's *La casa de los espíritus*, Traba's *Conversación al sur* and Roig's *L'hora violeta*, as this chapter has shown, each reveal the manifold ways in which sex and politics are inextricably intermeshed. *La casa de los espíritus* tends to genderize the political struggle to such an extent that the power struggle becomes universalized and therefore effectively muted. There are elements of gender occlusion in *Conversación al sur* as well, but these are ultimately framed within the specifically feminine perspective of the novel which, subtly but convincingly, suggests that the most enduring protagonists of the political wars which raged in the Southern Cone in the 1970s were the women. *L'hora violeta*, like Traba's novel, presents political experience from a feminine view-point and seems ultimately to promote an 'anti-political' message: love is more important than Communism or feminism. Despite their very different ideological perspectives, all three novels have one common theme: that of viewing the gender war as the unspoken centre of the political war between Left and Right.

---

[37] See above Chapter III, p. 84. It is striking that the three writers most renowned for their frank treatment of sexuality (Tusquets, Roig and Carme Riera) are Catalan, and this despite the fact that, as Roig has argued elsewhere, Catalunya is a sexually inhibited country; see Geraldine C. Nichols, *Escribir, espacio propio: Laforet, Matute, Moix, Tusquets, Riera y Roig por sí mismas*, pp. 174–83. See selection in *On Our Own Behalf: Women's Tales from Catalonia*, edited by Kathleen McNerney.

V

GENDER TROUBLE

In her essay 'Gender Trouble', Judith Butler argues that various types of discourse, ranging from the feminist to the psychoanalytic, while ostensibly destabilizing the subject 'as object of coherence', nevertheless tend to 'institute gender coherence' by other means, and in particular through 'the stabilizing metanarrative of infantile development'.[1] As she goes on to argue, the construction of coherence in this way 'conceals the gender discontinuities than run rampant within heterosexual, bisexual, and gay and lesbian contexts in which gender does not necessarily follow from sex, and desire, or sexuality generally, does not seem to follow from gender' ('Gender Trouble', p. 336). Butler's reading of sex and gender as not co-terminous leads her to a radical conclusion: 'If the inner truth of gender is a fabrication and if a true gender is a fantasy instituted and inscribed on the surface of bodies, then it seems that genders can be neither true nor false but are only produced as the truth effects of a discourse of primary and stable identity' ('Gender Trouble', p. 337).

The three texts studied in this chapter, each in their individual way, address the issues raised by Butler's notion of 'gender trouble'. Luisa Valenzuela's *El gato eficaz* reveals sexual gender to be a fluid, even ungraspable, reality by deconstructing binary pairs such as male/ female, white/black, and dog/cat. Cristina Peri Rossi's *La nave de los locos* likewise deconstructs the notion of a fixed sexual identity, in particular in the scenes in the novel which highlight how cross-dressing tends to dissolve the barriers between male and female. Rosa Montero's *Temblor* reverses the laws of the patriarchal world and creates a universe in which women hold the strings of power.

---

[1] 'Gender Trouble', *Feminism/Postmodernism*, edited and with an introduction by Linda J. Nicholson (New York and London: Routledge, 1990), pp. 324–40 (pp. 328–29).

LUISA VALENZUELA: *EL GATO EFICAZ*

In an instructive essay, 'Mis brujas favoritas', Luisa Valenzuela (1938: Argentina) begins by positing the possible existence of 'un lenguaje femenino en absoluto emparentado con aquellas azucaradas palabras con las que hemos sido recubiertas a lo largo de siglos' (p. 88).[2] Instead she proposes the notion, one familiar from Cixous's work, of an intrinsically feminine discourse. Lacan's notion of a 'gliding signifier', rather paradoxically, is used by Valenzuela as further ammunition for her theory: 'El célebre deslizamiento del significado por debajo del significante – hoy tan vital como lo fue en su momento el encuentro fortuito del paraguas con la máquina de coser – no es necesariamente el mismo para cada individuo, y con mayor razón para individuos de distinto sexo' (p. 89). Even Lacanian knowledge, it would seem, is not exempt from gender specificness.[3] Valenzuela then cites Lacan's perception of the phallus as the site of Lack (an idea that will recur in her novels), and argues that it is as a result of this Lack that 'la humanidad en pleno gira en torno a una carencia, con cada sexo instalado en ubicación opuesta en lo que al falo como hito se refiere. Razón por la cual se impone que la mujer refuerce su posición y recree su discurso. Para reorganizar su territorio' (p. 90).[4] Her novelistic activity will therefore be seen in terms of a reappropriation of the linguistic territory which for so many years has been the sole prerogative of men. The aim of her novels is to right the wrong association made by men between women, witches and hysteria: 'Brujas primero, histéricas más tarde: las que por sus bocas descargan todas las frustraciones impuestas a su sexo que es también su lenguaje' (pp. 90–91). By identifying with the witches of the past who have suffered under the dictatorship of men, Valenzuela aims to

---

[2] 'Mis brujas favoritas', in *Theory and Practice of Feminist Literary Criticism*, edited by Gabriela Mora and Karten S. Van Hooft, pp. 88–95.

[3] It is doubtful, however, that Lacan would have condoned this distinction since, for the French psychoanalyst, the 'question of phallocentrism is inseparable from the structure of the sign'; see Raman Selden, *A Reader's Guide to Contemporary Literary Theory* (Lexington: University of Kentucky, 1985), p. 14. Valenzuela's reference to the 'fortuitous encounter of the umbrella with the sewing-machine' is, of course, to Lautréamont's proclamation of creative artistic absurdity, a metaphor which was later adopted by the Surrealists.

[4] In a 1985 interview, Valenzuela links the Lacanian notion of the phallus to Lack and to the search: 'lo que siempre se busca es el falo. La búsqueda es la búsqueda de esa cosa mítica. Pero no es el falo como el órgano sexual masculino, es el falo como lo que no existe, el falo lacaniano. Lo que nadie tiene, la carencia absoluta. Es la búsqueda de una carencia'; 'Más caras de espejos, un juego especular. Entrevista-asociaciones con la escritora argentina Luisa Valenzuela', *RI*, 132–33 (1985), 511–19 (p. 516).

create what she calls a 'lenguaje hémbrico' (p. 91), a specifically feminine language. Many of these concerns are visible in her novel, *El gato eficaz* (1972). There are incidental coincidences with the theory and the metaphors of Lacanian and neo-Lacanian knowledge (especially in the almost obsessive preoccupation with libido, Lack and fluidity), but, most importantly, Valenzuela's text strives to create a new language which is anti-masculinist and embodies 'lenguaje hémbrico' in strategical and thematic terms, as we shall see.

El gato eficaz is set in a bleak New York urban landscape and describes the (paranoiac) thoughts which pass through the mind of an initially female narrator. As soon becomes evident, Valenzuela's novel is a postmodern text which eschews a narrative proper; scenes are presented obliquely and the protagonists of the episodes remain unspecified; and, to cap it all, the narrator is not fixed either by time, place or even gender.[5] *El gato eficaz* in effect uses a stream-of-consciousness perspective in order to build episodes around various universalist oppositions (light/dark, cat/dog, consciousness/unconsciousness, death/life, sex/death) which the narrative consciousness embellishes, and then deconstructs. *El gato eficaz* is, thus, as much a book about binary oppositions in language as anything else.[6] Its pursual of a poetics of discontinuity is deliberate since, as Valenzuela has pointed out in an interview: 'We are fragmented; nothing is univocal; there is no unity'.[7] This idea certainly applies to *El gato eficaz* in which cultural/linguistic polarisms such as male/female, light/dark, dog/cat, for example, fall to pieces before our eyes.

In the opening pages of *El gato eficaz* we find a narrator, who seems disembodied, observing the antics of the 'cats of death': 'Cómo me gusta vagar de madrugada por el Village y espiar a los gatosbasureros de la

[5] Linda Craig notes that *El gato eficaz* 'defies any attempt at synopsis' since it has 'virtually no plot and few, if any, stabilising elements'; see her 'Women and Language: Luisa Valenzuela's *El gato eficaz*', in *Feminist Readings on Spanish and Latin-American Literature*, eds. L. P. Condé & S. M. Hart, pp. 151–60 (p. 151).

[6] As Sharon Magnarelli argues, one of the principal structuring devices in Valenzuela's novel is the link between women, cats and discourse; *Reflections/Refractions: Reading Luisa Valenzuela* (New York: Peter Lang, 1988), p. 67. Apart from their archetypal connotations, it is only fair to clarify that cats also have a personal resonance for Valenzuela; she does impressions of cats, she has cats as pets, and her mother had more than twenty of them (!); Montserrat Ordóñez, 'Más caras de espejos, un juego especular. Entrevista - asociaciones con la escritora argentina Luisa Valenzuela', *RI*, 132–33 (1985), 511–19 (p. 515). In another interview Valenzuela suggests that cats represent 'una cara más bien positiva del mal, son el demonio casero, familiar, encantador'; Magdalena García Pinto, *Historias íntimas: conversaciones con diez escritoras latinoamericanas*, p. 225.

[7] Evelyn Picon Garfield, *Women's Voices from Latin America*, p. 153.

muerte: escarban loquihambrientos en los tachos hasta dar con la basura que bajo sus uñas pueda matar de un rasguño' (p. 7).[8] As we can see, a distinction is drawn between cats (associated with the night and death) and dogs (associated with the day and life). In the neologism 'loquihambrientos' we have a first glimpse of what will be a consistent trait of Valenzuela's discourse. Echoing Joycean word-play, Valenzuela fuses two words, 'loco' and 'hambrientos', in order to generate a new lexical item.[9] As Valenzuela explained in an interview, 'I begin a sentence with a word meaning one thing, then all at once, in the middle of the sentence, the word begins to signify something else'.[10] By breaking down the dualism of man-made language, Valenzuela is in effect striving to embody her notion of a new 'lenguaje hémbrico'. Indeed, the same type of deconstruction of difference is soon applied to the cat/dog opposition. The cats are subsequently associated with liquid waste and death:

> Como ya se ha dicho, los gatos de la muerte insertan bajo sus uñas cierta basura secreta para dar el zarpazo final. Algunas amas de casa avisadas se cuidan muy bien de tirar sus fetos al tacho o de sacarlos a la calle. En general los desintegran con el triturador de la pileta de la cocina y dejan a las cloacas hacer el resto. Se explica así lo que muchos creyeron ser el suicidio colectivo de los gatos de la muerte, en realidad un intento desesperado por nadar río abajo en procura de alguno de esos restos, vitales para el cumplimiento de su letal deber. (p. 12)

Only a few pages later in the novel the association is extended to include sexual desire:

> Mujeres al fin, ellas sufren los vejámenes y se quedan adheridas, también sangrantes ahora, también en carne viva hasta que los negros fornidos caen exsangües y es entonces cuando empieza el acto de amor. Una penetración total, un contacto perfecto vena a vena, la absoluta entrega y el jadeo continuo: masa sangrante y suspirante que una vez fueron dos – o tal vez más de dos porque cada persona es ella y sus desdoblamientos – y ahora es sólo una masa sangrante y suspirante, con ricos borbotones, al fin recompuesta en identidad única, entregada al amor que es el exterminio. Bien puedo acariciarlos sin que ellos lo noten y contribuir con mis lágrimas a la licuefacción final cuando los veo dichosos desaparecer por alguna alcantarilla. (p. 16)

[8] All references are to *El gato eficaz* (México: Joaquín Mortiz, 1972).

[9] For a good discussion of Joyce's word-play, see Hugh Kenner, *Joyce's Voices* (London: Faber and Faber, 1978).

[10] Evelyn Picon Garfield, *Women's Voices from Latin America: Interviews with Six Contemporary Authors*, p. 150.

A set of associations gradually emerges linking women to cats, to death, to sexual desire, and finally to liquid ('licuefacción', for example, combines the image of destruction with that of liquidity). Though Valenzuela's text had, thus, been concerned to establish the difference between the male and the female, through the images of dog and cat, now it seeks to dissolve that difference to produce 'una masa sangrante y suspirante' which has been 'recompuesta en identidad única'. Sexual difference has been elided to produce a liquid reality which in turns becomes purely waste matter ('los veo dichosos desaparecer por alguna alcantarilla').

The association Valenzuela establishes between desire and waste is reminiscent of Lacan's theory of the 'objet-petit-a'.[11] To describe the birth of desire in the human species, Lacan used the porte-manteau word 'Hommelette' which simultaneously puns on the French for 'man' and 'omelette'. One of Lacan's most imaginative commentators, Cathérine Clément, has described the Hommelette as a 'thin wafer, as flat and slippery as a crêpe but as lively as an amoeba' which is 'destined to coat the body of the newborn'. As she goes on, it is 'immortal – a product of separation but itself resistant to further division'.[12] Libido begins to grow within the Hommelette and seeks out objects of its own desire. The 'objet-petit-a', like a machine which unleashes desire, is also associated with waste for, as Clément suggests, 'the tiny object is also a fallen object. Something that has dropped out of the body along with the infant and the afterbirth: we thus come back to our Hommelette, which symbolizes the object of desire'. As she also observes, 'desire feeds on waste'.[13] The 'gatos de la muerte' fulfil a very similar function in Valenzuela's text to the 'objet-petit-a' in Lacan's text; while at once the object of desire, the cats of death are also emblematic of waste. A further parallel between Valenzuela's text and Lacanian knowledge suggests itself. For Lacan regarded the book as itself associated with waste, referring to publication in an untranslatable pun as 'poubellication', punning on 'poubelle' (rubbish).[14] A similar link is explored in *El gato eficaz*. As Sharon Magnarelli points out, the distinction made between cats and dogs throughout the narrative is also related to the physical aspects of writing: 'The white dogs evoke the blank, white page, the

[11] In her discussion of *El gato eficaz* with Evelyn Picon Garfield, Valenzuela specifically alludes to Lacan's notion of the 'dismembered body', but says that she wrote *El gato eficaz* before coming across this Lacanian idea which, we are therefore to presume, she reached independently; see *Women's Voices from Latin America*, p. 116.

[12] *The Lives and Legends of Jacques Lacan*, translated by Arthur Goldhammer (New York: Columbia University Press, 1983), pp. 96–97.

[13] Clément, *The Lives and Legends of Jacques Lacan*, p. 99.

[14] Clément, *The Lives and Legends of Jacques Lacan*, p. 100.

tabula rasa, pure and virginal, which promises potentially infinite and perfect worlds. But, the black cats, apparently necessary to the production of these worlds, in the form of writing, as black lettering, soon enter and besmirch and pervert the pure white page'.[15]

But what is perhaps most striking about *El gato eficaz* is how it focusses on trans-sexuality, a notion which Valenzuela has confessed to finding personally fascinating.[16] The clearest indication of this is, of course, the elusive gender of the narrator of *El gato eficaz*. When the novel opens, we are led to believe that the narrator is female. Eighteen pages later, however, the narrator decides to change sex. Page 18 ends as follows: 'Poco he de saber, no estoy contenta, no quiero ser araña, me voy a cambiar de sexo'. By page 19 this transformation has already taken place: 'Soy un joven atleta y apolíneo, bastante pornográfico. Perdí mi don de gatos y de gente, me tiro a la piscina desde el trampolín más alto, las niñas me contemplan, en el aire yo cambio de posturas, luzco un torso brillante, unos músculos tensos' (p. 19). More than a particular sex, the narrator seems to embody a genderless libido, his/her gender being no more, or less, than what Judith Butler calls a 'fantasy instituted and inscribed on the truth of bodies' (see above).

Often the narrator actively creates gender trouble, which leads on a primary level to a sense of the uncanny in Valenzuela's work, as critics have suggested.[17] Chapter 12, for example, begins with the statement: 'Hoy me quiero erigir en defensora de pobres y de ausentes' (p. 84). A group epitomizing absence, as the text goes on to point out, are men: 'Pero cuando logro olvidarme de mí misma las cosas van poniéndose mejores y pienso en los ausentes. Un gran ausente único que los resume a todos: el hombre, el principio viril, el macho de los machos' (p. 84). Here Valenzuela is clearly echoing Lacan's view of the male, or the phallus on his behalf, as an embodiment of Lack.[18] As Valenzuela suggests in a foot-note: 'Están los que se van, los que regresan, los que nunca estuvieron y sin embargo exigen su cuenta en esta vida' (p. 84). It is not in spite of but precisely because of absence that the male sex wields

---

[15] *Reflections/Refractions: Reading Luisa Valenzuela*, p. 71.

[16] See Dorothy S. Mull and Elsa B. de Angulo, 'An Afternoon with Luisa Valenzuela', *Hispania*, 69:2 (1986), 350–52 (p. 351).

[17] Gerald Martin, *Journeys Through the Labyrinth: Latin American Fiction in the Twentieth Century*, p. 355.

[18] As Lacan argues, 'it was the appeal of the void, in the ambiguous béance of an attempted seduction of the other by the means on which subject has come compliantly to rely and to which he is going to commit the monumental construct of his narcissism'; *The Language of the Self: The Function of Language in Psychoanalysis*, translated with notes and commentary by Anthony Wilden (New York: Delta, 1975), p. 9.

power in this life.[19] The interplay between Valenzuela's text and Lacanian knowledge is playful and sustained.

The narrator not only escapes traditional notions of gender, but also traditional notions of space. At one point in the narrative, for example, the narrator simply leaves his/her narratees and moves into a different time-space continuum. On page 72, the narrator says: 'Ahora los dejo que juegen solos como buenos muchachos, yo me busco otro juego. . .' and a few pages later speaks of its journey inwards: 'Me gusta la lectura para adentro, con peso en cada coma, una frase nueva en cada frase y un nuevo paso donde no cuente el tiempo. Voy para atrás, para adelante, huyo siempre de él ¿por qué me mira?' (p. 77). Replicating Freudian knowledge, *El gato eficaz* focusses on the interplay of *eros* and *thanatos*, a constant theme of her work, as Evelyn Picon Garfield points out.[20] Chapters 1–2, for example, conflate these two libidinal drives. Chapters 3–5 focus on the death drive, ranging from the death of an individual (Herbie Mann in Chapter 3) to the theme of infelicitous death ('Morir infelizmente', pp. 32–35). Chapters 6–10, for their part, concentrate on the sexual motif, covering themes such as Peeping Toms (pp. 46–48) and fornication games ('Juguemos al fornicón'; pp. 67–73). But these two narrative blocks are not mutually exclusive; in a parody of Freudian knowledge, sex turns into death, and vice-versa. As Z. Nelly Martínez puts it, 'la sexualidad y el instinto destructor recuperan su vigencia y organizan, desorganizando, un discurso que, significativamente, se despliega como espacio de ruptura constante y constante recomposición'.[21] The section 'Mascarable', for example, in which an unnamed man answers a request in a local newspaper for a man to make a threesome in bed ('Pareja joven y agradable busca muchacho de buena presencia p/ formar terceto') concludes with a scene in which the man murders the couple after sex (pp. 64–66).

The final section of the book (chapters 11–18) continues to explore the interconnections between sex and death, and begins gradually to introduce the motif of the self-witnessing mind. By a now unavoidable rhetorical chain, writing becomes itself associated with death, for the narrator is gradually transformed into a vampire whom the reader is exhorted, echoing the plot of a Gothic novel, to stab through the heart:

---

[19] As Lacan suggests: 'It is in the name of the father that we must recognise the support of the Symbolic function which, from the dawn of history, has identified his person with the figure of the law'; *The Language of the Self: The Function of Language in Psychoanalysis*, p. 41.

[20] *Women's Voices from Latin America*, p. 144.

[21] '*El gato eficaz* de Luisa Valenzuela: la productividad del texto', *RCEH*, 4 (1979), 73–80 (p. 75).

Yo no estoy escribiendo una novela, sino simplemente anotando con el poco de vida que me queda esta prosa mayor que es mi testamento. Buenas señoras, por lo tanto, que habéis tenido la paciencia de seguir hasta aquí mis magras líneas, o que habéis por azar abierto el libro en esta precisa página, cumplid fielmente con las disposiciones y venid en hilera a orar ante mi tumba.

Y clavadme la estaca que lleváis en el pelo en el lugar exacto donde mi corazón se encuentra. (p. 88).

The narrator's request is not merely facetious. It relates back to the notion of the need for the narrator to be destroyed in order for the text to be born. As Lacan suggests, 'the symbol manifests itself first of all as the murder of the thing, and this dream constitutes in the subject, the eternalization of his desire'.[22] By killing the narrator, changing thing into symbol, the reader's desire will be eternalized. A similar insight underlies the reference at the end of the same section: 'Este es mi testamento y leeremos como leen los abogados, dando a cada vocablo justo peso, sin invertir el orden de las cláusulas, equivocándonos. Por suerte alguien sabrá que el significado es otro y me leerá tan sólo en los reflejos. Será justicia' (p. 90). Valenzuela's text should be read not with the eyes of a lawyer, who looks for the literal sense, but with the eyes of a reader who will kill the text, thereby turning its words into symbol. It is only by misreading the text, by listening to its echoes and reflections rather than its literalness, than the meaning of the work can be born.

A similar idea re-emerges at the conclusion of the novel. Once more the narrator speaks of her testament: 'Esta es mi confesión y también mi legado: generaciones futuras sabrán hasta qué punto me he acercado a él para destruirlo, cómo maquiné en ascensores para llevarme su alma y estampar mi sello en el fondo de su carne para poder retirarme dignamente y dejar que el fuego lo consuma' (p. 117). The 'él' with which the narrator is obsessed at the conclusion of the novel (pp. 113–19), also doubles as the potential future reader who will murder the narrator and resurrect her:

Fatuo todo aquel que pretende retenernos y nos detiene un tiempo. Lo que no cambia es fatuo con pretensión de eterno y no yo ya que no soy yo misma me transformo en colores dentro de mi retina, gasifico mis formas y me sigo nombrando yo, mí, me, no por vieja costumbre que no tengo sino a falta de algo mejor y a la espera de un nuevo solidario como vos que descubra las claves de este juego y alínee las piezas – blancas perrovidas, negras gatomuertes – y retome los ciclos. Jaque mate otra vez, que me

---

[22] *The Language of the Self: The Function of Language in Psychoanalysis*, p. 84.

> mate de lejos. Me mate, memite, me imite: sólo en un renacimiento reside
> mi esperanza. (p. 119)

The narrator vaporizes, turning into light ('colores dentro de mi retina')
and into language ('yo me sigo nombrando yo, mí, me'). Now it is the
'vos', the addressee of the narrator, who will take the place of the 'él'
and the 'vosotros' referred to in the previous pages. The reader will enter
into the verbal play with the narrator, playing chess with her. Significant
too in this passage is the shifting nature of the primal image used
throughout the novel (white dog/black cat), which is now projected onto
the squares of the chess board. The reader will check-mate the narrator,
namely, stop her game and close her text. This check-mate is also the
point at which the narrator is murdered: 'que me mate de lejos'. This act
of murder (turning thing into symbol) is also an act of imitation ('Me
mate, memite, me imite'). Given the playful nature of the text at this
point, it is not surprising that (at least) two potential interpretations
suggest themselves. The narrator may on the one hand be projecting a
utopian (and violent) fusion of (her) self and (her male) reader, or she
may alternatively be adopting the role of the Sphinx who answers
Oedipus's question with a riddle whose import he does not fully
comprehend until too late.[23] The narrator seems to have left the reader
with no more than a mask of her being. As Valenzuela was fond of
saying, in a typically postmodernist gesture, drawing attention to the
quoted nature of all knowledge: 'Como decía Oscar Wilde, "Dadme una
máscara y os diré mi verdad" '.[24] Whatever our reading of the final scene
of the novel, it will ultimately be mediated by death: like a phoenix the
dead narrator will rise from the flames of her reader's passion.

CRISTINA PERI ROSSI: *LA NAVE DE LOS LOCOS*

La nave de los locos (1984) by Cristina Peri Rossi (1941: Uruguay) is a
playful, postmodern text which describes the (mis)adventures of a
character whose name is simply a letter of the alphabet, Equis, in a
variety of urban settings; the novel includes episodes describing sordid
sexual encounters, far-fetched dream-sequences, and Equis's philoso-
phizing about life and the universe with his companions, Vercingetorix

---

[23] Sharon Magnarelli, *The Lost Rib: Female Characters in the Spanish-American
Novel* (London and Toronto: Associated University Presses, 1985), p. 172.
[24] Dorothy S. Mull and Elsa B. de Angulo, 'An Afternoon with Luisa Valenzuela',
Hispania, 69:2 (1986), 350–52.

and Graciela. The novel has little narrative structure and is furthermore
punctuated by a backdrop-discourse which describes in meticulous, and
indeed factual, detail the celebrated, eleventh-century tapestry depicting
the creation of the world which is held in Gerona Cathedral, Spain.

The above brief description of *La nave de los locos*, in its emphasis
upon playfulness and the rejection of plot strategies, tends to confirm its
identity as a postmodern text. But there are other ways in which Peri
Rossi's novel is postmodern. In the epilogue to *The Name of the Rose*,
Umberto Eco underlines that the postmodern stance 'consists in
recognizing that the past, since it cannot really be destroyed, because its
destruction leads to silence, must be revisited: but with irony, not
innocently'.[25] Thus, the 'already said', following the postmodern move,
will be acknowledged, albeit playfully, ironically or parodically. Indeed,
the consciousness of being 'somehow or other belated, *nachträglich,
après coup*', a central motif of the postmodern text, is at the core of Peri
Rossi's *La nave de los locos*, which situates itself in an epigonic
relationship to a variety of other texts such as Sebastian Brant's
Narrenschiff (1494), Pío Baroja's *La nave de los locos* (1925), and
Katherine Anne Porter's *Ship of Fools* (1959).[26] All of these works
ultimately derive inspiration from the historical practice common in
Europe, and especially Germany, in the first half of the fifteenth century,
when ships were loaded with mad people and sent downstream in order to
unload their human cargo at another unsuspecting town; though rooted in
a particular historical event, the *Navis stultiferum* soon became a literary
topos emblematizing the uncertainties of man's life.[27] Some of the
intertextual relationships between Peri Rossi's novel and the texts
mentioned above are no doubt tenuous; with Porter's novel of the same
name, Peri Rossi's novel shares no more than the idea that this world 'on
its voyage to eternity' is a ship of fools, on which, as the North American
novelist suggests, 'I am a passenger'.[28] Some intertextual relationships,
however, go beyond simple allusion. With Brant's *Narrenschiff*, for

[25] Quoted by Matei Calinescu, *Five Faces of Modernity* (Durham: Duke University
Press, 1987), p. 277.
[26] This definition of a fundamental trait of the postmodern text is by A. J. McKenna,
'Postmodernism: It's Future Perfect', in *Postmodernism and Continental Philosophy*,
edited by Hugh J. Silverman and Donn Welton (Albany, N.Y.: State University of New
York Press, 1988), pp. 228–42 (p. 229).
[27] Michel Foucault, *Folie et Déraison: histoire de la folie à l'âge classique* (Paris:
Plon, 1961), pp. 10–16.
[28] *Ship of Fools* (Boston: Little, Brown and Company, 1962), 2nd printing, p. vii. The
connection between the two novels is suggested by Gerald Martin, *Journeys Through the
Labyrinth: Latin American Fiction in the Twentieth Century*, p. 355.

example, Peri Rossi's novel shares the theme of exemplifying the follies of mankind using visual as well as verbal metaphors. Brant's work, for example, is illustrated with woodcuts which accompany the moral lesson of each of the 111 chapters. Peri Rossi imitates this technique, but she does not do so innocently, since the central visual metaphor of her novel is the eleventh-century *Tapestry of the Creation* which hangs in Gerona Cathedral. Peri Rossi's allusion to Brant's self-professed aim of debunking the 'folly, blindness, error and stupidity of all stations and kinds of men', is thus refocussed feminocentrically since her novel strives to deconstruct the patriarchal notion of Godhead, which itself is the 'madness' of the world, as we shall see.[29]

The allusions to Baroja's novel of the same name are, likewise, complex. They involve the sense, common to Baroja's as well as Peri Rossi's text, that life is an unmapped, hazardous journey. The Ship of Fools, as the first chapter of Baroja's novel reminds us, is 'el barco de la Humanidad, que marcha por el mar proceloso de la vida, y en el cual se albergan los mayores disparates'.[30] Equally significant is the fact that Peri Rossi's novel contains its own metanarrative focussing on the creative process via the Creation tapestry, just like Baroja's novel which has a 'Prólogo casi doctrinal sobre la novela'. There is also a hint of gender trouble in Baroja's novel which gives a foretaste of its later exploitation in Peri Rossi's novel; *Chipiteguy*'s niece is looking for her uncle during the Carlist Wars, and she does so dressed as a boy.[31] For a variety of reasons, as we can see, Peri Rossi's *La nave de los locos* is a postmodern, pastiche novel since it involves, in Fredric Jameson's words, a 'restructuration of a certain number of elements already given'.[32]

Though constituting a departure in terms of its postmodern structure, *La nave de los locos*, however, does reflect some of the themes and techniques common in Peri Rossi's early work. As Gustavo San Román has pointed out with respect to her early work: 'Among her preoccupations are dreams, childhood and (often alternative) sexuality, among

---

[29] Sebastian Brant, *The Ship of Fools*, translated into rhyming couplets with introduction and commentary by Edwin H. Zeydel (New York: Columbia University Press, 1944).

[30] *La nave de los locos* (Madrid: Cátedra, 1987), pp. 99–100. Baroja's novel refers explicitly to Brant's woodcuts in the introductory chapter, pp. 99–101. There are, of course, differences between Baroja's realist and Peri Rossi's postmodern novel, the most salient being that while Baroja uses the life-as-a-madhouse theme to suggest that madness is female ('la Dama Locura andaba suelta por el mundo', p. 101), Peri Rossi uses the same *topos* to undermine the phallocentric myth of Creation.

[31] Baroja, *La nave de los locos*, p. 162.

[32] Quoted by Julian Pefanis, *Heterology and the Postmodern: Bataille, Baudrillard, and Lyotard* (Durham: Duke University Press, 1991), p. 6.

her strategies, a predilection for allegory and fantasy'.[33] But *La nave de los locos* is also typical of the European phase of Peri Rossi's work (beginning with her residence in Barcelona as from 1971), in which political themes are less apparent than in her earlier work. It is a defiantly postmodern, self-reflexive novel which consistently stands back from the main action of the novel in order to introduce a metafictional viewpoint, itself related to the subversion of the laws of gender, as we shall see.

In the split it institutes between the action proper and the metatext which accompanies it, Peri Rossi's novel bears a striking resemblance to the work of the Argentine novelist, Julio Cortázar.[34] In Cortázar's *Los premios* (1960) and *Rayuela* (1968), for example, there are two distinctive voices, one which treats and describes everyday reality – the adventures of Oliveira and La Maga in *Rayuela* and the lives of the travellers on the cruise-boat – and the metatext which comments like a subconscious chorus on the main action. In *Los premios*, for example, the description of everyday life on the cruise is punctuated at regular intervals by the lyrical voice of a cruise passenger, Persio, which is associated with the waves and which alludes obsessively to the discontinuous aesthetics of modern art.[35] A similar aesthetic method is adopted in *La nave de los locos*. The vicissitudes of the life of the protagonist, Equis, and his friends, Vercingetorix and Graciela, are interspersed with poetic sections which describe in great detail the Gerona Cathedral *Tapestry of the Creation*, which Equis is said to have seen once and greatly admired (p. 13).[36] The first of these begin with the centre of the tapestry where the Creator of the Universe is depicted (p. 68), and then goes on to describe the inner and outer circles surrounding the Creator (pp. 72–73), the angel on the right of God (p. 84), and then onwards passages which depict the gradual creation of the heavens and the earth (p. 96, pp. 112–14, p. 132, p. 150, p. 162,

---

[33] 'Fantastic Political Allegory in the Early Work of Cristina Peri Rossi', *BHS*, 67 (1990), 151–64. See also essay by same author, 'Satire with Children in Cristina Peri Rossi', *SpSt*, 11 (1990–91), 1–10.

[34] In recent interviews Peri Rossi has tended to play down Cortázar's influence on her work. They were good friends but as she suggests: 'Creo que realmente se ha exagerado la influencia de Cortázar'; S. Camps, 'Peri Rossi', *Quimera*, 81 (1988), 40–49. The friendship and mutual respect between the two writers was evident to the present author at a reading of their works held in Paris in May 1983. An objective appraisal of Peri Rossi's work would tend to suggest that there are artistic similarities as well.

[35] See Steven Boldy, *The Novels of Julio Cortázar* (Cambridge: C.U.P., 1980), pp. 12–13.

[36] References are to *La nave de los locos* (Barcelona: Seix Barral, 1989). There is an excellent translation by Psiche Hughes, *The Ship of Fools* (London: Allison & Busby, 1989).

p. 198). A further similarity with Cortázar's novel is that the metatextual interludes are printed in italic script. A structural similarity is that Equis in *La nave de los locos* and the characters in *Los premios* are involved in a voyage which, at one stage in *La nave de los locos* is a sea-voyage as well, making the parallel very marked (see the 'Diario de a bordo', p. 19). The last similarity is thematic, and this involves a similarity in the metaphysical portent or revelational properties of Peri Rossi's novel and the typical Cortazean text.[37]

In many ways, thus, *La nave de los locos* has some striking similarites with the postmodern Cortazean literary text. In *La nave de los locos*, however, there is perhaps a clearer sense of irony than in the Cortazean text. Great play is made, for example, of the gaping difference between the grand syntax of the Gerona Creation Tapestry and the sordid lives of the protagonists. As Lucía Guerra-Cunningham has pointed out, for example, the protagonist of the novel and the setting of the novel are decidedly bathetic: Equis is an 'héroe anti-épico que significativamente carece de un nombre', while the modern metropolis is presented as 'la antítesis y el contra-espacio de "El tapiz de la creación" '.[38] Just as significant is the fact that Peri Rossi's work also embodies a desire to trespass onto forbidden (male) territory. As she pointed out in a feminist conference held in Barcelona in June 1990, she began to write 'para romper una ley que querían imponerme de pequeña. Las mujeres tenemos demasiados derechos prohibidos. Y yo quería subirme a los árboles, usar pantalones, fumar, e imaginar historias'.[39] In the spirit of this quotation, Peri Rossi's work embodies a transgression of patriarchal law. This is particularly evident in the section in *La nave de los locos* entitled 'Eva', in which Peri Rossi introduces a feminist dimension into the standard postmodern text. Her specific target here is the Genesis myth which, as Christine Froula has shown, 'exiles women from symbolic activity', thus turning the woman writer into 'not civilization's legitimate inheritor but its outsider'.[40] Until that part of the novel, the various descriptions of the Gerona tapestry of the Creation have tended to centre on male figures in the Genesis story (which is itself a phallocentric

---

[37] In an interview Peri Rossi has suggested that her own work is more symbolic than Cortázar's: 'yo me siento mucho más simbólica que Cortázar'; S. Camps, 'Peri Rossi', *Quimera*, 81 (1988), 40–49 (p. 48).

[38] Lucía Guerra Cunningham, 'La referencialidad como negación del paraíso: exilio y excentrismo en *La nave de los locos* de Cristina Peri Rossi', *REH*, 13:2 (1989), 63–74 (p. 67).

[39] Rosa María Piñol, 'Nueve autoras de distintas culturas coinciden en asociar escritura y libertad', *La Vanguardia* (23 June 1990).

[40] 'Rewriting Genesis: Gender and Culture in Twentieth-Century Texts', *TSWL*, 7:2 (1988), 197–220 (pp. 197–98).

narrative), and had been recounted in an objective, third-person narrative. The opening section of 'Eva' is entitled 'Fragmento de *Eva, sus confesiones*', and switches to a first-person narrative:

> Inscrita desde que nací, en los conjuros tribunales de la segunda naturaleza, igual que los iniciados, experimento la imposibilidad de escapar a las ceremonias trasmitidas por los brujos a través de los años, de palabras y de imágenes; luego de someterme a los ritos y a las convenciones, a los juegos, a las danzas y a los sacrificios, no puedo retroceder. El castigo, para la iniciada que huye, es el desprecio, la soledad, la locura o la muerte. (p. 153)

Eve expresses a consciousness which is trapped within the myths and rituals of patriarchy. To escape from that system is to risk ostracism, 'madness or death'. The discourse of the first woman is characterised, above all, by self-censorship. Any conflict with patriarchy must be avoided. It is significant, likewise, that Eve's memoirs are referred to as unpublished, which confirms the novel's sense of the exclusion of women from power and voice. Eve's exile is thus a multivalent metaphor of the exile of womanhood within patriarchal society, the exile underwriting life in the modern, industrial world, and the exile experienced by writers (including Peri Rossi) who have fled totalitarian regimes.[41] Though distinct in political terms, each of these different types of exile is characterised by the unpower of silence.

Eve's voicelessness reappears in the excerpts from the illiterate versions of Adam and Eve written by a group of school children between the ages of seven and twelve. All confirm Eve's sin and exonerate Adam. The first example culled by Graciela is indicative of the rest: 'Adán vivía muy felis entre los arboles y las plantas asta que llegó la Eva y le hiso comer la manzana porque quería matarlo y reinar ella sola' (*sic*, p. 157). Most of the excerpts express misogyny: 'El estava solo y no la pasava muy bien porque no tenía con quien havlar pero cuando nació ella fue mucho peor' (*sic*, p. 157). A similar misogyny emerges when Graciela

---

[41] As Peri Rossi pointed out in an interview, *La nave de los locos* 'pretendía ser una novela sobre el exilio como metáfora o alegoría, como condición del hombre'; S. Camps, 'Peri Rossi', *Quimera*, 81 (1988), 40–49 (p. 40). Women writers in particular embody the allegory of exile, since their work is characterised by what Peri Rossi in the same interview calls 'exilio interno' (p. 44). All is not gloom and doom, however; Peri Rossi draws attention to the humour involved in her treatment of exile in the novel (p. 43), while one critic has referred to how Equis represents 'la modalidad *liberadora* del exilio' (my emphasis); see Lucía Guerra-Cunningham's important article, 'La referencialidad como negación del paraíso: exilio y excentrismo en *La nave de los locos* de Cristina Peri Rossi', *REH*, 13:2 (1989), 63–74 (p. 67).

asks her pupils to imagine Adam's daily life. As one schoolchild in
Graciela's class suggests: 'Adan trabajaba duro para mantener el hogar
plantaba patatas lechugas tomates arroz y de vez en cuando traía un
ciervo o un león para comer mientras esa vaga de Eva no hacia nada
porque ni iba al supermercado y además no tenía hijos que cuidar' (*sic*, p.
160). The first task set by Graciela on the virtues and foibles of Adam
and Eve predictably shows Adam as brave, honest, hardworking,
intelligent, responsible and obedient, while Eve is excessively curious,
prone to gossip, bad-tempered, lazy and frivolous (pp. 160–61).

The following section evokes a riddle of the fairy-tale structure,
according to which the suitor has to solve a riddle or successfully execute
a task, in order to deserve the hand of the king's daughter. The grand
riddle – the Oedipal complex – is mentioned in section XIX:

> En el sueño, había una pregunta que flotaba como un enigma, como
> aquellos acertijos que los reyes, enamorados de su hijas, proponían a los
> pretendientes.
> Príncipes, caballeros degollados en el insensato afán de resolver la oscura
> adivinanza que conservaba a las hijas para los padres. En el sueño, Equis
> escuchaba la pregunta: *¿Cuál es el mayor tributo, el homenaje que un
> hombre puede ofrecer a la mujer que ama?* (p. 163)

One is tempted to read fairy tales of this kind on a Freudian level, and see
the outcome of death for the suitor as an image of the castration which is
visited on the perpetrator of incest. This enigma returns to haunt Chapter
XXXI when Equis goes to a room with a prostitute but is unable to have
sex with her because of impotence, and then symbolically is castrated. As
he says to her, 'Hace mucho tiempo que no tengo una erección' (p. 188).
The question Equis heard in his dream concerning the 'greatest tribute'
that a man can give to 'the woman he loves' is not answered in the text in
the events which follow on from the dream, as, indeed, we might expect
in a postmodern text of this kind. Rather, the question is deconstructed.
From this point onwards, the various scenarios which appear debunk the
notion of traditional heterosexual love. The first scene concerns a
journey to London by a group of women who want an abortion (Chapter
XIX). Chapter XXI depicts Equis's unsuccessful attempt to have sex with
an ugly, wizened prostitute (her body is battered; she has scars which
look 'estampados como lacre' and large varicose veins; p. 187). The
novel ends with a scene from a sex show involving two transvestites. The
riddle mentioned at the beginning of this section – which is based on
Freud's theory of the evolution of the human personality – is trivialised
into an inquiry as to the sex of the participants. As the promotion reads:

Sensacionales travesties
¿Hombres o mujeres?
Vealos y decida usted
mismo (p. 189)

Cross-dressing, on a primary level, tends to deconstruct the notion of a
fixed sexual identity and, in this, Peri Rossi's text seems to advocate a
utopian love which is unisex, encompassing hetero- and homosexual
love.[42] In its search for sexual 'in-difference', however, *La nave de los
locos* runs the risk of *appearing* to go beyond the phallic order but being
in fact simply a confirmation of the existing phallocratic order, thereby
running a risk that critics have pointed to as existing in a paradigmatic
work on the text/sex relationship, namely, Roland Barthes's *Le Plaisir du
texte*. As Jane Gallop suggests, a propos Barthes's text, with words
which are potentially applicable to *La nave de los locos*, the 'wish to
escape sexual difference might be but another mode of denying
women'.[43] Ultimately, the decision will be the reader's. The message on
the billboard, 'DECIDA USTED MISMO', is thus to be seen as implicating
the reader directly in the process of gender discovery, a decision which
the text leaves open. Since the novel ends with a cross-dressing scene,
however, one thing at least is clear: *La nave de los locos* projects the
(rhetorical) question 'What is the greatest tribute and homage a man can
give to the woman he loves?' as not unanswerable, but simply a
misguided question to ask in the first place.

ROSA MONTERO: *TEMBLOR*

As the entry on Rosa Montero (1951: Spain) in Katharina M. Wilson's
An Encyclopedia of Continental Women Writers states, along with
Montserrat Roig and Esther Tusquets, Montero 'stands at the forefront of

[42] Peri Rossi's novel does not, however, explicitly advocate a lesbian utopia, unlike
her poetry in which the speaker 'increasingly feels the urge to mark herself as a woman
and, more precisely, as a lesbian'; *Women's Writing in Latin America*, edited by Sara
Castro-Klarén, Sylvia Molloy and Beatriz Sarlo, p. 207.
[43] Jane Gallop, 'The Body Politic', in *Thinking Through the Body* (New York:
Columbia University Press, 1988), pp. 91–118 (p. 113). The ambiguity of Barthes's
critical writings on the subject of gender has also been noted by Stephen Heath; see
Naomi Schor, 'Dreaming Dissymmetry: Barthes, Foucault, and Sexual Difference', in
Men in Feminism, edited by Alice Jardine & Paul Smith (New York and London:
Methuen, 1987), pp. 98–110 (p. 100). Cross-dressing as a metaphor of the undecidability
of sexual gender has been much used in feminist discourse; see Elaine Showalter,
'Critical Cross-Dressing: Male Feminists and the Woman of the Year', in *Men in*

the new women's narrative of democratic Spain'.[44] The relationship between the sexes has proved to be an enduring theme in Montero's work, ranging from the depiction of gender oppression in a sleazy Madrid nightclub in *Te trataré como a una reina* (1983) to sexual equality in the work-place in *Amado amo* (1988).[45] Montero's most recent novel, *Temblor* (1990), further explores the issue of sexual gender, this time depicting a universe in which the male-female balance of our patriarchal world has been turned on its head.

Temblor is set in a world which is recognisable from the brave, new worlds of science fiction, yet it is peopled by monsters and by men and women who are reminiscent of Neanderthal man. As Alma Amell suggests, Montero's novel enacts 'un viaje inverso por el tiempo, de una era futura a la prehistoria, ida y vuelta'.[46] It also involves a fairly conventional struggle between good and evil with the main protagonist involved in a quest which her Elder, Corcho Quemado, has entrusted to her, and in which her role is crucial if the world is to be saved. Perhaps most intriguing, this is a world which is rapidly disappearing before the eyes of its inhabitants. The first indication of this occurs early on in the novel:

> Cuando Agua Fría venía corriendo campo a través hacia el recinto de los Grandes, súbitamente una pizca del mundo se desvaneció. Sucedió en el horizonte, hacia la derecha, en una esquina de su campo visual; Agua Fría registró el cambio con el rabillo del ojo y se paró a mirar. Allí, a lo lejos, había un jirón de bruma gris, un pequeño parche, una nada pastosa en donde antes, Agua Fría estaba casi segura, se levantaba un árbol. (p. 11)[47]

The idea here seems to be as follows: if individuals are not given full citizen status, epitomised by a letter they receive from an official dressed in purple, then they will die what is called a 'muerte verdadera' (p. xx).

Feminism, pp. 116–32; and the critique of her position by Craig Owens, 'Outlaws: Gay Men in Feminism', *ib.*, pp. 219–32.

[44] *An Encyclopedia of Continental Women Writers*, Vol. II, p. 861.

[45] For a good introduction to Montero's work, see Joan L. Brown, 'Rosa Montero: From Journalist to Novelist', in *Women Writers of Contemporary Spain*, pp. 241–57. Brown isolates three main themes in Montero's work, which are the relationship between the sexes, the role of women and the abuses committed by those in power. See also Eunice Myers, 'The Feminist Message: Propaganda and/or Art', in *Feminine Concerns in Contemporary Spanish Fiction by Woman*, pp. 99–112.

[46] Review of *Temblor*, *EC*, 3.2 (1990), 150–51 (p. 150).

[47] All textual references are to *Temblor* (Barcelona: Biblioteca Breve, 1990), 7th edition. The popularity of Montero's novel is suggested by the fact that, from its publication in February 1990, until October of the same year, it went through 7 editions, and sold 80,000 copies.

In an unusual twist to Berkeley's theory of idealism ('esse percipi est'), once an individual dies, the physical surroundings which were once their home will themselves being to melt away. This is shown decisively in the case of Agua Fría's mother who dies a 'real death' and whose house and belongings are already beginning to disappear when her daughter pays her a visit: 'Su madre había fallecido y su mundo se esfumaba detrás de ella' (p. 22).[48] One reason proposed why the world is beginning to disintegrate is that the knowledge of the Elders is not being passed on. As Corcho Quemado suggests, 'el mundo se borra por todos los que mueren de muerte verdadera, sin aprendices a los que poder entregar su memoria' (p. 11). This transmission of culture to the new generation of which Agua Fría is part is language-centred. Thus, Agua Fría's initiation is completed once the origin of her name is explained to her.[49]

There are, however, some basic differences between *Temblor* and the archetypal science fiction tale. The most obvious difference is that the protagonist is a woman, although here, Montero's novel approaches the remiss of an offshoot of the science fiction novel, feminist SF.[50] Agua Fría is the centre of the action; she leads the tribe who adopted her to a

[48] It is likely that Montero would have come across an idea of this kind – namely, the relationship between the external existence of the world and the role that our perceiving consciousness has in creating that world – in Unamuno's works, and particularly, *Niebla* (1914), which demonstrates certain similarities with *Temblor*; an equally possible source would be Borges's *Ficciones* in which philosophical issues involving idealism and perception are raised; see John Sturrock, *Paper Tigers: The Ideal Fictions of Jorge Luis Borges* (Oxford: Clarendon, 1977).

[49] The types of names used by Montero in this novel are redolent of the names of the heroes and heroines of North-American Indians popularized in Westerns; the name of the individual, according to the Sioux Indians, for example, should express something about the individual's character or actions. This idea seems to have found its way into *Temblor*. Agua Fría's name, for example, derives from the glass of cold water that her mother drank immediately she was conceived (p. 13). Montero's novel is characterised by its allusive heterogeneity. At another point of the novel, there is a reference to how the Anteriores' bodies were consumed by vultures and eagles, a rite which emphasies their sanctity. This would appear to be an allusion to a custom prevalent among Buddhists in Bombay in which the holy men's bodies are left to be devoured by vultures in the Tower of Silence. Likewise, Agua Fría is told at one stage that 'las aguas de un mismo río son siempre distintas' (p. 26), which alludes to Heraclitus's fiftieth fragment: 'As they step into the same rivers, other and still other waters flow upon them'; Charles H. Kahn, *The Art and Thought of Heraclitus: An Edition of the Fragments with Translation and Commentary* (Cambridge: C.U.P., 1979), p. 53. *Temblor* seems to delight in these cannibalized allusions to cultural texts, whether popular or philosophical, and effects a postmodernist levelling of canonic texts.

[50] For a general background, see Penny Florence, 'The Liberation of Utopia or Is Science Fiction the Ideal Contemporary Women's Form', in *Plotting Change: Contemporary Women's Fiction*, ed. Linda Anderson (London: Edward Arnold, 1990), pp. 65–83.

secret realm where the mystery of the origin of the disintegration process will be revealed. Since her mission is successful and she finally destroys, against all the odds, the evil regime of the 'sacerdotisas', it is fair to argue that she exhibits all the traits normally associated with the hero-quester in patriarchal tales. Yet, Agua Fría, even in this her most masculinist side (the salvation of the world), shows feminine character-istics. She begins her quest as a twelve-year-old adolescent with barely emerging breasts (p. 14, p. 11), at the time of the death of both of her mother-figures (her natural mother, p. xx), and her spiritual mother (p. xx), and, to round off the allegory, at the time of her first menstruation (p. 16). Despite these defiantly female paradigms, her quest is related to the salvation of the universe; her menstruation echoes the growth within the universe and coincides with the setting of the sun: 'En el hechizo de esa luz muriente, Agua Fría permanecía de pie sintiendo manar entre sus ingles la sustancia roja de la vida. Después el sol se hundió en las nieblas de un horizonte líquido y descendieron las tinieblas' (p. 16). Agua Fría is, thus, a heroine about to save the world (p. 14), since she carries on the quest/secret/knowledge/mission which her mentor, Corcho Quemado, entrusts to her before her death (p. 18).

Temblor takes this feminocentric gesture one step further. It is clear, right from the beginning of the story, that sexual gender is one of the most important, if not *the* most important, issue. Montero's novel focusses specifically on sexual difference and projects the epistemologi-cal divide separating man from woman as the single most significant juncture wherein identity, human values and human courage to change life is located. On the second page of the novel, for example, the protagonist, Agua Fría, expresses a need to know the sexual identity of the Elder ('Anterior'), and proposes the possibility that gender was not a defining characteristic of the world in which the Anteriores lived (p. 10). Gender is also seen as significant in that the world-vision depicted through Agua Fría's eyes is matriarchal, in the sense that the ultimate power, expressed in social, economic and religious terms, is held by a select band of women. Women, this text suggests, are congenitally superior, civilized beings:

> Las mujeres estaban congénitamente incapacitadas para ejercer la violencia. Su biología las colocaba en un estado superior de la evolución espiritual. No se trataba de un impedimento físico: era una repugnancia heredada, esencial, definitiva. Un tabú inscrito en su memoria genética. Así como los peces no eran capaces de volar y los pájaros no podían sobrevivir bajo las aguas, así los varones permanecían atrapados por el primitivo y atroz instinto de la violencia, mientras que las mujeres carecían de esas debilidades sanguinarias. (p. 121)

The most striking example of the congenital advancement of women is the fact that the priestesses in the novel hold the power of hypnosis, which they use to devastating effect on their enemies, who are, more often than not, men. Hypnosis, since it is an example of mind over matter, shows how *Temblor* overturns one of the dogmatic metaphors of patriarchy which normally projects woman as manipulated matter and man as manipulative mind. Thus, Agua Fría's first encounter with a man confirms her contempt of the male species; when she first meets a man, she muses to herself: 'no era más que un varón' (p. 17). When she hears the way he refers to the sacred rites of the priesthood, and his cynical rejection of the Law (which is ironic given his name Respetuoso Orgullo De La Ley), Agua Fría brands him a heretic, and runs off (p. 20).

The sexual divide appears too in the area of power politics in the guise of castration which occupies an important role in Montero's novel. Women, metaphorically speaking, castrate men who have committed a crime, the crime normally taking the form of a man's desire to usurp the power of women. The men are not literally castrated; their castration takes the displaced form of the amputation of an arm. We learn mid-way through the novel that this is a traditional punishment for wayward males; one young man's stump went gangrenous after amputation and he died in agony, since the priestess refused to allow him any medical help (p. 127). When Agua Fría meets Pedernal, she finds he too has had his left hand amputated, and, as if to make the sexual metaphor plain, he is now wearing the attire of a priestess (p. 230). Indeed, so much so has he adopted his new-found sexual identity that he is prepared to betray Agua Fría and hand her over to the Gran Sacerdotisa, as we soon discover. The image of a castrated male specifically undercuts the thrust of patriarchy in that castration is traditionally the image of womanhood projected by the patriarchal mind. Montero's text thereby effects a revengeful reversion of this gender-laden image.

Temblor evokes an unsettling dialogue with the stereotypical view of primitive societies. This brave, new world, far from being the vision of the future which it is superficially intended to be, has far more similarities with the retrograde, primitive worlds dreamed up by anthropologists on behalf of Neanderthal man. That Montero is referring, perhaps innocently, to the discourse of anthropology is clear in the primary importance given to hunting, which is associated with those supernatural rites from which the women of the Uma tribe are excluded: 'Sus ritos eran complicados y herméticos, por lo menos para las mujeres, que no estaban autorizadas a acercarse al fondo de la cueva, allí donde, en medio de las tinieblas más espesas, los guerreros ejecutaban raras liturgias y realizaban las pinturas sagradas' (p. 182). Also reminiscent of the musings of the anthropologist is the scene which Agua Fría is hit fiercely over the head by her prospective husband, Zao, as a sign of his growing love for her; to get her revenge she bites his finger to the bone (pp. 202–03). The mixture of the future (permanently policed, supervised state of Talapot) and the past (cavemen living a brutish existence) evident in *Temblor* is clearly lifted from the dreamscape of the typical science fiction novel, and may have borrowed its muddied ideology as well.

There are indications, however, that Montero's novel strives to transcend its populist source, and this is glimpsed in its evocation of the origins of power. The world is ending, seemingly, because of the corruption of power, which is experienced as a punishment of the Gods, for which blame is apportioned to the priest caste, who are consequently murdered by the populace in their thousands. Yet, one distinctive feature of Montero's vision of Apocalypse Now is the specifically gendered nature of its origins. The result of cosmic disintegration is that the women have thereby grasped power from the hands of men. Thus Agua Fría begins to unsettle the roles of men and women in Renacimiento because she shows that she can hunt as well as any man: 'En Renacimiento todo era distinto. Hombres que daban lecciones magistrales a las mujeres, mujeres capaces de matar. . . como ella misma lo había hechos dos días antes. Y esa voluntad común de construir una sociedad absurdamente igualitaria' (p. 125). On one level, her entry into that world allegorizes the entry of the knowledge of feminism into the patriarchal universe, an intellectual osmosis which brings about a postmodernist levelling of previously cherished certainties relating to identity and gender. This is suggested, for example, when Bala asks Agua Fría why she has come to their tribe:

> – Eres una mujer extraña – dijo pensativamente –. Vistes de un modo extraño, tienes una cara extraña, hablas extrañamente y te comportas como no se comportaría ninguna mujer. ¿Qué buscas entre nosotros? ¿Por qué quieres vivir aquí? (p. 179)

Her arrival effectively reverses the 'immasculation', to use Judith Fetterley's term, whereby women are dominated by men;[51] she is a New Woman, or at least this is how it is seen in Renacimiento. But there is a paradox here. The chaos in the novel, which is nihilistic in the sense that it makes objects, such as trees, disappear and that it makes human union barren, could be seen as suggesting that the deepest fear expressed in the

---

[51] Judith Fetterley, *The Resisting Reader: A Feminist Approach to American Fiction* (Bloomington and London: Indiana University Press, 1978), p. xx.

novel is the unsettling of gendered identity; in a sense, *Temblor* might be read as a delineation of the potential harm wrought by gender trouble. This, in itself, could be seen as a surprising ideological substructure to be found in a novel authored by a woman. If one were to follow this line of reasoning, it might be possible to interpret the novel as a veiled allegory of evil produced by the spread of female power; the 'sacerdotisas' would therefore function as that element within society which has carried gender trouble too far, those strident (lesbian-?)feminists, perhaps, against whom the heterosexual female protagonist wages war and whom she finally vanquishes.[52] When seen in the light of its wariness of gender trouble, one would need to conclude that *Temblor* is, indeed, a conservative novel which projects the paradise of heterosexual sex (an idea which is promoted by Corcho Quemado [p. 13], as well as by Agua Fría on various occasions [p. 204], both of whom recall with fond affection the feeling of contentedness after sex with a male).[53] Further evidence of the distrust of gender trouble is provided by the suggestion, repeated at different times in the novel, that the apocalypse experienced by the inhabitants of the world has led to a low, if not non-existent, birth-rate. As the Gran Sacerdotisa suggests, wars and famines were made doubly pernicious because 'por alguna enigmática razón la humanidad ya no era tan fértil como antes' (p. 242). The reason for this, as we soon discover, is the corruption of the Woman-Priests who live in the Inner Circle. Once more, the text seems to suggest, an excess of power wielded by a small band of women leads to destruction. This may explain the horror evoked in the mind of the protagonist when she meets the androgyne. When Agua Fría asks whether he/she is a man or a woman, the androgyne replies: 'Ni yo mismo lo sé. Tengo pechos. También en el lado izquierdo, sólo que ése me lo vendo. Pero mi sexo es de varón. A veces me siento mujer, a veces hombre. La verdad es que ser una cosa o la otra me da lo mismo' (p. 143). Agua Fría's suspicions prove to be well-founded when the androgyne drugs her in order to sell her to bandits (pp. 147–48). Montero's text, as this episode reveals, expresses a deep-

[52] Roberto Manteiga, for example, suggests that Montero's work promotes a vision of women which is at odds with 'the writings of some of her more militant feminist contemporaries', 'The Dilemma of the Modern Woman: A Study of the Female Characters in Rosa Montero's Novels', in *Feminine Concerns in Contemporary Spanish Fiction by Woman*, pp. 113–23 (p. 123).

[53] Montero's use of the Science Fiction mode is thus not as feminist or radical as that of writers such as Joanna Russ and Ursula Le Guin who aggressively deconstruct images of manhood in their work; for further discussion of these two writers see Roz Kaveney, 'The Science Fictiveness of Women's Science Fiction', in *From My Guy to Sci-Fi: Genre and Women's Writing in the Postmodern World*, edited by Helen Carr (London: Pandora, 1989), pp. 78–97.

seated suspicion about androgyny and its corollary, gender trouble. It is for this reason that, as Juan Antonio Masoliver Ródenas points out, *Temblor* has a double-forked moralism since it is 'tanto una advertencia contra el dogma como contra la utopía'.[54]

To see *Temblor* as expressing a fear of gender trouble is a plausible reading, but it is not the only reading possible of Montero's novel. Crucial to an understanding of the novel is the dynamics of its conclusion. The ending in a sense is produced by a play on words 'bruma/Bruna'. The 'bruma', or mist, epitomises the evil against which the wits of the protagonist are pitted, the nothingness which threatens to eat up the whole of her existence. The conclusion of *Temblor* tends to suggest that Montero's personal use of the Science Fiction format follows contemporary trends in feminist SF which has, as Roz Kaveney suggests, 'tended far more to the Utopian side of the SF tradition'.[55] Thus, the appearance of Bruna, or indeed a simulacrum of Agua Fría's beloved dog, in the closing pages of the novel, triumphantly expounds the possibility of rebirth and the transcendence of the muddy forces of nothingness: 'Era una perra del mismo tamaño que *Bruna*, con su mismo vientre dilatado por los múltiples partos, las mismas orejas hirsutas, los tristes ojos caramelo, el delicado hocico. Era una perra que *tenía* que ser *Bruna*' (p. 247). Even if the dog who appears in the closing episode of the novel is not Bruna, Montero's text points to the viability of what Mircea Eliade calls a 'crisis and renewal' motif.[56] Bruna finally overcomes 'bruma'; life vanquishes the forces of nothingness.

As we have seen in this chapter, gender trouble, or the deconstruction of gender coherence, plays a crucial role in Valenzuela's *El gato eficaz*, Peri Rossi's *La nave de los locos* and Montero's *Temblor*. On the level of metaphor, gender trouble is evident in all three novels via the appearance of characters/narrators whose gender is unstable: the narrator in *El gato eficaz* who changes into a man and then back into a woman, the sex-show featuring transvestites which concludes *La nave de los locos* and the unnerving androgyne who kidnaps the protagonist of *Temblor*. On the level of textuality, however, these three novels produce different gender configurations. In *El gato eficaz* and *La nave de los locos*, for example,

54 '*Temblor*, de Rosa Montero', *Insula*, 525 (1990), 19–20 (p. 20).

55 Roz Kaveney, 'The Science Fictiveness of Women's Science Fiction ', in *From My Guy to Sci-Fi: Genre and Women's Writing in the Postmodern World*, edited by Helen Carr (London: Pandora, 1989), pp. 78–97 (p. 96).

56 *The Quest: History and Meaning in Religion* (Chicago: The University of Chicago, 1969), pp. 54–71. Eliade also notes the re-emergence of such motifs in modern literature, pp. 123–26. Montero's scene might also be seen as a rewriting of the conclusion of Unamuno's *Niebla* in which the dog, Orfeo, has the last word.

the dissolution of gender stasis is enacted on the level of textuality, since these two novels refuse to inscribe their narrative identities within a patriarchal master plot; they refuse to tell a 'straight' story. Their meandering textual weavings defy the plot-completion and character-fixing demanded by the phallocentric standard. *Temblor*, however, *does* re-enact a recognisably 'straight' plot which has a fixed set of values (which have been drawn from the patrocentric world of science fiction), and a gender-stable protagonist. By portraying the androgyne as a victim of its own ugliness, Montero unveils her distaste for the *temblor* of gender trouble. In conclusion, while *El gato eficaz*, *La nave de los locos* and *Temblor* may be treating the motif of gender trouble from different angles, each novel projects the drama of gendered identity as a central configuration of the changing times in which we live.

CONCLUSION

In the present study an attempt has been made to analyse the role played by five structuring devices or motifs (the *Bildungsroman*, the patriarchal prison, the fairy tale, sexual politics and gender trouble) in a selection of representative women's novels from Spain and Latin America written during the period 1936–the present day. We have seen that a central theme of the novels studied has involved demonstrating, in a graphic and experimental way, the varying ways in which patriarchy seeks to undermine the status of womanhood. Some novels focussed on the ways in which women's lives are structured according to a pre-established patriarchal plan (*Nada*, *La plaça del Diamant*, *Perto do coração selvagem*); others concentrated on the ways in which men imprison women in their domestic roles (*La amortajada*, *Album de familia*, *Los recuerdos del porvenir*); some novels sought to redress the balance through a re-evaluation of the fairy tale (*Primera memoria*, *El cuarto de atrás*, *El mismo mar de todos los veranos*), others explored the interpenetration of gender and politics (*La casa de los espíritus*, *Conversación al sur*, *L'hora violeta*), while still others sought to re-draw the map of sexual boundaries (*El gato eficaz*, *La nave de los locos*, *Temblor*). Though clearly implicated in the gender issues raised in these novels, the male reader is in a sense observing from the other side of the looking glass. Faced with the difference of women's writing, he may at times feel like Otávio in Clarice Lispector's *Perto do coração selvagem* when faced with Joana: 'Diga de novo o que é Lalande' he implores (see Chapter 1, p. 33).

The collection of essays *Men in Feminism*, edited by Alice Jardine and Paul Smith, offers another focus on men observing from the other side of the looking glass; this time the subject is feminism. If one judges by the praxis of the writers concerned, it is clear that three essential approaches to the matter are proposed, namely, self-emasculation (Stephen Heath), violent penetration (Paul Smith), or textual innocence (Andrew Ross).[1]

---

[1] Heath, 'Male Feminism', pp. 1–32; Smith, 'Men in Feminism: Men and Feminist Theory', pp. 33–46; Ross, 'Demonstrating Sexual Difference', pp. 47–53; see *Men in*

As the work of these three critics demonstrates, a man writing about feminism or women's writing runs the risk of stepping on property which is seen as out of bounds for his gender (a difficulty I encountered in a session on critical theory given at the Kentucky Foreign Language Conference in 1990), and it is only fair to make clear that the present study does not have intrusion of this kind as one of its aims. It is simply offered as a reversal of the writer-reader relationship which, for perhaps too long, has simply meant women reading men.

Feminism, edited by Alice Jardine and Paul Smith. Judging by the reactions to these essays by those female feminists whose responses appear in the book, Heath is admired, Ross tolerated and Smith criticised; see especially Elizabeth Weed, 'A Man's Place', pp. 71–77, and Elaine Showalter, 'Critical Cross-Dressing; Male Feminists and the Woman of the Year', pp. 116–32.

LIST OF WORKS CONSULTED

I. CRITICISM ON WOMEN AUTHORS STUDIED

Agosín, Marjorie, *Las desterradas del paraíso, protagonistas en la narrativa de María Luisa Bombal* (New York: Senda Nueva Editores, 1983).

Alegría, Fernando, *Nueva historia de la novela hispanoamericana* (Hanover, N.H.: Ediciones del Norte, 1986).

Amell, Alma, '*El temblor*', *EC*, 3.2 (1990), 150–51.

Anderson, Christopher L, & Lynne Vespe Sheay, 'Ana María Matute's *Primera memoria*: A Fairy Tale Gone Awry', *RCEH*, 14 (1989), 1–14.

Balderston, Daniel, 'History and Fantasy in *Los recuerdos del porvenir*', *BHS*, LXVI (1989), 41–46.

Bassnett, Susan (ed.), *Knives and Angels: Women Writers in Latin America* (London and New Jersey: Zed Books Ltd., 1990).

Bellver, Catherine G., 'Montserrat Roig: A Feminine Perspective and a Journalistic Slant', in *Feminine Concerns in Contemporary Spanish Fiction by Women*, edited by Roberto C. Manteiga, Carolyn Galerstein & Kathleen McNerney (Potomac, Maryland: Scripta Humanistica, 1988), pp. 152–68.

Bergmann, Emilie, 'Reshaping the Canon: Intertextuality in Spanish Novels of Female Development', *ALEC*, 12 (1987), 141–57.

Boschetto, Sandra M., 'Threads, Connections, and the Fairy Tale: Reading the Writing in Isabel Allende's *La casa de los espíritus*', in *Continental, Latin-American and Francophile Women Writers*, edited by Ginette Adamson and Eunice Myers (Lanham, MD: University Press of America, 1990), Vol. II, pp. 51–63.

Brown, G. G., *A Literary History of Spain: The Twentieth Century* (London: Ernest Benn Limited, 1972).

Brown, Joan L., 'One Autobiography Twice Told: Martín Gaite's *Entre visillos* and *El cuarto de atrás*', *HJ*, 7 (1986), 37–47.

Brown, J. L., and E. M. Smith, '*El cuarto de atrás*: Metafiction and the Actualization of Literary Theory', *Hispanófila*, 90 (1987), 63–70.

—————— (ed.), *Women Writers of Contemporary Spain: Exiles in the Homeland* (London and Toronto: Associated University Presses, 1991).

——————, 'Carmen Martín Gaite: Reaffirming the Pact Between Reader and Writer', in *Women Writers of Contemporary Spain*, pp. 72–92.

——————, 'Montserrat Roig and the Creation of a Gynocentric Reality', in *Women Writers of Contemporary Spain*, pp. 217–39.

143

————, 'Rosa Montero: From Journalist to Novelist', in *Women Writers of Contemporary Spain*, pp. 241–57.

Brushwood, John S., *The Spanish American Novel: A Twentieth-Century Survey* (London and Austin: University of Texas Press, 1975).

Camps, S., 'Peri Rossi', *Quimera*, 81 (1988), 40–49.

Castillo, Debra A., 'Never-ending story: Carmen Martín Gaite's *The Back Room*', *PMLA*, 102:5 (1987), 814–28.

Charlon, Anne, *La condició de la dona en la narrativa catalana (1900–1983)*, translated by Pilar Canal (Barcelona: Edicions 62, 1990).

Ciplijauskaité, Biruté, *La novela femenina contemporánea (1970–1985): hacia una tipología de la narración en primera persona* (Barcelona: Anthropos, 1988).

Cixous, Hélène, *Reading with Clarice Lispector*, edited, translated and introduced by Verena Andermatt Conley (London: Harvester-Wheatsheaf, 1990).

Clarasó, Mercè, 'The Angle of Vision in the Novels of Mercè Rodoreda', *BHS*, 57 (1980), 143–52.

Coddou, Marcelo (ed.), *Los libros tienen sus propios espíritus: Estudios sobre Isabel Allende* (México: Universidad Veracruzana, 1986).

Coelho, Novaes, 'A presença da "Nova Mulher" na ficção brasileira atual', *RI*, 50 (1984), 141–54.

Condé, L. P., & S. M. Hart (eds.), *Feminist Readings on Spanish and Latin-American Literature* (Lampeter: Edwin Mellen, 1991).

Cypess, Sandra M., 'The Figure La Malinche in the Texts of Elena Garro', in *A Different Reality: Studies on the Work of Elena Garro*, edited by Anita K. Stoll (London and Toronto: Associated University Presses, 1990), pp. 117–35.

————, 'Visual and Verbal Distances in the Mexican Theater: The Plays of Elena Garro', in *Woman as Myth and Metaphor in Latin-American Literature*, edited by Carmelo Virgilio & Naomi Lindstrom (Columbia: University of Missouri Press, 1985), pp. 44–62.

d'Ambrosio Servodidio, Mirella, & Marcia L. Welles (eds.), *From Fiction to Metafiction: Essays in Honour of Carmen Martín Gaite* (Lincoln: Society of Spanish and Spanish American Studies, 1983).

————, 'Esther Tusquets's Fiction: The Spinning of a Narrative Web', in *Women Writers of Contemporary Spain: Exiles in the Homeland*, ed. Joan L. Brown (London and Toronto: Associated University Presses, 1991), pp. 159–78.

Durán, Manuel, '*El cuarto de atrás*: imaginación, fantasía, misterio: Todorov y algo más', in d'Ambrosio Servodidio, Mirella, & Marcia L. Welles (eds.), *From Fiction to Metafiction: Essays in Honour of Carmen Martín Gaite* (Lincoln: Society of Spanish and Spanish American Studies, 1983), pp. 129–37.

Fitz, Earl, *Clarice Lispector* (Boston: Twayne, 1985).

————, 'Hélène Cixous's Debt to Clarice Lispector: The Case of *Vivre l'Orange* and *L'Ecriture féminine*', *RLC*, 251:1 (1990), 235–49.

Fox-Lockert, Lucía (see also Guerra-Cunningham), *Women Novelists in Spain and Spanish America* (Metuchen, N.J., and London: Scarecrow Press, 1979).

Franco, Jean, *Plotting Women: Gender and Representation in Mexico* (London: Verso, 1989).

Fuster, Joana, *Literatura catalana contemporània* (Barcelona: Curial, 1978).

Gálvez Lira, Gloria, *María Luisa Bombal: realidad y fantasía* (Potomac, Maryland: Scripta Humanistica, 1986).

García, Evelyne, 'Lectura: N. Fem. Sing. ¿Lee y escribe la mujer en forma diferente al hombre?', *Quimera*, 23 (September 1982), 54–57.

García Pinto, M., *Historias íntimas: conversaciones con diez escritoras latinoamericanas* (Hanover: Ediciones del Norte, 1988).

Glenn, Kathleen M., '*El cuarto de atrás*: Literature as *juego* and the Self-Reflexive Text', in d'Ambrosio Servodidio, Mirella, & Marcia L. Welles (eds.), *From Fiction to Metafiction: Essays in Honour of Carmen Martín Gaite* (Lincoln: Society of Spanish and Spanish American Studies, 1983), pp. 149–59.

———, '*El mismo mar de todos los veranos* and the Prism of Art', in *The Sea of Becoming: Approaches to the Fiction of Esther Tusquets*, ed. Mary S. Vásquez (New York: Greenwood Press, 1991), pp. 29–43.

Gold, Janet L., 'Reading the Love Myth: Tusquets with the Help of Barthes', *HR*, 55 (1987), 337–46.

Guerra-Cunningham, Lucía (see also Fox-Lockert), *La narrativa de María Luisa Bombal, una visión de la existencia femenina* (Madrid: Playor, 1980).

———, 'La referencialidad como negación del paraíso: exilio y excentrismo en *La nave de los locos* de Cristina Peri Rossi', *REH*, 13:2 (1989), 63–74.

Hart, Patricia, *Narrative Magic in the Fiction of Isabel Allende* (London and Ontario: Associated University Presses, 1989).

Hart, Stephen M., '*Ecriture féminine* and the Political Unconsciousness', *The Other Scene: Psychoanalytic Readings in Modern Spanish and Latin-American Literature* (Boulder, Colorado: Society of Spanish and Spanish-American Studies, 1992), pp. 63–85.

———, 'Esther Tusquets: Sex, Excess and the Dangerous Supplement of Language', *Antípodas*, 3 (1991), 85–98.

Johnson, Roberta, *Carmen Laforet* (Boston: Twayne, 1981).

———, 'Personal and Public History in Laforet's Long Novels', in *Feminine Concerns in Contemporary Spanish Fiction by Women*, edited by Roberto C. Manteiga, Carolyn Galerstein & Kathleen McNerney (Potomac, Maryland: Scripta Humanistica, 1988), pp. 43–53.

Jones, Margaret E. W., *The Literary World of Ana María Matute* (Lexington: The University Press of Kentucky, 1970).

———, 'Barcelona's Restrictive Space in *El mismo mar de todos los veranos*', *Ideas '92*, 7 (1990), 95–101.

———, 'Dialectical Movement as Feminist Technique in the Works of Carmen Laforet', *Studies in Honor of Gerald E. Wade* (Madrid: José Porrúa Turanzas, 1979), pp. 109–20.

Kantaris, Elia, 'The Politics of Desire: Alienation and Identity in the Work of Marta Traba and Cristina Peri Rossi', *FMLS*, 25 (1989), 248–64.

Kostupulos-Cooperman, Celeste, *The Lyrical Vision of María Luisa Bombal* (London: Tamesis, 1988).

Levine, Linda Gould, 'Carmen Martín Gaite's *El cuarto de atrás*: A Portrait of the Artist as a Woman', in d'Ambrosio Servodidio, Mirella, & Marcia L. Welles (eds.), *From Fiction to Metafiction: Essays in Honour of Carmen Martín Gaite* (Lincoln: Society of Spanish and Spanish American Studies, 1983), pp. 161–72.

Lindstrom, Naomi, 'Rosario Castellanos: Representing Women's Voice', *LF*, 5:2 (1979), 29–47.

——, *Women's Voice in Latin American Literature* (Washington, DC: Three Continents Press, 1989).

Magnarelli, Sharon, *The Lost Rib: Female Characters in the Spanish-American Novel* (London and Toronto: Associated University Presses, 1985).

——, *Reflections/Refractions: Reading Luisa Valenzuela* (New York: Peter Lang, 1988).

Mandrell, James, 'The Prophetic Vision in Garro, Morante, and Allende', *CL*, 42:3 (1990), 227–46.

Manteiga, Roberto C., Carolyn Galerstein, & Kathleen McNerney (eds.), *Feminine Concerns in Contemporary Spanish Fiction by Women* (Potomac, Maryland: Scripta Humanistica, 1988).

Marcos, Juan Manuel, *De García Márquez al postboom* (Madrid: Orígenes, 1986).

Martin, Gerald, *Journeys Through the Labyrinth: Latin-American Fiction in the Twentieth Century* (London: Verso, 1989).

Martínez, Z. Nelly, '*El gato eficaz* de Luisa Valenzuela: la productividad del texto', *RCEH*, 4 (1979), 73–80.

Masiello, Francine, 'Women, State, and Family in Latin American Literature', in *Women, Culture, and Politics in Latin America: Seminar on Feminism and Culture in Latin America*, ed. Emilie Bergman et. al. (Berkeley: University of California Press, 1990), pp. 27–47.

Masoliver Ródenas, Juan Antonio, '*Temblor*, de Rosa Montero', *Insula*, 525 (1990), 19–20 (p. 20).

McNerney, Kathleen, 'A Feminist Literary Renaissance in Catalonia', in *Feminine Concerns in Contemporary Spanish Fiction by Women*, edited by Roberto C. Manteiga, Carolyn Galerstein & Kathleen McNerney (Potomac, Maryland: Scripta Humanistica, 1988), pp. 124–33.

—— (ed.), *On Our Own Behalf: Women's Tales from Catalonia* (Lincoln and London: University of Nebraska Press, 1988).

Menton, Seymour, 'Las cuentistas mexicanas en la época feminista, 1970–1988', *Hispania*, 73 (1990), 366–70.

Meyer, Doris, ' "Parenting the Text": Female Creativity and Dialogic Relationships in Isabel Allende's *La casa de los espíritus*', *Hispania*, 73 (1990), 360–65.

Miller, Beth, 'Female Characterization and Contexts in Rosario Castellanos's *Album de familia*', *AmH*, 4:32–33 (1979), 26–30.

——, *Uma consciência feminista: Rosario Castellanos* (São Paulo: Editora Perspectiva, 1987).

Miller, Yvette E., & Charles M. Tatum, *Latin American Women Writers: Yesterday and Today* (Pittsburgh, PA: Latin American Literary Review, 1977).

Molinaro, Nina L., *Foucault, Feminism, and Power: Reading Esther Tusquets* (London and Toronto: Associated University Presses, 1991).

Mora, Gabriela, 'A Thematic Exploration of the Works of Elena Garro', in *Latin American Women Writers: Yesterday and Today*, edited by Yvette E. Miller & Charles M. Tatum (Pittsburgh, PA.: Latin American Literary Review, 1977), pp. 91–97.

————, & Karen S. Van Hooft (eds.), *Theory and Practice of Feminist Literary Criticism*, edited by Gabriela Mora and Karten S. Van Hooft (Ypsilanti, Michigan: Bilingual Press, 1982).

————, 'Narradoras hispanoamericanas: vieja y nueva problemática en renovadas elaboraciones', in *Theory and Practice of Feminist Literary Criticism*, pp. 156–174.

Morris, Celita Lamar, 'Carmen Laforet's *Nada* as an Expression of Woman's Self-Determination', *LF*, 1:2 (1975), 40–47.

Mull, Dorothy S. Mull, & Elsa B. de Angulo, 'An Afternoon with Luisa Valenzuela', *Hispania*, 69:2 (1986), 350–52.

Myers, Eunice, & Ginette Adamson (eds.), *Continental, Latin-American and Francophone Women Writers* (Lanham, MD: University Press of America, 1987).

————, 'The Feminist Message: Propaganda and/or Art', in *Feminine Concerns in Contemporary Spanish Fiction by Woman*, edited by Roberto C. Manteiga, Carolyn Galerstein & Kathleen McNerney (Potomac, Maryland: Scripta Humanistica, 1988), pp. 99–112.

Nichols, Geraldine L., 'The Prison House (and Beyond): *El mismo mar de todos los veranos*', *RR*, 75 (1984), 366–85.

————, *Escribir, espacio propio: Laforet, Matute, Moix, Tusquets, Riera y Roig por sí mismas* (Minneapolis, Minnesota: Institute for the Study of Ideologies and Literature, 1989).

Quinn, Kathleen, '*Tablero de damas* and *Album de familia*: Farces on Women Writers', in *Homenaje a Rosario Castellanos*, ed. Maureen Ahern & Mary Seale Vásquez (Valencia: Albatros, 1980), pp. 99–105.

Ordóñez, Elizabeth J., 'Reading, Telling and the Text of Carmen Martín Gaite's *El cuarto de atrás*', in d'Ambrosio Servodidio, Mirella, & Marcia L. Welles (eds.), *From Fiction to Metafiction: Essays in Honour of Carmen Martín Gaite* (Lincoln: Society of Spanish and Spanish American Studies, 1983), pp. 173–84.

Ordóñez, Montserrat, 'Más caras de espejos, un juego especular. Entrevista-asociaciones con la escritora argentina Luisa Valenzuela', *RI*, 132–33 (1985), 511–19.

Peixoto, Marta, '*Family Ties*: Female Development in Clarice Lispector', in *The Voyage In: Fictions of Female Development*, edited by Elizabeth Abel, Marianne Hirsch, and Elizabeth Langland (Hanover and London, University Press of New England, 1983), pp. 287–303.

Pérez, Janet, *Ana María Matute* (Boston: Twayne, 1971).

——, *Contemporary Women Writers of Spain* (Boston: Twayne, 1988).

——, 'Portraits of the *Femme Seule* by Laforet, Matute, Soriano, Martín Gaite, Galvarriato, Quiroga, and Medio', in *Feminine Concerns in Contemporary Spanish Fiction by Women*, edited by Roberto C. Manteiga, Carolyn Galerstein & Kathleen McNerney (Potomac, Maryland, Scripta Humanistica, 1988), pp. 54–77.

——, 'The Fictional World of Ana María Matute: Solitude, Injustice, and Dreams', in *Women Writers of Contemporary Spain: Exiles in the Homeland*, edited by Joan L. Brown (Cranbury: Associated University Presses, 1991), pp. 93–115.

Picon Garfield, Evelyn, *Women's Voices from Latin America: Interviews with Six Contemporary Authors* (Detroit: Wayne State University Press, 1985).

Piñol, Rosa María, 'Nueve autoras de distintas culturas coinciden en asociar escritura y libertad', *La Vanguardia* (23 June 1990).

Poniatowska, Elena, 'Marta Traba o el salto al vacío', *RI*, 132–33 (1985), 883–97.

Pope, Randolph D., 'Mercè Rodoreda's Subtle Greatness', in *Women Writers of Contemporary Spain*, ed. Joan L. Brown (London and Toronto: Associated University Presses, 1991), pp. 116–135.

Reed, Suzanne Gross, 'Notes on Hans Christian Andersen Fairy Tales in Ana María Matute's *Primera memoria*', in *Continental, Latin-American and Francophone Women Writers*, edited by Eunice Myers & Ginette Adamson (Lanham, MD: University Press of America, 1987), Vol. I, pp. 177–82.

Ribeira de Oliveira, Salange, 'The Social Aspects of Clarice Lispector's Novels: An Ideological Reading of *A Paixão segundo G.H.*', *La Chispa '87 Selected Proceedings*, ed. Gilbert Paolini (New Orleans: Tulane University, 1987), pp. 211–20.

Riera, Carme, 'Literatura femenina: ¿Un lenguaje prestado?', *Quimera*, 18 (April 1982), 9–12.

Riquer, Martín de (ed.), *Obras de Bernat Metge* (Barcelona: Universidad de Barcelona, 1959).

Robles Suárez, Juana (ed.), *La mujer por la mujer* (México: Pepsa Editores, 1975).

Rodríguez, Aleida Anselma, 'Todorov en *El cuarto de atrás*', *Prismal/Cabral*, 11 (1983), 76–90.

Rodríguez Monegal, Emir, 'Clarice Lispector en sus libros y en mi recuerdo', *RI*, 50 (1984), 231–38.

Rodríguez Peralta, Phyllis, 'Images of Women in Rosario Castellanos's Prose', *LALR*, 6:11 (1977), 68–80.

San Román, Gustavo, 'Fantastic Political Allegory in the Early Work of Cristina Peri Rossi', *BHS*, 67 (1990), 151–64.

——, 'Satire with Children in Cristina Peri Rossi', *SpSt*, 11 (1990–91), 1–10.

Saval, Lorenzo, & J. García Gallego (eds.), *Litoral femenino: literatura escrita por mujeres en la España contemporánea* (Granada: Litoral, 1986).

Serrano y Sanz, *Apuntes para una biblioteca de escritoras españolas desde el año 1401 al 1833* (Madrid: Atlas, 1975). Biblioteca de Autores Españoles Series, 4 vols.

Silva Velázquez, Caridad L., & Nora Erro-Orthman, *Puerta abierta: la nueva escritora latinoamericana* (México: Joaquín Mortiz, 1986).

Sobejano, Gonzalo, 'Direcciones de la novela española de postguerra', in *Novelistas españoles de postguerra*, edited by Rodolfo Cardona (Madrid: Taurus, 1976), pp. 47–64.

Sola, María, '*Conversación al sur*: Novela para no olvidar', *SiN*, 12:4 (1982), 67–71.

Spires, Robert C., 'Intertextuality in *El cuarto de atrás*', in d'Ambrosio Servodidio, Mirella, & Marcia L. Welles (eds.), *From Fiction to Metafiction: Essays in Honour of Carmen Martín Gaite* (Lincoln: Society of Spanish and Spanish American Studies, 1983), pp. 173–84.

Stoll, Anita K. (ed.), *A Different Reality: Studies on the Work of Elena Garro* (London and Toronto: Associated University Presses, 1990).

Swanson, Philip (ed.), *Landmarks in Modern Latin American Fiction* (London and New York: Routledge, 1990).

Terry, Arthur, *Catalan Literature* (London: Benn, 1972).

Thomas, Michael D., 'The Rite of Initiation in Matute's *Primera memoria*', *KRQ*, 25 (1978), 153–64.

Traba, Marta, 'Hipótesis sobre una escritura diferente', *Quimera*, 13 (September 1981), 9–11.

Triadú, Joan, '*La plaça del Diamant*, de Mercè Rodoreda', in *Guia de literatura catalana contemporània*, edited by Jordi Castellanos (Barcelona: Edicions 62, 1973), pp. 403–07.

Valenzuela, Luisa, 'Mis brujas favoritas', in *Theory and Practice of Feminist Literary Criticism*, edited by Gabriela Mora and Karten S. Van Hooft (Ypsilanti, Michigan: Bilingual Press, 1982), pp. 88–95.

Wilson, Katharina M. (ed.), *An Encyclopedia of Continental Women Writers* (New York and London: Garland Publishing, Inc., 1991), 2 vols.

II. GENERAL AND BACKGROUND STUDIES

Abel, Elizabeth, Hirsch Marianne & Langland, Elizabeth (eds.), *The Voyage In: Fictions of Female Development* (Hanover and London, University Press of New England, 1983).

Abrams, Fred, 'The Death of Zorrilla's Don Juan and the Problem of Catholic Orthodoxy', *RoN*, 6 (1964), 42–46.

Althusser, Louis, *Pour Marx* (Paris: Maspéro, 1966).

Alvarez, Sonia E., 'Women's Movements and Gender Politics in the Brazilian Transition', in *The Women's Movement in Latin America: Feminism and the Transition to Democracy*, edited by Jane S. Jaquette (Boston: Unwin Hyman, 1989), pp. 18–71.

Arenal, Electra, & Stacey Schlau, 'Strategems of the Strong, Strategems of the Weak: Autobiographical Prose of the Seventeenth-Century Hispanic Convent', *TSWL*, 9:1 (1990), 25–42.

The Basic Works of Aristotle, edited and with an introduction by Richard McKeon (New York: Random House, 1941).

Aristotle, *Poetics*, translated by Leon Golden (Tallahassee: University Presses of Florida, 1981).

Auslander Munich, Adrienne, *Andromeda's Chains: Gender and Interpretation in Victorian Literature and Art* (New York: Columbia University Press, 1989).

Baroja, Pío, *La nave de los locos*, edited by Francisco Fores Arroyuelo (Madrid: Cátedra, 1987).

Bergman, Emilie, *et al.* (eds.), *Women, Culture and Politics in Latin America: Seminar on Feminism and Culture in Latin America* (Berkeley: University of California Press, 1990).

Bernstein, J. S., 'Pascual Duarte y Orestes', *Symposium*, 22 (1968), 301–18.

Blattersby, Christine, *Gender and Genius: Towards a Feminist Aesthetics* (Bloomington and Indianapolis: Indiana University Press, 1989).

Blaye, Edouard de, *Franco and the Politics of Spain* (Harmondsworth: Penguin, 1976).

Boldy, Steven, *The Novels of Julio Cortázar* (Cambridge: C.U.P., 1980).

Briggs, Katherine M., *A Dictionary of British Folk Tales in the English Language Including the F. J. Norton Collection. Part A. Folk Narratives* (London: Routledge and Kegan Paul, 1970).

Bruford, W. H., *The German Tradition of Self-Cultivation: 'Bildung' from Humboldt to Thomas Mann* (Cambridge: C.U.P., 1975).

Butler, Judith, 'Gender Trouble', *Feminism/Postmodernism*, edited and with an introduction by Linda J. Nicholson (New York and London: Routledge, 1990), pp. 324–40.

Calinescu, Matei, *Five Faces of Modernity* (Durham: Duke University Press, 1987).

Cixous, Hélène, 'The Laugh of the Medusa', *New French Feminisms: An Anthology*, edited by Elaine Marks and Isabelle de Courtivron (Brighton: The Harvester Press, 1981), pp. 245–64.

Clément, Cathérine, *The Lives and Legends of Jacques Lacan*, translated by Arthur Goldhammer (New York: Columbia University Press, 1983).

Conde, Carmen, *Poesía femenina española (1950–1960)* (Barcelona: Bruguera, 1971).

Crow, Mary (ed.), *Woman who has Sprouted Wings: Poems by Contemporary Latin American Women Poets* (Pittsburgh, PA: Latin American Literary Review Press, 1987).

Cruz, Sor Juana Inés de la, 'Respuesta de la poetisa a la muy ilustre Sor Filotea de la Cruz', *Obras completas de Sor Juana Inés de la Cruz* (México: Fondo de Cultura Económica, 1957), vol. IV, pp. 440–75.

Danahy, Michael, *The Feminization of the Novel* (Gainesville: University of Florida Press, 1991).

Derrida, Jacques, *De la grammatologie* (Paris: Minuit, 1967).

Deyermond, Alan, 'Spain's First Woman Writers', in *Women in Hispanic Literature: Icons and Fallen Idols* (Berkeley, Los Angeles and London: University of California Press, 1983), pp. 27–52.

Durand, Frank, 'The Reality of Illusion: *La desheredada*', *MLN*, 89 (1974), 191–204.

Eliade, Mircea, *The Quest: History and Meaning in Religion* (Chicago: The University of Chicago, 1969).

Fetterley, Judith, *The Resisting Reader: A Feminist Approach to American Fiction* (Bloomington and London: Indiana University Press, 1978).

Florence, Penny, 'The Liberation of Utopia or Is Science Fiction the Ideal Contemporary Women's Form', in *Plotting Change: Contemporary Women's Fiction*, ed. Linda Anderson (London: Edward Arnold, 1990), pp. 65–83.

Foucault, Michel, *Folie et Déraison: histoire de la folie à l'âge classique* (Paris: Plon, 1961).

Freud, Sigmund, *Werke aus den Jahren 1925–1931* (London: Imago, 1948).

Froula, Christine, 'Rewriting Genius: Gender and Culture in Twentieth-Century Texts', *TSWL*, 7:2 (1988), 197–220.

Furman, Nelly, '*A Room of One's Own*: Reading Absence', *Woman's Language and Style*, edited by Douglas Butturff & Edmund L. Epstein (Akron, Ohio: University of Akron, 1978), pp. 99–105.

Gallop, Jane, 'The Body Politic', in *Thinking Through the Body* (New York: Columbia University Press, 1988), pp. 91–118.

Gilbert, Sandra M., & Susan Gubar, *The Madwoman in the Attic. The Woman Writer and the Nineteenth Century Literary Imagination* (New Haven: Yale University Press, 1979).

Gilead, Sara, 'Magic Abjured: Closure in Children's Fantasy Fiction', *PMLA*, 106:2 (1991), 277–93.

Goodman, Katherine, *Dis/Closures: Women's Autobiographies Between 1790 and 1914* (New York: Peter Lang, 1986).

Hart, Stephen M., *Spanish, Catalan and Spanish-American Poetry from "modernismo" to the Spanish Civil War* (Lampeter: Edwin Mellen Press, 1990).

Heath, Stephen, 'Male Feminism', in *Men in Feminism*, edited by Alice Jardine and Paul Smith (New York and London: Methuen, 1987), pp. 1–32.

Herrmann, Claudine, *The Tongue Snatchers*, translated by Nancy Kline (Lincoln & London: University of Nebraska Press, 1989).

Irigaray, Luce, *Ce Sexe qui n'en est pas un* (Paris: Minuit, 1977).

Jordan, Barry, *Writing and Politics in Franco's Spain* (London and New York: Routledge, 1990).

Kahn, Charles H., *The Art and Thought of Heraclitus: An Edition of the Fragments with Translation and Commentary* (Cambridge: C.U.P., 1979).

Kaplan, Cora, *Sea Changes: Essays on Culture and Feminism* (London: Verso, 1984).

Kaplan, Sydney Janet, 'Varieties of Feminist Criticism', in *Making a Difference: Feminist Literary Criticism*, edited by Gayle Greene & Coppélia Kahn (London: Methuen, 1985), pp. 37–58.

Kaveney, Roz, 'The Science Fictiveness of Women's Science Fiction ', in *From My Guy to Sci-Fi: Genre and Women's Writing in the Postmodern World*, edited by Helen Carr (London: Pandora, 1989), pp. 78–97.

152LIST OF WORKS CONSULTED

Kenner, Hugh, *Joyce's Voices* (London: Faber and Faber, 1978).

Kirkpatrick, Susan, *"Las Románticas": Women Writers and Subjectivity in Spain, 1835–1850* (Berkeley: University of California Press, 1989).

Lacan, Jacques, *The Language of the Self: The Function of Language in Psychoanalysis*, translated with notes and commentary by Anthony Wilden (New York: Delta, 1975).

Lazzaro-Weis, Carol M., 'From Margins to Mainstream: Some Perspectives on Women and Literature in Italy in the 1980s', in *Contemporary Women Writers in Italy: A Modern Renaissance*, edited by Santo L. Aricò (Amherst: The University of Massachusetts Press, 1990), pp. 197–217.

Mainer, José-Carlos, 'Las escritoras del 27 (con María Teresa de León al fondo)', *Homenaje a María Teresa de León* (Madrid: Universidad Complutense, 1989), pp. 13–39.

McKenna, A.J., 'Postmodernism: It's Future Perfect', in *Postmodernism and Continental Philosophy*, edited by Hugh J. Silverman and Donn Welton (Albany, N.Y.: State University of New York Press, 1988), pp. 228–42.

Millett, Kate, *Sexual Politics* (New York: Doubleday and Co., 1970).

Moi, Toril, *Sexual/Textual Politics* (London: Methuen, 1983).

———— (ed.), *French Feminist Thought: A Reader* (Oxford: Basil Blackwell, 1987).

Molloy, Silvia, *At Face Value: Autobiographical Writing in Spanish America* (Cambridge: Cambridge University Press, 1991).

Nelson, Cary, 'Men, Feminism: The Materiality of Discourse', in *Men in Feminism*, edited by Alice Jardine & Paul Smith (New York and London: Methuen, 1987), pp. 153-72.

Norris, Christopher, *Deconstruction: Theory and Practice* (London: Methuen, 1982).

O'Connor, Patricia, *Gregorio and María Martínez Sierra* (Boston: G. K. Hall, 1977).

————, *Dramaturgas españolas de hoy: Una introducción* (Madrid: Espiral Fundamentos, 1988).

Owens, Craig, 'Outlaws: Gay Men in Feminism', in *Men in Feminism*, edited by Alice Jardine and Paul Smith (New York and London: Methuen, 1987), pp. 219-32.

Pefanis, Julian, *Heterology and the Postmodern: Bataille, Baudrillard, and Lyotard* (Durham: Duke University Press, 1991).

Pratt, Annis, *Archetypal Patterns in Women's Fiction* (Brighton: Harvester Press, 1982).

Prescott, W. H., *The Conquest of Mexico* (New York: Henry Holt and Company, 1922).

Propp, Valdimir, *The Morphology of the Folk Tale*, revised edition (Austin & London: University of Texas Press, 1968).

Rich, Adrienne, *On Lies, Secrets and Silence: Selected Prose. 1966–78* (New York: Norton, 1979).

Rodgers, Eamon, 'Galdós's *La desheredada* and Naturalism', *BHS*, 45 (1968), 285–98.

Ross, Andrew, 'Demonstrating Sexual Difference', in *Men in Feminism*, edited by Alice Jardine and Paul Smith (New York and London: Methuen, 1987), pp. 47–53.

Scholes, Robert, *Fabulation and Metafiction* (Urbana: University of Illinois Press, 1979), p. 26.

———, 'Reading Like a Man', in *Men in Feminism*, edited by Alice Jardine & Paul Smith (New York and London, Methuen, 1987), pp. 204–18.

Schor, Naomi, 'Dreaming Dissymmetry: Barthes, Foucault, and Sexual Difference', in *Men in Feminism*, edited by Alice Jardine & Paul Smith (New York and London: Methuen, 1987), pp. 98–110.

Selden, Raman, *A Reader's Guide to Contemporary Literary Theory* (Lexington: University of Kentucky, 1985).

Showalter, Elaine, 'Critical Cross-Dressing: Male Feminists and the Woman of the Year', in *Men in Feminism*, edited by Alice Jardine and Paul Smith (New York and London: Methuen, 1987), pp. 116–32.

Skidmore, Thomas E., & Peter H. Smith, *Modern Latin America* (Oxford: Oxford University Press, 1989).

Smith, Paul, 'Men in Feminism: Men and Feminist Theory', in *Men in Feminism*, edited by Alice Jardine and Paul Smith (New York and London: Methuen, 1987), pp. 33–46.

Smith, Paul Julian, *The Body Hispanic: Gender and Sexuality in Spanish and Spanish American Literature* (Oxford: Clarendon Press, 1989).

Spender, Dale, *Man Made Language* (London: Routledge and Kegan Paul, 1980).

Spivak, Gayatri, *In Other Worlds: Essays in Cultural Politics* (New York and London: Methuen, 1987).

Sturrock, John, *Paper Tigers: The Ideal Fictions of Jorge Luis Borges* (Oxford: Clarendon, 1977).

Todd, Janet, *The Sign of Angellica. Women, Writing and Fiction, 1660–1800* (New York: Columbia University Press, 1989).

Todorov, Tzvetan, *The Fantastic: A Structural Approach to a Literary Genre*, translated from the French by Richard Howard (Cleveland: The Press of Case Western Reserve University, 1973).

Valentí i Fiol, E., 'Carles Riba i la seva traducció de l'*Odisea*', *ER*, IX (1961), 127–37.

Valls, Fernando, 'El eterno juego del sueño y de la vida', *La Vanguardia* (1 March 1991).

Weed, Elizabeth, 'A Man's Place', in *Men in Feminism*, edited by Alice Jardine and Paul Smith (New York and London: Methuen, 1987), pp. 71–77.

Winnett, Susan, 'Coming Unstrung: Women, Men, Narrative and Principles of Pleasure', *PMLA*, 105:3 (1990), 505–18.

Woolf, Virginia, *A Room of One's Own* (London: Hogarth, 1942).

INDEX

Agustini, Delmira 2, 4
Albert, Catarina 2, 3
Alberti, Rafael 4
Album de familia 2, 46, 140, 146, 147
Aldecoa, Ignacio 4
Aldecoa, Josefina R. 4
Alegría, Claribel 5
Aleixandre, Vicente 113
Alice in Wonderland 64, 65, 72
Allende, Isabel 3, 54, 89, 91–99, 115, 143, 144, 146
Allende, Salvador 91, 92
Alós, Concha 5
Althusser, Louis 89–91, 149
Amado amo 132
Amor es un juego solitario, El 78
Amortajada, La 2, 36–45, 140
Andersen, Hans Christian 68, 148
Andromeda 37, 150
Aragon, Louis 113
Arderiu, Clementina 4
Aristotle 1, 35, 150
Artemio Cruz 39
Atencia, María Victoria 5

Baroja, Pío 125, 126, 150
Barthes, Roland 30, 131, 145
Beatrice 75
Beauvoir, Simone de 45, 46
Bécquer, Gustavo 113
Belli, Giaconda 5
Berkeley, George 113
Bildungsroman 9–12, –and Laforet 13–19, –and Lispector 28–35, –and Rodoreda 19–28
Blue Beard 76

Böhl von Faber, Cecilia 2, 3, 11
Bombal, María Luisa 2, 36–45, 143, 145
Bonjour, tristesse 113
Borges, Jorge Luis 133
Brant, Sebastian 125, 126
Brecht, Bertolt 87
Bullrich, Sylvia 5

Caballero, Fernán (pseudonym of Cecilia Böhl von Faber, q.v.) 3, 11
Carroll, Lewis 65, 71, 72
Cartagena, Teresa de 2
Casa de Bernarda Alba, La 15
Casa de los espíritus, La 3, 91–99, 115, 140, 143, 146
Castellanos, Rosario 2, 36, 45–53, 145, 146, 147, 148
Castro, Juana 5
Castro, Rosalía de 2
Català, Victor (pseudonym of Catarina Albert, q.v.) 3
Cela, Camilo José 63
Cervantes, Miguel 47, 51
Cien años de soledad 97
Cinderella 16, 17, 38, 63, 80
Circe 113, 114
Cixous, Hélène 4, 7, 10, 28, 30, 34, 35, 117, 144, 150
Clarín 95
Conversación al sur 2, 99–107, 115, 140, 149
Cortázar, Julio 54, 127, 128, 150
Cross, St John of the 112
Cruz, Sor Juana Inés de la 2, 3, 36, 45, 51, 52, 62, 150
Cuauhtemoc 48, 51

155

Cuarto de atrás, El 3, 12, 64, 65, 71–78, 86, 87, 140, 143, 144, 145, 146, 147, 148, 149

Dante, Alighieri 75, 113
Darío, Rubén 38, 48, 77
De la grammatologie 79, 150
Derrida, Jacques 59, 79, 150
Death in Venice 113
Desheredada, La 16, 151, 153
Deuxième Sexe, Le 45
Diosdado, Ana 5
Don Juan Tenorio 39, 149
Don Quijote 47
Dos Passos, John 101
Dostoevsky, Fedor Mikhailovich 10, 45

Eco, Umberto 125
Eliade, Mircea 138, 151
Entre visillos 71, 143
Essai sur l'origine des langues 79

Fagundez Telles, Lygia 5
fairy tales 63–65, –and Allende 97, –and Garro 56, –and Martín Gaite 71–78, –and Matute 65–70, –and Rodoreda 22–23, –and Tusquets 78–87
Falcón, Lidia 110
Familia de Pascual Duarte, La 63, 150
Ferré, Rosario 5
Ficciones 133
Fortunata y Jacinta 95
Foucault, Michel 81, 125, 147, 151
Franco, Francisco 13, 64, 71, 76, 77, 87, 107, 150, 151
Freud, Sigmund 9, 26, 111, 114, 122, 130, 151
Fuentes, Carlos 39
Fuertes, Gloria 5

García Lorca, Federico 15
García Márquez, Gabriel 54, 91, 97, 146
García Morales, Adelaida 5
Garro, Elena 2, 36, 53–62, 93, 144, 146, 147, 149

Gato eficaz, El 2, 116–24
gender trouble 116, –and Montero 131–39, –and Peri Rossi 124–31, –and Valenzuela 117–24
Girondo, Oliverio 43
Goethe, Johann Wolfgang von 11
Gómez de Avellaneda, Gertrudis 2
Gómez Ojea, Carmen 5
Grande, Almudena 84
Guido, Beatriz 5

Hansel and Gretel 76
Heraclitus 133, 151
Herrmann, Claudine 34, 151
Hitler, Adolf 15
Homer 80, 113, 114
Huidobro, Vicente 43

Ibarbourou, Juana de 2, 4
Iliad 113
Irigaray, Luce 10, 34, 86, 151
Isabel I 76, 77

James, Henry 6
Janés, Clara 5
Jara, Marta 5
Jones, Ernest 10
Joyce, James 25, 32, 119, 152

Kafka, Franz 75
Karenina, Anna 45, 51

Lacan, Jacques 117, 118, 120, 121, 122, 123, 150, 152
Laforet, Carmen 2, 12–19, 34, 65, 66, 145, 147, 148
Lange, Norah 11, 43
Lautréamont, Comte de 117
Lawrence, D.H. 88
Lázaro, Maribel 5
Le Guin, Ursula 137
'Lección de cocina' 36, 45–53
Léon, María Teresa de 4, 152
lesbian desire 83–84, 109, 131
Lévi-Strauss, Claude 79
Lewis, C.S. 80
L'hora violeta 3, 107–15, 140

Little Mermaid, The 64, 67, 68, 69, 70, 80, 82
Lispector, Clarice 2, 12, 28–35, 112, 140, 144, 148
López de Córdoba, Leonor 2
López de Gómara, Francisco 48
Lynceus 1
Lynch, Marta 5

Machado, Antonio 85
Malinche, La 57
Mallarmé, Stéphane 38
Mann, Thomas 113, 150
Maragall, Joan 113
Martín Gaite, Carmen 3, 64, 65, 86, 143, 144, 145, 146, 147, 148
Martín-Santos, Luis 64, 85
Martínez Sierra, Gregorio 4, 152
Martínez Sierra, María de la O 4, 152
Marx/Marxism 89, 90, 92, 93, 94, 95, 96, 98, 101, 102, 103, 110, 149
Mastretta, Angeles 5
Matto de Turner, Clorinda 2
Matute, Ana María 2, 64–70, 86, 143, 145, 147, 148, 149
Mayas, the 31
Mayoral, Concha 5
Medio, Dolores 5, 65, 148
Méndez, Concha 2, 4
Mendoza, María Luisa 5
Mercaderes, Los 70
Merlin, Condesa de 11
Metge, Bernat 22, 148
Mexican Revolution 53
Millett, Kate 10, 44, 88, 98, 152
Mismo mar de todos los veranos, El 3, 65, 78–87, 115, 140, 145, 147
Mistral, Gabriela 2, 4
Moix, Ana María 5, 12, 147
Montero, Rosa 3, 116, 131–39, 144, 146
Morejón, Nancy 5
Mozart, Wolfgang Amadeus 111
Mulder, Elizabeth 73
Mythologies 30

Nada 2, 12–19, 34, 66, 140, 147
Name of the Rose, The 125

Narrenschiff 125
Nave de los locos, La 3, 116, 124–31, 145, 150
Neruda, Pablo 92
New Criticism 47
Niebla 74, 133
'novela rosa' 73, 74, 78

Ocampo, Silvina 5
Ocampo, Victoria 11
Odyssey, The 40, 153
Oedipus 1, 64, 124, 130
Oliver, Maria-Antònia 5
Orestes 64, 150
Orozco, Olga 5
Ozores, Ana 45

Pardo Bazán, Emilia 2
Parra, Teresa de la 43
patriarchal prison 36–37, –and Bombal 37–45, –and Castellanos 45–53, –and Garro 53–62
Pedro Páramo 43
Penelope 40, 113, 114
Pérez Galdós, Benito 16, 95
Peri Rossi, Cristina 3, 7, 99, 124–31, 138, 139, 144, 145, 148
Perseus 37
Perto do coração selvagem 2, 12, 28–35, 112, 140
Peter Pan 65, 68, 80, 86
Pinar, Florencia 2
Pirandello, Luigi 74
Pizarnik, Alejandra 5
Plaça del Diamant, La 2, 12, 13, 19–28, 34, 35, 140, 149
Plaisir du texte, Le 131
Pombo, Pilar 5
Poniatowska, Elena 5
popular culture 49, 76, 77
Porter, Katherine Anne 125
postmodernism 118, 124, 125, 126, 128, 133
Prado, Adélia 5
Premios, Los 127, 128
Primera memoria 2, 12, 64–70, 86, 87, 140, 148, 149
Propp, Vladimir 63, 152

Prosas profanas 77
Puss in Boots 64

Quiroga, Elena 5, 65, 148

Rama, Angel 4
Ramona, adéu 108
Rapunzel 80
Rayuela 127
Recuerdos del porvenir, Los 2, 36, 53–62, 140, 143
Regenta, La 95
regressus ad uterum 26, 114
Respuesta de la poetisa a la muy ilustre Sor Filotea de la Cruz 36, 52, 53, 150
Riba, Carles 4, 113, 153
Rich, Adrienne 18, 153
Riera, Carme 5, 86, 115, 147, 148
Rodoreda, Mercè 2, 13, 19–28, 34, 144, 148, 149
Roig, Montserrat 3, 86, 89, 107–15, 131, 143, 147
Room of One's Own, A 7, 8, 151, 153
Rossetti, Ana 5
Rousseau, Jean-Jacques 11, 79
Rulfo, Juan 43, 54
Russ, Joanna 137

Sabina, María 5
Sagan, Françoise 113
Science Fiction 132–38, 151, 152
Sei personaggi in cerca d'autore 74
sexual politics 88–91, –and Allende 91–99, –and Roig 107–15, –and Traba 99–107
Shakespeare, Judith 8
Shakespeare, William 8, 80, 113
Ships of Fools 125
Simó, Isabel-Clara 5
Sleeping Beauty 56
Snow Queen, The 80, 82
Snow White and the Seven Dwarfs 57, 58, 63, 64, 81
Sommers, Armonía 5
Spanish Civil War 13, 14, 15, 19, 20, 24, 25, 27, 65, 66, 67, 107, 108, 115

Sphinx 124
Spivak, Gayatri 99–100, 153
St George and the Dragon 67
Storni, Alfonsina 2, 4
subaltern 48, 99, 100, 104, 106
Swift, Jonathan 80

Tales of Narnia 80
Tapestry of the Creation 126, 127
Te trataré como a una reina 132
Temblor 3, 116, 131–39, 146
Temps de les cireres, El 108
Teresa de Avila, Santa 2, 3, 51, 52
Theseus 85
Thousand and One Nights 80
Tiempo de silencio 64, 85
Todorov, Tzvetan 71, 75, 144, 148, 153
Tom Thumb 76
Traba, Marta 3, 4, 86, 89, 90, 99–107, 115, 145, 148, 149
trans-sexuality 121, 126, 131, 137, 138
Tristes tropiques 79
Tusquets, Esther 3, 7, 64, 65, 78–87, 115, 131, 144, 145, 147

Ulysses 113, 115
Unamuno, Miguel de 74, 133

Valentí, Helena 5
Valenzuela, Luisa 2, 116–24, 138, 139, 146, 147, 149
Varada tras el último naufragio 78
Villena, Isabel de 2
Virgin Mary 58

Waves, The 113
Woolf, Virginia 7, 8, 21, 40, 46, 58, 111, 113, 153
White Rabbit 82
Wilde, Oscar 124
Wizard of Oz, The 65

Zayas, María de 2
Zola, Emile 62
Zorrilla, José 39, 144